# THE SOCRATIC
# PARADOXES
# AND THE
# GREEK MIND

# THE SOCRATIC PARADOXES AND THE GREEK MIND

MICHAEL J. O'BRIEN

THE UNIVERSITY OF NORTH CAROLINA PRESS
CHAPEL HILL

TO ANNE AND DAVID

# PREFACE

The title of this book links one man's doctrines[1] with the genius of his nation. Since the book is more concerned with Plato than with Greek cultural history, its principal emphasis lies on the Socratic paradoxes rather than on the Greek mind. My main purpose in writing it was to examine and to explain a difficult aspect of Platonic moral philosophy and not to make large statements about Greek thought and culture. But I could not do the first without involving myself somewhat in the second. The question inevitably arose, "To what, apart from the private genius of Socrates and Plato, can we attribute the ethical paradoxes?" The problem had been raised by others, but it had been solved, I found, in a way that I could not accept. Hence the long introductory discussion, in Chapters 1 and 2, of the Greek mind. This last phrase is simply the

1. Two men's doctrines, in a sense. The Socratic paradoxes are part of the philosophy of Plato, in whose dialogues they are for the most part espoused by the character Socrates. They are "Socratic" because of this last circumstance and because of the historical fact it reflects, that the real Socrates had held them in some form.

briefest and most convenient of the many locutions which have been used by scholars[2] to suggest that Greeks from Homer on had their own peculiar way of looking at moral questions, an ingrained "intellectualism" which Plato inherited. I do not myself believe that taken in this sense the phrase corresponds to the facts. What I do believe, and have tried to prove, is that Platonic ethics was a natural, although a brilliant and individual, stage in the evolution of Greek thought. In this sense, the Greek mind is the source of the Socratic paradoxes.

The greater part of the book is devoted to an analysis of Platonic dialogues. As I worked on these chapters, I found that the fundamental and recurrent question was that of Plato's development. The line between those who think that Plato's views changed radically over the years and those who think that they remained essentially the same is one of the deepest cleavages in classical philology. My own conviction, which I have argued in detail, is that the word "development" has too often been the easy and obvious solution to difficulties which might better have been solved otherwise. It is not zest for polemic which has prompted my many detours into the scholarly literature to make this and other points, but simply the belief that a sharp statement of conflicting views is usually the best way to clarify issues.

My interest in this subject was first aroused by Professor Whitney J. Oates, under whose direction, and that of Professor Antony E. Raubitschek, I wrote a doctoral thesis at Princeton in which many of the arguments of this book were first developed. I thank both men for their good advice, and Professor Oates in particular for his unfailing interest in the progress of my work since then. Professor Gregory Vlastos read an early draft of parts of the manuscript and took the time to offer detailed commentary. Others have read the whole manuscript, or large parts of it, and have given me the benefit of their advice and interest, especially Professors Geoffrey Kirk, Helen North, and Henry Immerwahr. Discussion with my students in a graduate course given at Yale in 1961-62 helped me give shape to some of my theories. A Morse Fellowship from Yale in

2. See, for example, E. R. Dodds, *The Greeks and the Irrational* (Berkeley and Los Angeles, 1951), p. 17.

1963-64 gave me the time to pursue the project nearly to its end. I enjoyed for most of that year the hospitality of the American Academy in Rome and the privileges of its library. For this I owe warm thanks to Mr. Richard Kimball, who was then director, to Mrs. Kimball, and to many others at the Academy, of whom I will mention in particular the executive secretary, Miss Margherita Rospigliosi, and the librarian, Mrs. Inez Longobardi. I am also grateful for the courtesies extended by the German Archaeological Institute and the Vatican Library. Professor Berthe Marti, who surrendered her Academy study to me while she was away, provided me with needed space to sort out notes and a quiet place to write. Dr. J. P. Webb will recall a summer when I used one room of his house at Central Lake, Michigan, for the same purpose. Finally, my wife, who typed most of the manuscript, has used her own knowledge of Greek and her good sense of style to help me clarify my argument in a number of places. She has also shown patience and good humor when they were needed.

M. J. O'B.

University College, Toronto
February, 1967

# CONTENTS

# ABBREVIATIONS

| | |
|---|---|
| *AJA* | *American Journal of Archaeology* |
| *AJP* | *American Journal of Philology* |
| *ASSPh* | *Annuaire de la Société Suisse de Philosophie* |
| Bergk | *Poetae Lyrici Graeci,* ed. Theodor Bergk, Parts 2 and 3, 4th ed. (Leipzig, 1882). Reprinted with indices by H. Rubenbauer, 1914-15. |
| *CJ* | *Classical Journal* |
| *CP* | *Classical Philology* |
| *CQ* | *Classical Quarterly* |
| *CR* | *Classical Review* |
| Diels-Kranz | *Die Fragmente der Vorsokratiker,* ed. Hermann Diels, rev. Walther Kranz, 8th ed., 3 vols. (Berlin, 1956). |
| Edmonds | *Fragments of Attic Comedy after Meineke, Bergk, and Kock,* ed. J. M. Edmonds, 3 vols. in 4 (Leiden, 1957-61). |

| | |
|---|---|
| *HSCP* | *Harvard Studies in Classical Philology* |
| *JHI* | *Journal of the History of Ideas* |
| *JHS* | *Journal of Hellenic Studies* |
| *JP* | *Journal of Philology* |
| Kock | *Comicorum Atticorum Fragmenta*, ed. Theodor Kock, 3 vols. (Leipzig, 1880-88). |
| Lewis and Short | Charlton T. Lewis and Charles Short, *A Latin Dictionary* (Oxford, 1879). |
| Liddell-Scott-Jones | Henry G. Liddell and Robert Scott, *A Greek-English Lexicon*, rev. Henry S. Jones, 9th ed. (Oxford, 1940). |
| *Mus. Helv.* | *Museum Helveticum* |
| Nauck | *Tragicorum Graecorum Fragmenta*, ed. August Nauck, 2nd ed. (Leipzig, 1889). |
| *R.-E.* | Pauly-Wissowa-Kroll, *Real-Encyclopädie der classischen Altertumswissenschaft* |
| *REA* | *Revue des Études Anciennes* |
| *REG* | *Revue des Études Grecques* |
| *Rhein. Mus.* | *Rheinisches Museum* |
| *R. Philos.* | *Revue Philosophique* |
| Schroeder | *Poetae Lyrici Graeci*, ed. Theodor Bergk, Part 1: *Pindari Carmina*, rev. Otto Schroeder, 5th and 6th eds. (Leipzig, 1900 and 1923). |
| *TAPA* | *Transactions and Proceedings of the American Philological Association* |

# THE SOCRATIC
# PARADOXES
# AND THE
# GREEK MIND

# INTRODUCTION

The central doctrines of Platonic ethics have always seemed, at first sight, an affront to common sense. That virtue is knowledge and vice ignorance, that no man does wrong on purpose or desires evil, are propositions that invite facile refutation. They are, one could argue, absurd. If we always chose what we knew, or at least believed, to be right, no effort would be required to transform good judgment into right action. There would be one problem in personal moral achievement, to learn right from wrong; one aim in moral education, to teach it to others. Once instructed in ethics, we could take lightly all our worst desires: knowledge would make them impotent. But all experience and good sense demonstrate the opposite. We all do wrong on purpose; we desire evil; we are tempted and we hesitate; and if we are virtuous in the end, it has been only by continual effort.

So much said, it remains hard to believe that Plato could have been wholly unaware of the plain facts of experience, and this in itself is good cause to believe that he taught not absurdities but paradoxes. Even a cursory review of the dialogues shows what scholars have generally acknowledged—the question is complex. In the first place, if virtue were knowledge in an unqualified sense, then all virtues should be reduced to wisdom. Instead, Plato speaks of courage and temperance as distinct from wisdom. While insisting that they depend upon knowledge for their full perfection in a way that goes beyond popular conception, he does not reduce them to knowledge. At times, in fact, he speaks as if they were opposed and as if an excess of one weakened the other. In the second place, the ethical paradoxes, naively interpreted, would imply that education in virtue is merely instruction in right and wrong. But the education described in the *Republic* is more than a course in ethics; it includes a training of the emotions. In the third place, Plato does not limit the sources of wrongdoing to ignorance, but includes disorders of the body and of the lower parts of the soul. These disorders are sometimes classified as ignorance too, e.g. at *Republic* 444a ff. and *Timaeus* 86b ff. But the word is used there in no ordinary sense. It is the ignorance of a man who is aware of what is right but whose awareness is clouded at the moment of choice.

These three concessions to what the ordinary cultivated Athenian would have regarded as good sense, and what the modern reader will judge to be quite conventional notions of morals and education, create their own problem. They seem at first so inconsistent with the ethical paradoxes that we are driven to assume either a flat contradiction in Platonic thought or else a development accompanied by radical change. Since the paradoxes are most in evidence in the earliest dialogues, and the more conventional views come to prominence later, one might suppose that Plato in his maturity abandoned the more startling and less tenable ideas of his youth. One might, on the other hand, try to reconcile what seems irreconcilable, and so salvage the essential unity of Plato's thought. Both interpretations have been defended, the first with more assiduity than the second.

It is the object of this book to re-examine the whole problem of the ethical paradoxes, their role in Plato's thought, the allegiance he gave to them at different periods of his career, and their relation to the common ethical views held by his predecessors and contemporaries. Before attacking this complex problem, I think it advisable to clarify the procedure of this study by laying down a few broad principles which I have tried to follow in writing it. Though the best Platonic criticism has always respected these, it is worth the trouble to define them at the outset, if only because a disproportionate amount of scholarship flourishes by refusing to accept their implications. Most misunderstandings of the ethical paradoxes, I believe, can be traced to this fact.

The first and most obvious principle is that Plato's individual ethical doctrines cannot be grasped except as parts of his whole moral philosophy. The ethical paradoxes, in particular, must be seen in the full context of Platonic thought before they can be understood. Detached from it they are nonsense. Placed in the context of some modern systems they exemplify "the error," as Grote puts it, ". . . of dwelling exclusively on the intellectual conditions of human conduct, and omitting to give proper attention to the emotional and volitional."[1] But it is not fair to assume that Plato ought to have separated the grounds of conduct into the intellectual and the volitional because some later philosophers did so, and to find fault with a doctrine of his because in the light of such a separation it makes bad sense is equally unfair. Moral experience can be analyzed in different ways, and the analysis implied in the statement that virtue is knowledge is not that of Aristotle, or Augustine, or John Stuart Mill. The statement makes sense only if understood as a part of Platonic thought.

The first step in criticism, then, is philological, to discover, by examining the dialogues, what sort of analysis Plato has made of moral experience. The philosophical critic can then discuss its worth, and the historian of philosophy can compare it with others. But the philologist's work is primary, and this study, although not entirely philological in the above sense, is mainly so; its first purpose is to explain how Plato analyzed the rational and irrational influences upon moral choice. All this implies that Platonic ethics is a coherent body of thought, or at least that the critic should accept

1. George Grote, *Plato and the Other Companions of Sokrates* (London, 1865), 1.399.

its coherence as a working hypothesis. In saying this I do not mean to deny all development in Plato, or to suggest that drafts of the *Republic* and the *Laws* were in his cabinet when he published the *Protagoras*. I mean only that this development, at least in his theory of virtue, is more like an organic growth than a *volte-face*, and that in his early dialogues he had already reached a certain maturity of view. Only a detailed study of the relevant passages can establish this without a question in the face of many arguments to the contrary. The central chapters of this book are devoted to that effort.

Such respect toward Plato as a thinker requires patience toward him as a writer. The dialogues are not meant to stand together as a body of treatises; if they embody a system, they present it unsystematically. Scholars cannot evade the implications of Plato's indirect and suggestive way, though they may protest the trouble it creates for them. "You can tell us what other people think, but not what you think," says Glaucon to Socrates at *Republic* 506b8 ff., and the modern Platonic scholar, who often feels himself to be in Glaucon's position, cannot but sympathize. The difficulty he faces is essentially that posed by the literary form of the Platonic dialogue. Our second principle, therefore, is that to understand philosophical content in Plato the reader must pay special attention to the mode of its expression.

The importance to Platonic studies of this question of literary form has been well explained by Victor Goldschmidt.[2] The study of Plato, as he has said, still labors in the shadow of the doxographers, who sought in the philosophers a dogmatic system, a collection of theses ranged under clear headings, lending itself to orderly summary and explanation. But the Platonic system proved difficult to define in the face of the diversity and even apparent contradiction in its formulas. The nineteenth century, in bringing to it the idea of evolution, injected order into its apparent chaos and then furnished an independent basis for chronological sequence in the study of stylistic change as practiced by Campbell, Ritter, and others. But this and other criteria of chronology have been able to establish no more than relative dates for three or four large groups of works, and theo-

2. Victor Goldschmidt, "Sur le Problème du 'Système' de Platon," *Rivista Critica di Storia della Filosofia*, 5 (1950), 169-78.

ries of development have varied in details. Their more fundamental defect is that they have too seldom paid attention to the form of the dialogue, which is not a treatise, and in whose atmosphere of irony and allusiveness a scholar who merely quarries for *dogmata* has no proper place. Goldschmidt's own conclusion is that the dialogue as a literary *genre* has yet to be explained in regard to its history, its purpose, and its laws of composition. One thing is certain, "Il y a dans les *Dialogues* autre chose que des affirmations."[3]

3. *Ibid.*, pp. 173-75. Goldschmidt's book, *Les Dialogues de Platon, Structure et Méthode Dialectique* (Paris, 1947), is an effort to discover, by a detailed analysis of each dialogue, some general laws of form which he thinks are inseparable from the method of dialectic itself (p. 33). Typically, the book eschews chronological presentation.

One of Goldschmidt's predecessors was René Schaerer, whose book *La Question Platonicienne* (Neuchatel, 1938) maintains that the dialogue is not a literary device used to embellish ideas that might have been expressed as well otherwise; on the contrary, the ideas made explicit in it do not exhaust its meaning (p. 13). The dialogue is not Plato speaking to us but Socrates, e.g., speaking to Protagoras (p. 44) or Charmides or Theaetetus. The path to objective truth is different for each (p. 66) and will end closer to the goal for some than for others. Generally speaking, moreover, no dialogue presupposes another, as successive treatises would. The proper analogy is the successive sketches by a painter of one subject from different angles (p. 81). The philosopher works not for any one verbally exact conclusion, but for the long-cultivated and intimate familiarity with his subject out of which will come in the end the flash of truth (pp. 86-89. Cf. *Letter VII*, 341cd). Since the dialogues are literary portrayals of individual efforts to reach that goal, they contain it implicitly and in some fashion reveal it to us, but not directly or fully. Schaerer's notion that dialogue is a cousin to drama is not peculiar to him. Cf. Dorothy Tarrant, "Plato as Dramatist," *JHS*, 75 (1955), 82-89, especially 89. Wm. Chase Greene invokes the same analogy in speaking of the *Republic*, at the beginning of his article, "The Paradoxes of the *Republic*," *HSCP*, 63 (1958), 199-216; he even extends it to the details of *prologos, stichomythia, rhesis, stasimon,* and *anagnorisis* (pp. 199-202). These are not the first or the only critics to realize that Platonic philosophy is partly expressed in the form and movement of the dialogue. There have always been some who could read a dialogue as not merely literature or merely philosophy. No one can look at Jowett's slight introduction to his translation of the *Laches* without seeing that the dialogue has struck him as a totality, and that the art of it has reinforced the thought (Benjamin Jowett, *The Dialogues of Plato* [New York, 1871], 1.70). The first volume of Paul Friedländer's *Platon* records that scholar's early break with the older tradition of Bonitz, who had discussed the philosophy of the *Phaedo* after remarking that he was about to disregard its artistic composition. "Many years ago," says Friedländer, "I put an exclamation mark beside this sentence, and out of this exclamation mark grew my interpretation of Plato" (trans. H. Meyerhoff [London, 1958], p. 232).

By and large, however, partial explanations have prevailed. Total lack of feeling for the dialogue form is rare, and was perhaps seen at its worst in an 18th century view, in the dismissal of Platonic philosophy as a chaos by Jacob Brucker, *Historia Critica Philosophiae* (2nd ed.; Leipzig, 1766-67), 1.665. But

Those who find explicit Platonic doctrines everywhere in the dialogues must share the field with those who in certain early works claim to find none at all. Early in the century, Wilamowitz lent his great authority to the belief that some of the early dialogues are rounded and purposeful as art and biography, but of no philosophical importance.[4] More recently, Ernst Hoffmann has proposed that the *Ion, Hippias Minor, Protagoras, Laches, Lysis,* and *Charmides* form a group of prephilosophical "Kunstwerke." These six, he says, show little or no promise of the high purpose and serious doctrine of the *Phaedo,* the *Gorgias,* and the *Republic.* They illustrate the Socratic way of life, but they are best classified as comedies in prose, and at times they become pure persiflage.[5]

The biographical aspect of many dialogues cannot be denied. Most obvious in the *Apology, Crito,* and *Phaedo,* it is still discernible in the lifelike portraits of Socrates in the *Laches, Symposium, Protagoras,* and elsewhere. But absolute fidelity to biographical detail is not compatible with artistic freedom or philosophical independence. One way to resolve this dilemma is to suppose an early and largely biographical series of dialogues which gradually gives way to a later series expounding Plato's own philosophy. William Chase Greene has proposed such a transition, and he implies that it coincides with the gradual way in which Plato's Socrates comes to monopolize the talk. Greene also suggests that Plato's early works were based on notes of Socratic conversations.[6] John

---

the old assumptions of men used to reading philosophical treatises are still common. It is taken for granted not only that words are used with rigorous consistency in different works, but also that conclusions must be explicit. Therefore, any proposition which looks like a dogma is assumed to be one, even though expressed conditionally, or ironically, or as a question.

4. See below, Chapter 3, note 11; Chapter 4, notes 8 and 23.

5. Ernst Hoffmann, "Die Literarische Voraussetzungen des Platonverständnisses," *Zeitschrift für Philos. Forschung,* 2 (1947), 465-80, especially 476. This point of view, in one form or another, is common. Joseph Moreau, *La Construction de l'Idéalisme Platonicien* (Paris, 1939), pp. 2 ff., has criticized what he believes is a widespread tacit agreement to leave the early dialogues to the literary critics and the later ones to the philosophers. He cites as an example the division of labor in the Budé ed. of Plato, in which A. Croiset and L. Bodin have edited the *Protagoras* as a work of art and have said that it contains no Platonic philosophy properly so called ([Paris, 1923], p. 3). Other early dialogues receive similar treatment in that series.

6. Wm. Chase Greene, "The Spoken and the Written Word," *HSCP,* 60 (1951), 45-46.

Burnet and A. E. Taylor extended this Socratic period of Plato far beyond the usual limits and made it encompass the Theory of Ideas itself.[7] They found an argument in the demands made on Plato by truth and personal loyalty to his teacher. He could not have treated Socrates "without scruple, to the point of putting into his mouth all sorts of theories invented by Plato himself."[8] The Burnet-Taylor view has generally and rightly been rejected. Not only would its suppositions force us to accept Xenophon's *Oeconomicus* as biographical, but it contradicts what Aristotle says about the origin of the Theory of Ideas.[9] The limits of Socratism may be incapable of definitive settlement, and with them the exact degree to which Plato's early dialogues are biography, but some of the arguments used to prove that these are scrupulously historical can be rejected. One argument used by Taylor and others is that in nearly all the early dialogues, except the shortest, the conversation wanders, as actual talk does, over a wide field of topics.[10] But if it can be proved, as I shall try to do for three or four dialogues, that the talk is as balanced, as purposeful, and as painstakingly contrived as in a play of Sophocles, then its claim to be a mere essay in recollection shrinks.

In spite of the difficulty of the subject, there is wide recognition that the early dialogues at times practice a deliberate silence concerning subjects of the highest importance about which Plato had already formed some views.[11] This might seem a strange way for philosophy to be written, but it is not incompatible with Plato's

7. See the introduction to John Burnet's ed. of the *Phaedo* (Oxford, 1911), and A. E. Taylor's *Socrates* (London, 1935) throughout.

8. A. E. Taylor, *Plato, the Man and His Work* (4th ed.; London, 1937), p. 25.

9. See W. D. Ross (ed.), *Aristotle's Metaphysics* (Oxford, 1924), I, xxxiii ff.

10. Taylor, *Plato*, p. 25.

11. See, aside from those scholars already mentioned, Paul Shorey, *The Unity of Plato's Thought* (Chicago, 1903), p. 15; T. Gomperz, *Griechische Denker* (2nd ed.; Leipzig, 1903-09), 2.261; Moreau, *Construction*, p. 9; W. Jaeger, *Paideia*, trans. G. Highet (New York, 1939-44), 3.91; A. Koyré, *Introduction à la Lecture de Platon* (New York, 1945), p. 27; J. Sulliger, "Platon et le problème de la communication de la philosophie," *ASSPh*, 11 (1951), 155-75; V. de Magalhâes-Vilhena, *Socrate et la Légende Platonicienne* (Paris, 1952), p. 211; John Gould, *The Development of Plato's Ethics* (Cambridge, 1955), p. 41; Reginald Hackforth, *Plato's Phaedrus*, Translated with introduction and commentary (Cambridge, 1952), p. 163.

expressed views on the subject of writing. At *Phaedrus* 276c Socrates says that the man with knowledge of the just, the noble, and the good will not commit his "seeds" to writing in the vain hope that they will be able to defend themselves and teach the truth satisfactorily. He goes on to identify the philosopher's serious work as teaching, and calls writing his pastime. *Letter VII* puts this in different words: there is no treatise by Plato on any of the subjects he seriously studies, for these cannot be expressed adequately in writing (341c-e, 344c).[12]

This clear warning against reading the dialogues as treatises does not mean that the interpretation of Plato's written works is a futile game. It only confirms what the attentive reader of Plato will already have realized: the dialogues display the conflict and interaction of minds and beliefs, not a logical procession of connected truths. In some works, it is true, the dramatic technique is used less than in others. Much of the *Republic* could be rewritten as a monologue. Even in dialogues where there is a conflict of ideas there are many passages in which it is grossly unequal. The contribution of Polemarchus, for example, to the *Republic* is mainly to state some common misconceptions and allow them to be crushed; he is no match for Socrates. But Polemarchus is not the model for all of Socrates' opponents. This would be clear enough from the *Parmenides*, but it should be kept in mind also in reading those dialogues in which Socrates apparently wins his arguments.

In the *Protagoras*, for example, the clear superiority of Socrates in debate must not be taken as a vindication of all his arguments, since even he is perplexed and unsatisfied at the conclusion. Pro-

---

12. Neither the *Phaedrus* nor *Letter VII* can be used, of course, to demonstrate the *kind* of structure I will find in some early dialogues. Their passages about the limitations of the written word, in fact, also apply to the *Republic*, where reticence is practiced (e.g. about the Good) but where the structure is quite different.

P. Merlan's article, "Form and Content in Plato's Philosophy," *JHI*, 8 (1947), 406-30, argues that Plato not only wrote inconclusive dialogues but avoided positive teaching in general, and even held his personal convictions subject to ultimate doubt. But this view takes too little account of the different effects to be expected from the written and the spoken word (*Phaedrus* 276a) and of the difference between opinion and knowledge. The dialogues fail to be definitive because they cannot transmit knowledge, only the impetus to it.

tagoras says that courage is a product of natural endowment and good upbringing, while Socrates says it is knowledge. But in the comprehensive discussion of virtue in the *Republic*, the views of both have a place. In the *Laches* too, it would only betray a misconception of Plato's method to inquire whether he speaks through Laches, Nicias, or Socrates. Socrates has the last word, and it is he who defines the unsolved problem with which the dialogue ends, but Plato's own views are found in the arguments of no single character. The dialogue has a plot in which separate parts of the truth maneuver to a stalemate. Plato's own thought is expressed in the design of the dialogue, but that expression is literary as well as philosophical and so requires the exercise of literary perception.

In dialogues like the *Protagoras* and the *Laches* Plato's own views are not made explicit. But in many passages elsewhere the words of one speaker, usually Socrates, are, in effect, Plato's words. In such passages there is little real conflict of minds, and the expository intention overbalances the dramatic, though dramatic forms are always kept. But even these passages need critical attention; if we know Plato is speaking we must still decide in what sense he speaks. He is full of inconsistencies that would be inexcusable in a writer who claimed to give a systematic and verbally consistent account of his beliefs. But since we cannot attribute such a motive to him, our interpretation of ambiguous or paradoxical statements must take into account the context.

The third principle, therefore, is that different treatments of the same subject, especially definitions and divisions, should be compared with great caution and without any prejudice in favor of verbal consistency. Plato habitually addresses himself to the point at issue without reference to comments he may have made elsewhere on the same subject. The reason for this method is evidently a conviction that definitive verbal statements of truth are not to be found. So Plato's definitions are provisional. They are, in fact, never true definitions, if by a definition we mean a description that must be memorized and in all relevant contexts either reiterated or presupposed. As a result, cross reference is hazardous. To write of Plato's term ἀνδρεία as one might write of Spinoza's term *sub-*

*stantia* will force the critic who has begun with an assumption of verbal consistency to end with a charge of doctrinal inconsistency. No common definition can underlie Plato's different uses of the word ἀνδρεία, and when he uses that word in different senses even in the same dialogue the explanation must be a lack of verbal scruple and not a development in theory.[13] Other examples of his free way with words are not hard to find. Although there is no doctrine on which he lays more stress than the involuntariness of wrongdoing, yet in the *Laws*, soon after stating it (860d), he makes a distinction between voluntary and involuntary crimes (869e). Only context makes it clear that he is drawing the conventional legal distinction between intent and absence of intent.[14] So too he had spoken earlier of voluntary and involuntary deceit (730c). He calls two kinds of ignorance the "greatest" in separate dialogues, but here too the context reveals two distinct criteria.[15] In one dialogue, the *Gorgias* (467d6-e1), the term βούλησις seems to take on a technical meaning, but it is elsewhere used in a looser sense.[16] Finally,

13. Courage ( ἀνδρεία ) is provisionally defined in the *Republic* as the power to preserve the right opinion about what is and is not to be feared (430b). But elsewhere it is often a quality either independent of reason or actually hostile to it. At *Rep.* 375a, the term ἀνδρεῖος is applied to horses, dogs, and other animals. Yet at *Laches* 197a Nicias had rejected this use of the word on the ground that animals had no share in reason. Callicles, in the *Gorgias*, thinks of courage as a quality which aids the intelligent man to achieve the unlimited indulgence of all his desires (491ab). We expect Callicles to hold such views, but we find that Socrates himself occasionally uses the term "courage" in its Calliclean sense. At *Gorgias* 463a the rhetorician, who practices not an art but a form of flattery, is said to be shrewd and courageous; at *Meno* 88b the possibility is allowed that courage can sometimes be senseless; at *Rep.* 426d it is a quality of men who are ready to serve sick and badly governed states. In all three passages the speaker is Socrates. Glaucon's hypothetical unjust man has all the good things in life except virtue; he succeeds through courage, strength, and his resources in friends and property (*Rep.* 361b). Similar references to courage are made by the Athenian Stranger in the *Laws* (630ab ff., 661d-662a, 696b, 963e). "So kann Platon nur als Greis geschrieben haben," says H. Raeder, *Platons Philos. Entwickelung* (Leipzig, 1905), p. 399. Yet this judgment overlooks the usage of the *Gorgias*, *Meno*, and *Republic*. Plato, who regularly yields to common usage when no point would be made by not yielding, can be discriminating with words when it suits his purpose. Hence Socrates, who credits rhetoricians with courage at *Gorgias* 463a, goes on to insist in the same dialogue that courage is inseparable from knowledge and the good (495de).

14. See below, Chapter 6, note 17.

15. See below, Chapter 6, note 13.

16. See *Laws* 863b9, *Lysis* 208e, *Rep.* 445b, *Gorgias* 511b.

even the definitions of the virtues in *Republic* 442b-d are later qualified as a mere "sketch" (504d4-7).

Plato's divisions, like his definitions, serve only the needs of the moment. Four passages, concerned with defects of soul that incline a man to wrongdoing, offer what seem to be entirely different theories of vice. These are *Sophist* 227d ff., *Timaeus* 86b ff., *Republic* 444a ff., and *Laws* 860c ff., and in each the method of division reflects the purpose in hand. They are, therefore, not meant to be measured closely against one another. The passage in the *Timaeus*, in which the viewpoint is scientific and medical, is also remarkable in speaking of all vices as effects of temporary physical disorder or permanent physical defect. Its treatment of wickedness as a matter of body chemistry disregards moral responsibility and seems tacitly to replace moral effort with mechanical causation. But it only observes the principle of keeping to the point: a discourse on the physiological aspects of vice need only advert to the influence of the body on itself and on the reason. That reason in turn can influence the body is the presupposition of the whole program of education in the *Republic*.

Passages dealing with the parts of the soul and its powers show the same shifts of emphasis. The second part of the soul in the *Republic*, the θυμοειδές, is pre-eminently the seat of anger and courage. In the *Phaedrus* this part, represented by the good steed, in the metaphor of the soul as a chariot, is the source of shame and ally of temperance. Both dialogues discuss the struggle against temptation, the *Republic* in the story of Leontius, the *Phaedrus* in the struggle of charioteer and horses. In the first, the θυμοειδές is angry at the desires; in the second, the good steed is merely overwhelmed with shame. This difference is probably due to the political analogy in the *Republic*. The θυμοειδές corresponds to the soldier-police class; since this class curbs dissidents by anger and violence, the θυμοειδές is said to do the same to the desires. In the *Phaedrus* no such analogy inhibits the more normal view that what curbs desire is shame. By the same analogy it is sometimes said that courage is needed to suppress desires, although it is more common to make this act one of temperance.

To sum up, this book brings to the problem of the Socratic ethical paradoxes three major principles of inquiry. Because of the great distance which separates Plato's philosophical assumptions and methods from ours, none of the three is easy to apply. Yet the attempt must be made if the brilliant and original moral philosophy created by Plato under Socrates' influence is to be properly understood. The principles are as follows: (1) Each of Plato's ethical doctrines, being the partial expression of a whole philosophical analysis, can be understood only in reference to the others and to the whole. This seems a truism, but in studies of the ethical paradoxes it has seldom been fully appreciated. (2) Plato's literary art does not merely embellish his philosophical doctrine, but radically affects its expression; to discover what he means requires both philosophical and literary perception. (3) There are no fixed definitions and divisions, and so statements must be interpreted by reference to context. Plato's expositions, as the passages cited above show, fulfill limited intentions and solve particular problems, and they are not meant to form a verbally consistent group of propositions. But once the conditions of their expression are known, they reveal a consistent philosophy.

In the third chapter I shall consider the sense in which, for Plato, virtue is knowledge, and in later chapters the sense in which it is not. The former sense is primary, the latter secondary; on that proposition this whole study rests. Right action is primarily rational action. The ruling faculty in man in the proper order of things is reason, and that which ultimately determines his right actions is the guidance that his reason offers him in the form of knowledge. In any single act of choice all three of the soul's parts, λογιστικόν, θυμοειδές, ἐπιθυμητικόν, i.e. the principles of reason, anger, and desire, and the body acting through them, may influence the issue. Control, however, rests with reason, since the dispositions determining the action of each of the other two parts are effects of the exercise or omission of rational discipline. That reason controls choice is true in another sense too: every conscious choice is the effect of a rational judgment at the moment of decision. Uncontrolled passion leads men into error only by preventing reason from coming to a true practical judgment, and disciplined emotion leads men to do right only because it allows reason to judge truly. Vice is ultimately ignorance, and virtue is knowledge or true opinion.

It is worth noting that the decision to make reason central and make irrational forces depend on it is not required by moral experience itself. One might place the irrational and inexplicable elements of human nature at the center and make reason depend upon them. However true it is to say that what we choose is what we know, it is also true that what we know is both what we have chosen to know and what blind opportunity has allowed us to know. One who analyzes as Plato does and makes reason central must admit that all influence does not radiate outward from the center; much of it has its source near the circumference. But although Plato's analysis has no advantage over the other in symmetry, it is not arbitrary, but is demanded by his ontology. Reason is central because it is better than unreason; the principle of order is central because order is better than chaos. What determines Plato's analysis is his intention to speak of actual moral experience as that which may become ideal moral experience, and so the ultimate principle of that analysis is Plato's apprehension of the Good. Since the good life is the perfectly rational life, in which man's behavior is perfectly ordered and his highest faculties of mind are freed for the contemplation of the Ideas and of the Good itself, moral experience is said to be centered in reason.

A philosopher who accepts this point of view and tries to explain it has to struggle against apparently ingrained ways of thinking and speaking.[17] Most people assume that knowledge is only one among many sources of moral action; that some men are reasonable, but others are brave, and others are temperate; that among these attributes there is no necessary connection; that, in fact, few people possess all the virtues. By the same token, ignorance is only one among many sources of moral error; some men are too stupid to do what is right, but others are simply incontinent or hot-tempered.[18]

17. Recent scholarship has seen many mistaken attempts to prove that the doctrines in question, paradoxical to us, were not so to the Greeks. These are discussed in Chapter 1.

18. Aristotle may have been the first to accuse the early works of Plato of being naive in this respect. At *Nic. Ethics* 1145b23 ff. he criticizes the view

The basic ethical doctrines of Plato, which seem to deny obvious facts, are paradoxes. It is only as his discussion of them slowly reveals the full ethical philosophy of which they are a part that they become plausible.

These paradoxes are: no one does wrong willingly; no one wishes evil; virtue can be taught; virtue is an art like medicine or carpentry; virtue is knowledge; vice is ignorance. Not all of these have equal status. The first two can be called firm doctrines; the others are either persistent issues or working assumptions taken with reservations. All, however, are found to be true in some sense.

In the *Apology* Socrates pleads that a man would not corrupt his associates willingly, because by having corrupt associates he would cause injury to himself (25c). The remark is a crude foreshadowing of Plato's later explanations of the doctrine that wrongdoing is involuntary. The same point is made in the *Meno*, but with a general application, in the assumption by Socrates that to wish evil is equivalent to desiring evil for one's self. Nowhere in the *Meno* does he justify the assumption, but we find the grounds for it in the *Gorgias* (467d6 ff.) and throughout the *Republic* (see especially 612b). In the *Gorgias* he explains that he uses the word βούλησις to refer to the ends of activity and not to the means. That

---

of Socrates that when knowledge is present it rules action. His wording suggests that he is refuting *Protag.* 352b5 ff., and his objection is that the Socratic doctrine implies that incontinence does not exist. Grote's criticism, already quoted, of Socratic and Platonic ethics amounts to the same thing (see note 1). Thomas Maguire's book entitled *Essays on Platonic Ethics* (Dublin, 1870) is in large part a critique of Grote's interpretations. Maguire contends that "acting through ignorance does not mean in Plato merely acting in the absence of knowledge. . . . Ignorance [is] something positive, viz. the presence of disturbing influences" (p. 51). When Léon Robin, in *Platon* (Paris, 1935), p. 322, refers to "les causes concrètes de cette ignorance, qui nous rend méchants" and cites *Timaeus* 86b as one of Plato's efforts to define these while remaining faithful to Socratic rationalism, his supposition is the same: Plato always equated the moral aspect of desire, fear, pain, and pleasure with the effect which each has on the judgment.

Renford Bambrough, "Socratic Paradox," *Philosophical Quarterly*, 10 (1960), 289-300, has a generally good discussion of the nature of paradoxical statement and of the particular grounds for the disagreement between Aristotle and Plato on the voluntariness of wrongdoing. I doubt, however, that the language of contemporary ethical philosophy is as apt for interpreting Plato as Bambrough assumes, especially the distinction between factual belief and moral and emotional attitude (p. 298). Cf. the criticism of Gould in Chapt. 7, n. 2, below.

all moral error is unwilling and that no one wishes evil means that no man wishes the ultimate effect of wrongdoing, the destruction of happiness. This doctrine is then simply an assertion that all conscious human activity is rational. In other words, the form of all practical judgment is the apprehension of something as a good: to choose is to judge that the action chosen will effect a good end. The doctrine further implies that conscious choice is never ultimately irrational. To choose an action seen as absolutely evil is unthinkable. Philosophers who find this possible suppose a mutual independence of value-judgment and choice which Plato would have repudiated. For him the practical judgment and the choice are two sides of one coin; each implies the other. Plato puts it more simply, but paradoxically: no one does wrong on purpose; no one wishes evil.

Socrates makes frequent use in the dialogues of the analogy between virtue and the arts and sciences, but he is aware that there is something misleading in it. In the *Gorgias* (460b) he argues that the man who has learned what is just must be a just man, because the man who has learned carpentry, music, or medicine is thereby a carpenter, musician, or physician. The whole argument of the *Hippias Minor* rests on his use of the analogy. But in this dialogue the analogy breaks down; in any art the expert is the man who can err on purpose, but it is unthinkable that the virtuous man should do wrong on purpose. At the dialogue's conclusion Plato clearly intimates that the art of virtue is unique in that no one who has it breaks its rules intentionally. He does not say, however, why this should be true of one art and not of others. The paradox of the *Hippias Minor* reappears near the beginning of the *Republic*, where it is demonstrated by analogy that if justice is in all respects like the other arts it will include the ability to do wrong efficiently (334a10).

The *Laches* takes a long step towards solving the paradox. Socrates first proves against Laches that courage cannot be any particular art, such as the military art or swimming, because when two men stand up equally well under stress, we judge the less skillful man to be braver. Nicias then proposes that courage is a science of ultimate ends, not of means or of intermediary ends. His proposal is defeated on the grounds that it provides for no distinction among the virtues. Plato will solve this problem in the *Republic* by finding the basis for the distinction of virtues in the lower soul and the basis for their unity in the dominance of reason. But in doing so he will accept in substance the proposal of Nicias: virtue is one and its unity lies in the fact that it centers upon a knowledge of ultimate ends. This doctrine not only preserves the analogy of virtue and the arts but solves the paradox of the *Hippias Minor* and of *Republic* 334a10. An art and science of ultimate ends will not enable its possessor to reject those ends in the way that skill in medicine would enable him to poison his patients. One can poison in the belief that it will bring ultimate good; one cannot knowingly reject the ultimate good itself. The art of medicine differs from the art of virtue because the first is an art of means, the second an art of ends. In other words, the paradox that virtue is an art and a science is solved by joining it to the other paradox that no man wishes evil.

Connected with these is the persistent issue: Can virtue be taught? The question is answered only after it is understood by those who discuss it. The *Meno* finds evidence for both sides. Virtue seems to be knowledge, wholly or in part, and the possibility of teaching it is therefore likely; but no one teaches it. What the *Meno* does not discuss is whether virtue is more than knowledge and whether, accordingly, it requires more than instruction. The *Protagoras* comes closer to giving an answer. The arguments of Socrates and Protagoras contain the main elements of a solution, but they are never combined. Virtue is knowledge, says Socrates, and yet no one teaches it or learns it. Everyone teaches it and learns it, says Protagoras, but it is not knowledge—at least courage is not. Socrates comments that both of them have one foot on each side of the fence, and the dialogue ends. The *Republic* answers the question whether virtue can be taught, not explicitly, but by offering a practical scheme for teaching it.[19] The teaching is not in-

---

19. In the allegory of the ship of state in the *Republic*, one mark of stupidity in the mutinous crew is their denial that the art of navigation can be taught (488b7).

struction alone, however, but instruction combined with discipline of the lower impulses. The reason is that virtue is not knowledge alone, but knowledge exercising rational control over the passions. Virtue as it appears in the *Republic* has three components: knowledge (or right opinion), natural temperament, and the discipline which the former imposes on the latter.

The doctrines that stress the unity of man's nature under reason and the unity of his activity under knowledge are paradoxes because they give only half the truth. They look to an ideal that is only partly fulfilled in the actual. Human nature is not only one; it is multiple too. Human activity is not only unified; it is also divided. The doctrine that virtue is one in knowledge must be balanced by the doctrine that virtue is also courage, temperance, and justice. The conviction that right action lies in the full dominance of reason must be balanced by the recognition that some control must lie with the second part of the soul, the "spirited element" (τὸ θυμοειδές). These statements do not contradict each other: they merely express different levels of analysis. To preserve the former figure, the doctrines that man's nature is composite and that man's virtue is multiple are both one step closer to the periphery of Platonic theory. At the center of that theory, in the doctrines that virtue is knowledge and that man's activity is rational, all disorderly influences are transformed into ignorance, the absence of knowledge. Beyond the center they assume positive qualities and can be distinguished. Man's nature extends from center to circumference, and its principles of activity are divided by Plato into three segments of that radius. These are the so-called parts of the soul—the rational, the spirited, and the appetitive. Reason, the first of these, shapes the soul by a discipline which a man may impose on himself or see imposed on him by a teacher or ruler. But in so disciplining the spirited and appetitive principles, reason imparts to them certain permanent dispositions. These are the virtues of courage and temperance, called virtues because they are the effects of reason imposing order upon irrational powers. Virtue is therefore both one and many: the one virtue of wisdom creates the subsidiary virtues of courage and temperance, through which it preserves in the soul that order which is the virtue of justice. These subsidiary virtues in turn preserve wisdom by thwarting the disorderly impulses. There exists between the first two parts of the soul, therefore, a kind of mutual dependence. Reason controls the θυμοειδές; it renders it vigorous against threats to the integrity of human nature but docile to reason itself. The θυμοειδές, in turn, acting according to the rule of reason, lends its vigor to subdue the excessive desires of the ἐπιθυμητικόν and to meet hostile forces from outside. In these crises it shows the emotions of fear and fearlessness: it fears shame and dishonor and is fearless before pain. In a sense, therefore, the source of moral action is not reason alone, just as virtue is not knowledge alone.

These doctrines, which are here presented in systematic and compressed shape, are found scattered through dialogues composed over the course of many decades. It would be wrong to assume, and impossible to prove, that they appeared full-blown in Plato's mind at the beginning of his career and persisted without change until the end. No thinker with a productive life as long as Plato's could have been utterly resistant to change. On the other hand, to make a chart of his development based upon silences and upon verbal inconsistencies is, for reasons explained above, equally unwise. These general cautions aside, some of the chapters which follow will clarify in detail the reasons why one can treat Plato's moral philosophy as a single and coherent body of thought rather than as a series of quite separate theories, each implying the rejection of what is essential to the others. This body of doctrine undoubtedly grew in complexity over the years, but in its basic intellectualism, and in its fidelity to the Socratic paradoxes, it remained one.

So alien are these paradoxes to the philosophical assumptions current in our day that the question inevitably arises: How did they strike Plato's Greek readers? To a useful extent, the education, the prejudices, and the interests of the cultivated Athenian of the late fifth and early fourth centuries are known to us. We know the language he spoke; we have a substantial part of the literature he heard and read; with diligence we can even discover some of the great intellectual issues which stirred his time, and, not least, the Greek terms in which they were expressed. It should be possible, therefore, within limits, to put oneself in the position of an educated Athenian of the year 400 B.C. The attempt to do so is not frivolous. If we hope to judge Plato's exact meaning, his originality, and the influences upon him of earlier Greek thought, an effort must be made to recapture the relevant aspects of the culture for which he wrote. An attempt to do this will occupy the next two chapters. The purpose of this historical background is twofold. In the first place, it will enable us to judge how receptive Plato's audience would have been to the paradoxes which astonish and offend us. But more than this, it is meant to throw light on a number of important terms, issues, and theories current before Plato, which have left a deep and as yet imperfectly understood impress on his whole ethical philosophy. It therefore provides a necessary background for the subsequent examination of the dialogues themselves.

# 1. THE PARADOXES

## AND

## GREEK "INTELLECTUALISM"

The Greek which Plato learned as a child and later used to express his own philosophy came to him weighted with the thought of Homer, Hesiod, the historians, and the writers of tragedy. Through it, their influence lay heavy upon him. He could not, for example, speak of moral questions without using their ethical vocabulary. More than that, he freely accepted from his predecessors ethical norms that he might have rejected. The *Apology* itself is less a defense of lofty eccentricity than a proof that Socrates has upheld in truer fashion than his judges the virtues they all profess to honor.[1] Since we honor those virtues ourselves, a cultural and linguistic essay on that aspect of Socrates' defense would lack interest, though it might help us estimate its author's debt to Greek tradition. But doctrines that we find paradoxical exert a fascination in proportion to their strangeness; one wonders

1. He is wise, brave, pious, just, and in money matters more than temperate (*Apol.* 20d, 28b ff., 30a, 32bcd, 31c).

how far they are Platonic and how far merely Greek. That question has an obvious bearing on Plato's originality.

There is widespread agreement among historians of Greek philosophy that the intellectualism of Socrates and Plato, so strange to us, has deep roots in the Hellenic mind. According to E. R. Dodds, "the so-called Socratic paradoxes, that 'virtue is knowledge,' and that 'no one does wrong on purpose,' were no novelties, but an explicit generalized formulation of what had long been an ingrained habit of thought."[2] In fact, the notion that what surprises us in these paradoxes would only have struck other Greeks as a systematic expression of what they had all learned to believe from childhood has become, in one form or other, a commonplace.[3] Its prevalence is a result of the modern historical sense, and it rests in a general way on the sound principle that no author entirely escapes the influence of his own culture and his own language. Nevertheless, it can fairly be said that Greek intellectualism, as it is now taught, is a myth. Like any other myth, it has many points of contact with reality, but what measure of truth it contains is distorted by fundamental misconceptions about Greek language and Greek thought. These have bred generaliza-

2. E. R. Dodds, *The Greeks and the Irrational* (Berkeley and Los Angeles, 1951), p. 17.

3. The theory that intellectualism typified Greek ethics from the beginning was the thesis of a book by Max Wundt, called *Der Intellektualismus in der Griechischen Ethik* (Leipzig, 1907). Wilhelm Nestle adopted it in "Intellektualismus und Mystik in der Griechischen Philosophie," *Neue Jahrbücher für das Klassische Altertum*, 49 (1922), 137-57. He regards Plato's "intellectualization" of ethics as "genuinely Greek" and the fulfillment in doctrine of the native genius of the Greek race (pp. 138,144). The latter he contrasts with the barbarian love of fantasy and the voluntarism of the Romans. The theory has continued to gain adherents in recent years. G. C. Field, *Plato and His Contemporaries* (2nd ed.; London, 1948), p. 105, says, concerning the belief that if we know what is good, nothing more is needed to make us do it, "this is not a peculiarity of Plato or of Socrates, but is simply a natural development of the assumptions of Greek thought and Greek language." Lionel Pearson and Bruno Snell have adopted the theory in qualified form. Pearson, in his book *Popular Ethics in Ancient Greece* (Stanford, 1962), p. 52, says that "throughout Greek literature a man's moral worth is estimated largely in terms of his intelligence. . . [Plato] does not mark a revolutionary change in Greek thought." Snell, in "Das Frühste Zeugnis über Sokrates," *Philologus*, 97 (1948), 132, mentions as common knowledge, requiring no supporting evidence, that "schon der frühgriechischen Ethik ist ja das 'Wissen' bestimmend für das richtige Handeln." Among later authors, however, he excludes at least Euripides from this generalization.

tions which rest like a fog over the intellectual history of early Greece and prevent, among other things, a just appraisal of Plato's debt to his predecessors. This debt is real and undeniable, and is nowhere more evident than in his ethical paradoxes. An effort will be made in the next chapter to show that those paradoxes are best understood as the juncture of several lines of fifth-century philosophical and religious thought. But the present state of the question requires that we first prove what scholars of an earlier age might have thought unnecessary, that the Socratic paradoxes were paradoxes.

Undeniably, much in Greek literature seems to prove the opposite. A mountain of evidence can be brought forward to attest to the "ingrained habit of thought" mentioned above. Any student of Greek literature before Plato, for example, soon learns that words like σοφία, γνώμη, σωφροσύνη, ἀφροσύνη, ἄνοια, and ἀμαθία frequently have a moral reference. The σοφία of the Seven Wise Men is practical and moral. It is expressed in admonitions to observe the mean, honor one's father, not to marry above one's station, avoid excessive pleasures, guard one's tongue while drinking, and obey the laws.[4] The word σοφία keeps these ethical connotations in many passages of Pindar. Wise men, he says, bear nobly the power given by god; they praise moderation, and they do not aspire too high.[5] This usage is not confined to Pindar. Theognis claims that he wishes to keep "the rule of wisdom" in his praise and blame of wine, and he joins virtue with wisdom as if they formed a compound idea; Xenophanes attributes to himself a wisdom that can produce a well-ordered state; and Heraclitus says that wisdom lies in speaking the

4. Diels-Kranz, I, p. 63. The apophthegms are those of Cleobulus, nos. 1, 2, 18; Solon, nos. 1, 3; and Chilon, nos. 2, 19. The meanings of σοφία are discussed by Bruno Snell, *Die Ausdrücke für den Begriff des Wissens in der Vorplatonischen Philosophie*, Philologische Untersuchungen, no. 29 (Berlin, 1924), 1-20.

5. Pindar, *Pyth.* 5.12 ff., frag. 216 (Schroeder, 204 in Bowra's ed. of Pindar), *Olymp.* 3.44-45. Cf. *Isth.* 7.42 ff., *Olymp.* 5.26. However, even a σοφός can be led astray by a troubled heart, so as to commit murder (*Olymp.* 7.30-31). When Solon came to visit Croesus, the Athenian's reputation for σοφία had persuaded the king that he would know more about true happiness than other men (Herodotus, 1.30). In Aeschylus' *Prometheus Bound*, an admonition to yield to Zeus is called σοφὴ εὐβουλία and its opposite ἄνοια (1038, 1079). The chorus of the same play, speaking of Io's fate, calls the man σοφός who said that one should marry in one's own station (887-93).

truth, in heeding nature, and in acting according to its requirements.[6]    ϒ Ɩ ς 𝛼 𝑜 𝑟𝑦

In all these passages the word used is σοφία or σοφός, but these
are not the only terms to have both intellectual and moral connotations. Γνώμη, says Theognis, is the gods' best gift to man; it enables him to rise above insolence and arrogance. A good man holds
fast to it always and so can endure good fortune and ill. This
"straight judgment" is rooted in his breast, and his thoughts are
just.[7]

Σωφροσύνη, good sense or soundness of spirit, is sometimes an intellectual, sometimes a moral virtue. At *Iliad* 21.462, where Apollo
says he would not be σαόφρων to fight with Poseidon on behalf of
mere mortals, it seems to have no moral overtones. It does, however, at *Odyssey* 4.158, where Telemachus is too σαόφρων to speak
out boldly before Menelaus. At *Odyssey* 23.13 and 30 it is expressed in proper behavior, specifically in not mocking one's lady
or betraying one's father's secret plans.[8] At Herodotus 1.4 it is the
good sense not to make a fuss over abducted women, and the contrary adjective is ἀνόητος. In Attic the moral connotations of σώφρων
are dominant; it means, in the definition of Liddell-Scott-Jones,
"having control over the sensual desires, temperate, self-controlled,
chaste." But the other meaning, "intelligent" or "sensible," used in
a way that has no implication of moral goodness, is found even in
Attic.

The gap between the two meanings of σωφροσύνη seems at its
widest when we compare Aristophanes' *Clouds* 1071-74, where τὸ
σωφρονεῖν is the privation of pleasure, with Euripides' *Cyclops* 336-
38, where οἱ σώφρονες are said to have the good sense to eat and
drink freely, and to recognize no god but their bellies. The peasant
at Euripides' *Electra* 50 ff. refers to the moral ambiguity of the
word in Attic when he says that those who would criticize him as
a fool for not touching Electra measure τὸ σῶφρον by false standards.

6. Theognis, 876, 790 (where the reading is admittedly uncertain); Xenophanes 21 B 2 (Diels-Kranz); Heraclitus 22 B 112 (Diels-Kranz). The σοφία attributed by Simonides to Pittacus is practical (frag. 5, Bergk).

7. Theognis, 1171 ff., 319 ff., 395-96.

8. At Phocylides, frag. 9 (Bergk), σωφροσύνη is a moral quality, associated
with κόσμος and opposed to light-mindedness.

On the other hand, the two meanings come together when σώφρων is used of one whose modest demeanor expresses the good sense of behaving like a mere man and not a god.[9]

Immoral behavior, on the other hand, is ἀφροσύνη, ἄνοια, or ἀμαθία. The first is applied to the behavior of Penelope's suitors,[10] and the fact that Achilles is not ἄφρων is said to have a bearing on how he will treat Priam, at *Iliad* 24.157. At *Iliad* 5.761 Hera describes Ares, who she says is behaving lawlessly, as ἄφρονα, and Ares uses the same word of Athena at 5.875. The word ἄνοια can also be applied to wrongdoing, as at Euripides' *Hippolytus* 398. In the same author's *Electra*, when Orestes recoils at the imminent prospect of carrying out Apollo's command to kill his mother, the word he applies to the offending oracle is ἀμαθία. Electra replies, "If Apollo is foolish, then who are wise?" (971 ff.)

One could multiply examples, but it should be already clear that Greek words which the dictionaries define as "wise" or "foolish," with their synonyms and derivatives, are used with great frequency to mean or imply "morally good" or "morally bad." The Greeks sometimes speak as if the knowledge of what one should do were the most important, if not the only, requisite of moral behavior. How far our estimate of their intent is accurate will appear later in this chapter.

When we examine the causes of this prominence of wisdom, one reason stands out with special clarity. This is the ancient appeal to the motive of profit or happiness, or to the fear of punishment.

9. For this last meaning, see Euripides' *Philoctetes*, frag. 799 (Nauck), and Sophocles' *Ajax*, 118-133. At Antiphon the Sophist 87 B 58 (Diels-Kranz), σωφροσύνη is the prudent self-restraint which checks impulses that, if indulged, would lead to one's own harm. Here also, the two meanings of σωφροσύνη are reconciled, but in a nontheological context. The word σώφρων means "sensible" at Euripides' *Orestes*, 1509, and at Sophocles' *Philoctetes*, 304. Verb, noun, and adverb all appear with meanings corresponding to this in other passages in Attic. See, for example, Thucydides, 3.44, 4.60, 4.61, 4.64, 6.11, 1.80, 3.43, 1.32; and Sophocles' *Philoctetes*, 1259. When σωφροσύνη means "good sense" or "intelligence" it often carries the connotation of "caution." Hence the phrase ἀλόγως σωφρονοῦσιν (Thucydides, 6.79.2), and the tendency of extremists, recorded by Thucydides (3.82.4), to attack those who possessed this virtue as cowards. There is a useful treatment of this whole subject in Helen North's article "A Period of Opposition to *Sôphrosynê* in Greek Thought," *TAPA*, 78 (1947), 1-17.

10. *Odyssey*, 16.278, 24.457. The context of ἄφρων at Odyssey, 23.12 also suggests the connotation of blameworthiness. See below, n. 60.

The fool does not mark the consequences of his crimes and omissions; the wise man does, and so he is virtuous. This is the natural interpretation of _Odyssey_ 22.374, where Odysseus, having killed all the suitors but having spared Medon, tells him to lay to heart and tell others that good deeds are far better than wicked ones. He has saved him to show him how true this is. The suitors, who ignored it, were both knaves and fools (2.282). So were his own companions, those "fools (νήπιοι), who ate up the cattle of Hyperion the Sun; but he took from them their day of return" (1.8-9). The punishment explains the epithet. The prudent man, like Chryses the priest, honors the gods in prayer and sacrifice and so can expect their help in trouble; if he is Hector, doomed to death, he can at least command their sympathy) (_Iliad_ 1.40, 22.170). When Athena stops Achilles from drawing his sword on Agamemnon, she does so with a promise of tripled gifts. He obeys her with the comment that obedience to the gods is the better course; it brings divine favor (1.212-217).

Hesiod, castigating Perses, the "fool" (νήπιε, _Works and Days_ 286), harps constantly on the theme that the unjust man lives to regret his crime, surrounded as he is by the watchful eye of Zeus and his thrice ten thousand spirits. "He does harm to himself who harms another, and a wicked plan is worst for the planner." Those, on the other hand, who give straight judgments find that their city flourishes and their people prosper.[11] Maxim supports poetry in presenting virtue as the wiser course. "Incontinence brings hurt," said Thales, and Solon advised, "Flee pleasure, which begets pain."[12]

To find human motives reduced in a systematic way to the pursuit of interest or glory and the avoidance of pain or loss, we must turn to Thucydides. In this respect the historian, in spite of all differences of religious belief and intellectual subtlety, is the heir of Hesiod. Turning his unsentimental and penetrating gaze on the partisans of Athens and Sparta alike, he finds that their motives, in peace and war, in plague and revolution, are essentially the same.

11. Hesiod, _Works and Days_, 217 ff., 225 ff., 252 ff., 265 ff., 280 ff., 286.
12. Diels-Kranz, I, pp. 63-64.

The Athenians, for example, acknowledge three motives to be at the root of their imperialism: fear, honor, and self-interest. All of these they regard as honorable and universal. The Lacedaemonians vote to make war on Athens, professedly to punish a wicked city for its injustices and to come to the aid of deserving allies, but they are in reality more swayed by their fear of Athenian power.[13] Within the society of Athens itself, as Pericles describes it in the Funeral Oration, public virtue is supported by the sanctions of punitive law and the good opinion of one's peers, by the knowledge that the happiness and liberty of the citizens depend upon their courage in war, and by the prizes awarded for merit. "For where the rewards of virtue are the greatest, there too are the best citizens."[14]

It is only natural that the plague, in disrupting all the sanctions and rewards to which Pericles appeals, should have produced widespread immorality and lawlessness (2.53). The account of the Funeral Oration and that of the plague, which follows closely, are meant to produce more than an effective dramatic juxtaposition. They throw a searching light on the motives for public-spirited behavior in Athens. An efficient and happy society, founded on intelligent self-interest, broke down when it no longer seemed intelligent to be just. Thucydides' account of the moral effects of the plague makes it evident that these resulted from a nullification or reversal of the same motives that made Athenians law-observing in peacetime. The fear of being brought to account no longer prevented crime; on the other hand, fear of infection caused abandonment of some victims. A sense of honor led the scrupulous to nurse their sick friends and die of the contagion. Virtue brought no more profit than vice. The religious and irreligious perished alike, and so terror of the gods no longer deterred malefactors (2.51-53). All these motives were acknowledged in the Funeral Oration before their orderly relationship was disrupted by the accident of an epi-

13. Thucydides, 1.75.3, 1.76.2, 1.88, 1.23.6. The Corinthians, on embassy to Athens before the war, insist that their cause is just but emphasize too that it is in Athens' interest to support them. Justice and expediency again coincide in their speech at the second council of Lacedaemon (1.123-24).

14. Thucydides, 2.46.1. Cf. 2.37.3, 2.43.2-5. Pearson, *Popular Ethics*, p. 163, calls the Funeral Oration "perhaps the most extreme example, before Plato, of the so-called intellectualist approach to ethics."

demic. Even religious piety, ignored by Pericles, is no new thing, since it is introduced here as a species of fear.[15]

The lowering of public spirit which plague and invasion had brought about in Athens was met by Pericles, in characteristic fashion, with an appeal to patriotism and a shrewd reminder that

15. Thucydides' analysis of Athenian morality is only obscured by the common assumption that δέος at 2.37.3 (τὰ δημόσια διὰ δέος μάλιστα οὐ παρανομοῦμεν) is different in kind from δέος as used elsewhere in the History. For example, E. F. Poppo, De bello Peloponnesiaco, libri octo (2nd ed.; Leipzig, 1866-83), translates διὰ δέος as "propter reverentiam" and cites, with evident approval, Krueger's explanatory phrase "sittliche Scheu" ( K. W. Krueger [ed.], [3rd ed., fasc. 1; Berlin, 1860], ad loc.), E.-A. Bétant, Lexicon Thucydideum (Hildesheim, 1961; reprint of 1843 ed.), 1.227, translates it as "ob reverentiam." B. Jowett's English version of Thucydides (2nd ed.; Oxford, 1900), 1.128, reads "a spirit of reverence pervades our public acts." A. W. Gomme, A Historical Commentary on Thucydides, II (Oxford, 1956), 112, says, "δέος does not occur elsewhere in Thucydides in this sense of 'proper fear,' 'respect' = αἰδώς, αἰσχύνη . . . but there is no difficulty." J. de Romilly, in "La Crainte dans l'Oeuvre de Thucydide," Classica et Mediaevalia, 17 (1956), 119-27, an article which demonstrates the major role played by δέος in Thucydidean psychology, ethics, and politics, nevertheless makes a special case of this passage, where "une seule fois, dans son oeuvre, δέος désigne une crainte morale" (p. 126).

But if Thucydides chose to write δέος rather than αἰδώς (a word used only by the Spartan Archidamus, at 1.84.3), he may well have done so to preserve that economy of conception and of terminology which marks his whole work. If so, there is no need to attribute to Pericles a notion of δέος at variance with the normal Thucydidean one. Reluctance to accept this seems to rest on the belief that Pericles would never, on this solemn and public occasion, have suggested that the Athenian at home acted from the same motives as the Athenian abroad. Hence "reverentia" at 2.37.3, but "fear" at 1.75.3. Yet we do an injustice to the Funeral Oration if we stress its idealism at the expense of its clarity and candor. Pericles acknowledges, even emphasizes, the role in Athenian society of the familiar motives of honor and self-interest (compare 1.75.3 with 2.37.3 and 2.43.2 ff.); even though he loftily dismisses niggling calculations of profit, his objection is not to the principle but to the tone and manner of putting it into practice. To make him speak of a "spirit of reverence [that] pervades our public acts" (Jowett) is to substitute for the Greek term, which has a well-recognized place in Thucydides' thought, an English term whose meaning in this nonreligious context is far from clear. There are some good comments on this passage in Victor Ehrenberg's Sophocles and Pericles (Oxford, 1954). He explains δέος as "fear of legal punishment or social disgrace" (p. 40).

Revolution achieved in Corcyra what plague had brought about in Athens. The normal bonds of law and tradition, which had identified public order with the welfare of the individual, were broken, and chaos ensued. Desire for profit and honor, which in the Athens of Pericles' Funeral Oration were channeled towards the common good, drove the Corcyrean factions instead to abandon the common welfare and pursue every moment's pleasure (3.82.8). Fear, no longer the support of oaths, reinforced treachery, since it was accounted safer to be first in violating a pledge.

the security of the state is the best guarantee of each citizen's welfare. Once again, more bluntly than in the Funeral Oration, altruism is the higher self-interest.[16]

In international affairs, this kind of intellectualism takes the form of _Realpolitik_. Diodotus, who urges forgiveness for the majority of the rebellious Mytilenians, waves aside the question of justice and says that sensible men (εἰ σωφρονοῦμεν) will consider only their own advantage in these affairs (3.44.1). It is policy, he insists, rather than pity, which should lead the wise statesman to limit punishment to the most guilty (3.48). He closes his address with an epigrammatic rejection of folly (3.48.2). The Spartans too, though addicted in their policy decisions to preachments about justice and an adherence to legal form, are actually as self-serving as the Athenians. This, at any rate, is Thucydides' interpretation of the trial of the Plataeans, a travesty staged by Sparta to lend color to their attempt to insure the loyalty of Thebes.[17]

Although Thucydidean ethics has its seeds in Homer and Hesiod, in the historian the intellectualist bias has carried all else before it, including religious reverence and the disinterested sentiments of friendship and compassion. It will not do to make his the canonical Greek view. This _caveat,_ moreover, requires something more than a few reservations about the unique ruthlessness of his "sensible" statesmen. It is sometimes assumed that the Greek ideal was at first a self-centered σοφία, with immediate personal profit or pleasure as the end, and later became a higher σοφία, serving profit or pleasure delayed, purified of crassness, and extended to the group. This would, in a sense, be moral progress: it is the way of civilized men to behave lawfully, generously, and loyally. Their behavior, moreover, need contain no genuinely altruistic motive. The Athenian described in the Funeral Oration served himself best in his loyalty to the state. So did the citizen of Plato's _Republic_, who

16. Thucydides, 2.60. There is a distant and ironic echo of Pericles' argument in the words of the turncoat Alcibiades, addressed many years later to the Spartans: τό τε φιλόπολι οὐκ ἐν ᾧ ἀδικοῦμαι ἔχω, ἀλλ᾿ ἐν ᾧ ἀσφαλῶς ἐπολιτεύθην (6. 92.4).

17. Thucydides, 3.68.4-5. This incident alone justifies the remark of the Athenian ambassador to Melos, himself an exponent of ruthless self-interest, that the Lacedaemonians call the pleasant noble and the expedient just (5.105.4).

lived a life in harmony with his own deepest desires and looked forward to a happy after-life. Nevertheless, to portray the evolution of Greek ethics as a progress in the management of self-interest would be a half-truth. Intelligence is always important in Greek moral thought, but, with a few exceptions like Thucydides and Plato, men with a devotion to consistency and philosophical rigor, it nowhere supersedes or absorbs other virtues. A balanced estimate of the importance of intelligence or wisdom in Greek ethics requires a look at some of the literature in which it plays a different role from that just sketched.

Other virtues were not always thought of as expressions of wisdom; in fact, they were at times opposed to it. Friendship, pity, kindliness, loyalty, and shame all held a strong and independent place in Greek moral sentiment. They were sometimes defended for their practical value: one can normally expect that favors will be returned and loyalty rewarded. But to make this a universal motive requires that we force unlikely implications on many Greek texts and do violence to others. At times Greek moral sentiment simply takes no account of self-interest and may even demand that it be abandoned.[18] This can take the form of an attack on σοφία.

18. Many readers will accept this without argument or documentation. Yet it must be defended in the face of statements like, "the belief that human beings should be treated as ends-in-themselves rather than as means is totally un-Greek" (Arthur W. H. Adkins, " 'Friendship' and 'Self-Sufficiency' in Homer and Aristotle," *CQ*, N.S. 13 [1963], 33). According to Adkins, friendly behavior in Homer, for example, is not by nature altruistic. It "makes, and is intended to make, the other person a φίλον object on whose help one can rely when one needs it" (p. 36). But Adkins offers us a sociological analysis which attempts also to be a study in motivation. For a sociologist, or a biologist, it may be true to say, "the possessive affection [that Homeric man] feels for what is φίλον is based on the need and desire for self-preservation" (p. 33). Friendship normally benefits society and the human species. But any individual, however tactful, who thought of his friends solely as means to his own self-preservation or advantage would have been accounted a false friend by most Greeks. Sophocles and Euripides both have plays written on this assumption (see text below).

Bruno Snell, in *Discovery of the Mind*, trans. T. G. Rosenmeyer (New York, 1960), has drawn us a slightly more qualified picture of the self-serving Greek who helps others on the principle *do ut des* (p. 168). Snell makes friendship, justice, and compassion logical and historical developments of the love of profit, happiness, and glory, aided by certain religious taboos. Of friendship he says, "Side by side with our earlier concept of morality as profit deferred to the future, we now have a new idea—profit extended to the many. In the circle of one's relatives and friends, the *philoi*, profit becomes a common cause;

Three authors will suffice as illustrations. The first, Homer, stands at the head of Greek literature, while the others, Sophocles and Euripides, wrote in the age of the sophists, when wisdom in the service of self-interest was a well-recognized ideal.

Achilles, in spite of Athena's successful appeal to his desire for profit at the beginning of the *Iliad*, is more often the very model of the uncalculating man. His conduct in abandoning his comrades and retiring to his tent, because of an affront suffered at Agamemnon's hands, might seem to fit easily into an ethics of personal glory and aggrandizement. But no scheme as simple as that will explain Achilles' character. In the ninth book he turns down with scorn Odysseus' long catalogue of the gifts offered by Agamemnon, and he rejects Phoenix's admonition that, if he delays, he may have to fight with no prospect of gifts at all. But he is moved by Ajax's simple reminder of their friendship. Odysseus, who appeals artfully to his sense of self-interest, evokes from Achilles only injured pride and a ringing declaration that he will sail the next day. His response to Phoenix already implies some doubt, and finally, he concedes to Ajax that he will stay, though he will not fight yet.[19] This is a small foreshadowing of his loyalty to the dead Patroclus, which, though cruel and perverse in its expression, proves that Greek friendship could outlast the usefulness of the one befriended. Achilles regards it as an absolute commitment that not even death can annul.[20] His treatment of Hector's corpse is an outrage to pity and shame, but his courtesy toward old Priam in the last book is proof that ordinarily he honors those virtues too. Priam's first words, "Remember your own father," invoke a motive which is beyond profit or even friendship. Profit there is, in the ransom offered

---

no one harms his neighbor" (p. 167). But this interpretation links by an extraneous logic motives which the Greeks regarded as autonomous and often, in their literature, set in conflict.

19. *Iliad*, 9.357-61, 618-19, 650-55. Cedric H. Whitman, *Homer and the Heroic Tradition* (Cambridge, Mass., 1958), is quite right in saying that "the embassy does not fail entirely to move Achilles" (p. 190). But his great stress on Phoenix's speech leaves unexplained the relevance of what he calls "the brief and touching appeal of Ajax" (*ibid.*). The influence of what Phoenix says cannot be denied; yet it is Ajax who, by stressing the claims of friendship (lines 630, 642), produces a definite change in Achilles' plans.

20. *Iliad*, 22.389-90; 23.19-23, 69-70, 95-96, 179-80.

for the corpse and accepted;[21] but in the scene of courtesy and compassion between the two men, this note of prudent self-interest is of small weight. Of even less weight is fear of divine punishment for outraging a suppliant. As an institution, the supplication of enemies no doubt required the support of profit and fear, but Homer presents Achilles' action in another light, and so reveals a kind of nobility which is not reducible to any Thucydidean category.

Elsewhere in Homer it is often hard to find disinterested motives which are not accompanied by some expectation of profit. But a mixture of motives is not an identification of them. So, for example, we can find genuine altruism in the open-handed hospitality of Eumaeus in the *Odyssey*, which comes from compassion and not only from fear of Zeus (14.389). He is faithful, moreover, to the absent and presumably dead Odysseus in spite of pessimism about his prospects of a reward (14.61 ff., 14.137-47). Philoetius too, though he nurses a faint hope of Odysseus' return and, by implication, of his own reward, appears more concerned by the likely sufferings of his master than by his own profit or loss (20.197 ff.). Both of these servants link their own prosperity with Odysseus', but the bond of loyalty is for neither of them basically prudential.

Achilles, the uncalculating and generous man, is only the first example of a familiar type in Greek literature. His spirit reappears in the *Philoctetes* of Sophocles, produced in 409 B.C. In this play the young Neoptolemus, Achilles' gallant and instinctively generous son, has accompanied Odysseus to Lemnos in an attempt to bring to Troy the bowman Philoctetes, whose presence is essential to a Greek victory. Since the Greeks, years before this, had abandoned Philoctetes, wounded and in pain, he cannot now be brought to Troy by means other than deceit and constraint. To these means Neoptolemus commits himself at the instruction of Odysseus, but he soon finds his chosen course of action unbearable. In dramatizing his ordeal, the *Philoctetes* opposes the claims of wisdom to those of friendship and justice, and puts the former in the meanest possible light.[22] Since the antagonists in this drama are the cleverest

21. *Iliad*, 24.44-45, 486; 23.594.
22. This may seem an oversimplification, since there is the added compli-

of the Greeks and the son of Achilles, it is natural that it should
derive its intellectual tension from the antitheses of candor and
falsehood, friendship and cleverness. In this way, Sophocles repeats
for the late fifth century a theme present in the *Iliad*.[23] But his play
belongs to an age of philosophical analysis, and it enacts the conflict of ideas as well as of men. One of these ideas is σοφία. On
Odysseus' lips the word is a boast or an excuse, but Neoptolemus
and Philoctetes rarely refer to it without contempt.[24] In spite of
this, a playwright bound to a consistent intellectualism would have
represented the young man's defiance of Odysseus as a revulsion
from mere cleverness in favor of a higher wisdom or a higher self-
interest.[25] No Platonist, knowing that the just is inseparable from
the wise, could have rested content with the line in which Neoptolemus says of his actions, "If they are just, they are better than wise"
(1246). But justice in this play is not a higher wisdom, nor are
friendship and pity, motives aroused in Neoptolemus by the sight of
a man helpless, dishonored, and betrayed.[26] Throughout the play,

---

cation of a struggle in Neoptolemus between loyalty to his comrades and loyalty to Philoctetes (cf. 94 and 911). But the larger struggle is between him
and Odysseus, or—in different terms—between his own nature and what he
has learned from Odysseus. This takes the form of a conflict of friendship and
justice against "wisdom."

23. See *Iliad*, 9.312-313 (echoed weakly at *Philoctetes*, 108), and other passages from the *Iliad* cited above. Achilles as a model of friendship is alluded.
to at 434 of this play. We are, moreover, constantly reminded that Neoptolemus has inherited Achilles' nature. See lines 3-4, 79, 874, 902 ff., 940, 971,
1066, 1284, 1310 ff. Odysseus, on the other hand, is the child of Sisyphus
(1311), and the σοφὸς παλαιστής (431), whose brother in spirit is Thersites,
also a σοφός (440 ff.).

24. An exception is 423. But see 431-32, 1015, 1246. Cf. ἐσωφρόνησας at
1259. In Odysseus, σοφία subserves an unscrupulous desire for gain or mastery
(81-85, 111), which is foreign to Neoptolemus' native instinct (94-95).

25. Line 1244, which might in another context be read as a contrast between cleverness and moral wisdom, can only mean here that Odysseus' threat
is nonsense.

26. It is Neoptolemus' "terrible pity" which moves him to take the side of
Philoctetes (965-66), and later to abandon any hope of glory at Troy or
honor among the Achaeans (1404-1405). This last motive was originally
strong in Neoptolemus (119). Philoctetes appeals to his sense of reputation
at 967-68, but his primary and more emphatic appeal, even
in those passages, is to pity. Pity, moreover, is the motive which Neoptolemus
himself acknowledges at 965 and 1074, to which is added his shock at the
inherent baseness and injustice of the deed (108, 1228, 1234, 1251). His
phrasing at 906 and 908, even if it implies (which it need not) concern for
his public repute, and his admission of shame at 120, cannot prove that anxiety for his reputation played a dominant role in his change of mind.

the most insistent moral note is expressed in the word φιλία and its cognates. As introduced by Philoctetes and repeated emotionally through the scene of his first appearance, these words are already weighted with dramatic irony.[27] The tension they introduce is moral as well as emotional, since Neoptolemus feigns a friendship for Philoctetes which the latter accepts. The young man's pledge of friendship (585-86, 671), added to pity for a suppliant (930), and his innate revulsion from deceit will soon outweigh in his mind all considerations of expediency and σοφία. In the end, the two men become genuine friends, and Neoptolemus, in giving up all his plans, accepts the demands of that friendship as absolute.[28] The resulting impasse cannot be solved short of divine intervention.

In the same decade Euripides produced his *Orestes*, a play equally untrammeled by ethical intellectualism. It deals with the troubles of Orestes shortly after he has killed in vengeance his mother Clytemnestra. Maddened by his ordeal and threatened with violent punishment at the hands of an angry city, he looks in vain to his uncle Menelaus for help. While Menelaus temporizes, Orestes is supported instead by the friendship of Pylades and the loyalty of his sister Electra. Together they plan to revenge themselves upon the disloyal Menelaus by killing his wife Helen and seizing his daughter Hermione. Only the intervention of Apollo averts catastrophe.

The "wise man" in this play is Menelaus, who declines to concern himself with Orestes, now under imminent sentence of death, though bound to him by ties of blood and gratitude.[29] Wisdom is Menelaus' touchstone, and the words σοφία and σοφός are a mannerism of his speech.[30] But in practice his "wisdom" produces hesitation, caution, sensitivity to threats, and inaction.[31] Though contemptible, Menelaus retains a certain shallow dignity. The ultimate caricature of the σοφός is not he but Helen's Phrygian slave, who

27. See lines 224, 228, 229, 234, 237, 242. The theme of φιλία recurs at 361, 390, 421, 434, 469, 492, 511, 530-31, 558, 586-87, 665, 671-73, 705, 1004, 1018, 1121, 1128, 1145, 1290, 1301, 1375, 1383, 1385, 1467.

28. Lines 1375, 1383, 1385, 1402.

29. *Orestes*, 244, 453, 482, 719.

30. *Ibid.*, 397, 415, 488, 490, 491, 710, 716.

31. *Ibid.*, 537, 626, 635, 696 ff., 748.

cowers before Orestes in terror at the latter's threatened violence.[32] This barbaric figure, half comical and half pitiful, turns out to be a man with a philosophy of life, which he sums up in the statement that sensible men always choose self-preservation. "Well-spoken," says Orestes, "Your intelligence saves you."[33]

In this play, as in the *Philoctetes*, the claim of friendship is absolute for those who accept it. "I am not wise," says Orestes, "but am a true friend to my friends" (424). Pylades exemplifies this ideal even better, by remaining loyal in the face of death (1072). In the judgment of Menelaus, to talk of death was simply not σοφόν (415). Pylades would have granted the point and yet rejected the course of action it seemed to imply, since in his moral world, and in that of his two comrades Orestes and Electra, what must be avoided at all costs is not folly but treachery.[34] The three comrades become so completely obsessed by the principle, "Help your friends, destroy your enemies,"[35] that they utterly abandon discretion and self-criticism. In the end, when they turn on Hermione, who though a useful tool for their vengeful plan is also a true friend and kin to them all, their guiding principle proves self-negating (1329 ff.). To destroy their enemies they must destroy their friends too. In the *Orestes*, therefore, Euripides means to glorify neither Pylades' friendship nor Menelaus' wisdom; the one is destructive, the other contemptible. But that is beside the point here. What matters is that the play shows that a Greek like Pylades could accept loyalty and altruism without first transmuting them into "wisdom" or a higher self-interest. Theognis had summed up this kind of loyalty long before Euripides made it the substance of his drama. May

32. This has already been remarked by Nathan A. Greenberg in his article "Euripides' *Orestes*: An Interpretation," *HSCP*, 66 (1962), 188.

33. *Orestes*, 1509, 1523, 1524. Orestes' contemptuous remark serves equally well to characterize the Phrygian himself and Menelaus. See especially line 415.

34. See lines 719, 740, 1057, 1087, 1228, 1237. Contrast Tyndareus who, provoked by Menelaus' canting use of σοφία, phrases his own attack on Orestes in the terms of ethical intellectualism (493 ff.). On the other hand, Orestes' use of σώφρων at 558, and Pylades' use of it at 1132, both express the normal Attic sense of "modest" or "chaste" and imply no more intellectualism than does Charmides' explanation of σωφροσύνη as αἰδώς (Plato, *Charmides* 160e). At line 1180, τὸ συνετόν is practical intelligence rather than moral insight.

35. See lines 748, 794, 450, 454-55, 652, 665-66, 727-28, 735, 802-3, 804-6, 1095-96, 1155, 1192, 1605.

heaven fall upon me, he said, if I will not come to the aid of those who love me and be to my enemies a sorrow and great pain.[36]

It hardly needs to be said that the passages quoted above imply no systematic denigration of σοφία as word or ideal on the part of Sophocles or Euripides. Other plays might be quoted to disprove that claim. The *Philoctetes* itself knows σοφός as a complimentary epithet, used of Nestor (423). What the passages show is merely that there is no ineluctable tendency in the Greek mind toward ethical intellectualism. A Greek found it perfectly possible to speak of pity as the unwise choice, of friendship as the imprudent course, and of cowardice as intelligent. He was not harried by the Socratic compulsion to ask himself at every moment, "Is not intelligence always a good thing?" It was at times a bad thing, and that was all there was to it.[37] The common man and the poet do not ordinarily pursue consistency any further. When they acknowledge, as they often do, the separateness of wisdom and cunning or wisdom and polymathy, they are as apt to do so by twisting language into paradox as by distinguishing terms. So Euripides, at *Bacchae* 395, has τὸ σοφὸν δ'οὐ σοφία. The apparent recalcitrance of words can always be overcome to serve the needs of context, the insights of genius, and the linguistic requirements of a new age. Because of the last, most words show stages of development, and for a number of them development means a descent, in successive

36. Theognis, 869-72. Disinterested φιλία is also prominent in the *Iphigeneia in Tauris*, where Orestes and Pylades are prepared each to sacrifice his own life for the other (605-608, 674 ff.). There may be a touch of enlightened self-interest in Pylades' remark at 678 ff. that he wants to escape the reproach of disloyalty, but this motive is distinctively subordinate in emphasis. The chorus of Greek women, with only a vague and uncertain promise of ultimate rescue, shows selfless friendship for Iphigeneia by its complicity in the escape at 1075. Cf. *Medea*, 85-86, which implies disapproval of selfishness.

Altruism finds a place as well in fifth century political and ethical thought. Democritus advises the strong to help the weak (Diels-Kranz, 68 B 255), and though the advantage of reciprocal help is not overlooked, this is far from being the central motive. Pity and comradeship are more important. The point is made by Eric A. Havelock, *The Liberal Temper in Greek Politics* (New Haven and London, 1957), p. 144. In short, unless the Greeks deceived themselves utterly, they did not always act, or expect others always to act, from self-interest.

37. Nestle, therefore, is misleading when he generalizes from Pindar's usage of σοφία and says, "Weisheit und Tüchtigkeit gehören für Pindar *als echten Griechen* untrennbar zusammen" (Wilhelm Nestle, *Vom Mythos zum Logos* [2nd ed.; Stuttgart, 1942], p. 164. My italics).

contexts, from honor to opprobrium. The word σοφός is used more than once in Herodotus to mean "cunning" or "clever," a use which already divests it of the ethical connotations it so often has elsewhere.[38] It is only one step from this usage to Sophocles' phrase at *Philoctetes* 1015, ἐν κακοῖς σοφόν. A parallel logic has produced Thucydides' word κακοξυνετώτερος, Euripides' phrase λίαν φρονεῖν, and, finally, the epigram of Cleon reported by Thucydides, which fully and consciously sheds the intellectualist bias: ἀμαθία τε μετὰ σωφροσύνης ὠφελιμώτερον ἢ δεξιότης μετὰ ἀκολασίας.[39]

If it was possible for a Greek to reject prudent self-interest outright as a moral ideal and to put friendship or pity in its stead, then neither wisdom nor profit held the unchallenged dominance in Greek ethics commonly attributed to them. That much is clear. But it would be a mistake even to concede that when wisdom *was* honored it was always thought to serve profit or pleasure. The importance of practical wisdom should not blind us to the fact that a Greek could value knowledge solely for its own sake. This conception of a wisdom which served no further end became fully ripe in Plato and, as later chapters will show, is integral to his doctrine of the philosophic life. In quite a different form, it appears also in the *Oedipus Tyrannus* of Sophocles, a play which delineates one man's passage from ignorance to knowledge. By no accident, this is also a passage from happiness and power to misery and degradation. Oedipus, haunted by oracles that predict his fall into monstrous crimes, is at first fool enough to think he can evade his fate and prove the god in error. He is forced to a wisdom that Sophocles recommends to us all and which Pindar preached in his own way: the greatest man is less than god. Yet in Sophocles' play this wisdom has nothing to recommend it but its own intrinsic value. It bears no promise of profit, of happiness, or, as yet, of di-

38. Herodotus, 2.121.ε.5, 1.68.1, 3.4.2, 3.85.1, 3.127.2, 5.21.2, 5.50.2, 5.23.2. Snell discusses the appearance of this meaning in *Die Ausdrücke*, p. 14.

39. Thucydides, 6.76.4, Euripides' *Iphigeneia in Aulis*, 924, Thucydides, 3.37.3. Passages which contradict intellectualist suppositions are to be found everywhere. I append a few: Sophocles' *Electra*, 345-46 and 1027 (scorns the good sense of being a traitor and a coward); Euripides' *Alcestis*, 1093 (praises a foolish act); Xenophon's *Memorabilia*, 1.6.11 (Antiphon calls Socrates just but not wise); Anonymus Iamblichi, 89.3.1 (Diels-Kranz) (implies that one can be wise but unjust).

vine favor. Its merit is simply that the possession of it ennobles a man who formerly was sunk in illusion. The play, moreover, does not suggest that Apollo would have revoked his oracle had Oedipus been humbler or more pious. His folly is in this respect unlike that of Odysseus' men or the suitors, who caused their own ruin. *Oedipus Tyrannus* could not have ended, as the *Antigone* does, with a declaration that wisdom is the greatest part of happiness (1347-48). Instead, we have the cry at lines 316-17, "How terrible to be wise, when wisdom brings no profit." The speaker is Teiresias, and he speaks of himself. But, like much else in this play, the lines are ironic and proleptic, and apply ultimately to the king. *Oedipus Tyrannus*, like the other literary evidence cited in the last few pages, shows that insurmountable difficulties await any attempt to reduce all Greek ethics to a rule of practical wisdom.

The contention that the Greeks always connected good morals with intelligence rests not only on arguments from Greek literature but also on linguistic proofs. These are in a way more formidable, because they deal with the very categories of Greek thought. They profess to show that classical Greek from the time of Homer was so committed in vocabulary and idiom to ethical intellectualism that only a dislocation of ancient habits of speech and thought could have produced any other theory. On this view, the emergence of Socrates was natural, almost inevitable. These linguistic arguments have earned such wide credence that they deserve to be met directly.

We begin with a group of phrases from Homer, all of which include forms of οἶδα. In none of them can οἶδα be translated as "know," its usual meaning; it requires instead some word or phrase expressing emotion, will, or sentiment. We would otherwise find in our English versions of Homer the anomalous phrases: "with kindly knowledge," "with savage knowledge," "with friendly knowledge," and so forth.[40] The common, almost universal reaction to these idioms is put neatly by Wilhelm Nestle, who says, "It seems

---

40. Some of the phrases in question are: ἄρτια ᾔδη (*Il.* 5.326), οἶδε θέμιστα (5.761), ἤπια εἰδείη (16.73), ἄγρια οἶδεν (24.41), αἴσιμα εἰδώς (*Od.* 2.231, 5.9), φίλα εἰδότες ἀλλήλοισιν (3.277), πεπνυμένα εἰδώς (4.696, 7.11), ἀποφώλια εἰδώς (5.182), ἀθεμίστια ᾔδη (9.189), λυγρὰ ἰδυῖα (11.432), ἤπια οἶδε (13.405), ὀλοφώϊα εἰδώς (17.248), κεδνὰ ἰδυῖαν (23.232).

indeed almost like an unconscious anticipation of the Socratic doctrine that virtue is knowledge, when what we call 'disposition' appears in Homer as 'knowledge'."[41]

Inquiry into the usage of other Greek words not only seems to
support Nestle's judgment but even invites one to extend it to
authors other than Homer. Throughout classical Greek, terms like
νοῦς, νοεῖν, γνώμη, γιγνώσκω, φρένες, φρονεῖν, φρόνησις, and φρόνημα must
often be translated by words denoting emotion or volition. The
prime example here is νοῦς or νόος, "mind." In Homer, the Phaea-
cians have a "god-fearing mind"; the Cyclopes do not. Ajax and
Achilles have "cruel minds." Hesiod speaks of Pandora's "shameless mind." In all these passages, the word means "character" or
"disposition" rather than "intellect."[42] Elsewhere it means "desire"
or "will."[43] The Homeric and Hesiodic usages persist in later Greek.
The Νοῦς of Anaxagoras both knows everything and arranges
everything, and the word in Herodotus can mean "purpose" or "intention." Examples could be multiplied.[44]

*[margin annotation: οἶδα]*

41. Nestle, *Vom Mythos zum Logos*, p. 33. He had earlier stated the same
view in his article "Intellektualismus," *Neue Jahrb.*, 49 (1922), 138. But that
interpretation had already found its way into the article on εἴδω by B. Giseke
in H. Ebeling's *Lexicon Homericum* (Leipzig, 1880-85), 1.354, where it took
the form of a curious aside on the shortcomings of Homer *philosophus*. It is
also found in E. Buchholz, *Die Homerischen Realien*, III (Leipzig, 1884),
200-207, in whose eyes Homer is a "Socrates ante Socratem" (p. 201). It is
repeated by E. R. Dodds, *The Greeks and the Irrational*, pp. 16-17; by Hermann Fraenkel, *Dichtung und Philosophie des Fruehen Griechentums*, Philological Monographs Published by the American Philological Association, no. 13
(New York, 1951), pp. 116-17; by Max Wundt, *Der Intellektualismus*, p. 10; by
Joachim Böhme, *Die Seele und das Ich im Homerischen Epos* (Leipzig, Berlin,
1929), p. 48; and by Paul Shorey, "On the Implicit Ethics and Psychology of
Thucydides," *TAPA*, 24 (1893), 75.
42. *Odyssey*, 6.121, 9.176; *Iliad*, 16.35, 23.484; *Works and Days*, 67.
43. *Iliad*, 23.149, 8.143, 16.103, 20.25; *Odyssey*, 22.215. The verb νοέω
expresses volition at *Odyssey*, 2.122 and *Iliad*, 24.560.
44. Anaxagoras, 59 B 12 (Diels-Kranz); Herodotus, 1.109.2. Pindar has
εὐμενεῖ νόῳ at Pythian, 8.18, and Aeschylus has ἄγναμπτον νόον at *Prom. Bound*,
164. At Sophocles' *Electra*, 913, νοῦς means "character" or "inclination."
A detailed discussion of the history of these words is found in Kurt von
Fritz, "Νοῦς and Νοεῖν in the Homeric Poems," *CP*, 38 (1943), 79-93, and
"Νοῦς, Νοεῖν, and their Derivatives in Pre-Socratic Philosophy (Excluding
Anaxagoras)," *CP*, 40 (1945), 223-42, and *CP*, 41 (1946), 12-34. See also R.
Schottländer, "Nus als Terminus," *Hermes*, 64 (1929), 228-42; Joachim
Böhme, *Die Seele*, pp. 52 ff.; and Pearson, *Popular Ethics*, pp. 55 ff. Von
Fritz speaks of "the inextricable connection of an intellectual element with
an element of volition in the concept of νόος" (*CP*, 38, p. 82). Böhme finds
three meanings of νόος, "Seele," "Verstand," and "Plan." (p. 53).

The φρένες, the seat of knowledge in some passages of Homer, are often the seat of the emotions too, such as fear, anger, and joy. The word in Homer also means "will" or "character."[45] Later authors show the same range of usage. Fear grips the φρένες at Aeschylus' *Suppliants* 379 and 513, and at Euripides' *Phoenissae* 1285; hatred at Aeschylus' *Eumenides* 986; and pleasure at Euripides' *Heraclidae* 939. The word means "will" at Sophocles' *Antigone* 993. The same variety of meaning characterizes φρονεῖν, φρόνησις, and φρόνημα.[46]

Γιγνώσκω and γνώμη combine the intellectual and the volitional. The verb means "form a judgment," "take a stand," or "decide," at Herodotus 9.2.2, Xenophon's *Anabasis* 6.1.19, Lysias 22.2, and Herodotus 1.74.4.[47] Γνώμη frequently means "opinion," "judgment," or "resolution," as at Herodotus 1.40; "purpose," as at Herodotus 3.119.2; "will," as at Aeschylus' *Prometheus Bound* 543 and 1003; and "wish," in the common phrase κατὰ γνώμην.[48]

The meanings of compound words confirm the impression given by the simple forms. Εὔνους, δύσνους, θηλύνους, εὔφρων, πρόφρων, ὀλοόφρων, δαΐφρων, (from δάϊς), δύσφρων, περίφρων (as at Aeschylus' *Suppliants* 757), κρατερόφρων, ταλασίφρων, φιλόφρων, and αὐτόγνωτος can all refer to attitude, emotion, or character rather than to intellect; and for most the former reference is the normal one.

45. See *Iliad*, 1.333, 2.301 (knowledge); 1.555 (fear); 16.61 (anger); 13.493 (joy); 15.194 (will); 24.40 (character).

46. The verb φρονεῖν refers to intention at *Iliad*, 9.310 and 17.286; to disposition in phrases like φίλα φρονέων (*Iliad*, 4.219), κακὰ φρονέουσι (*Iliad*, 22.264), ὀλοὰ φρονέων (*Iliad*, 16.701), and φρονεῖς εὖ (Euripides' *Medea*, 823); and to character at Sophocles' *Philoctetes*, 1006. The phrase μέγα φρονεῖν refers to spirit or will rather than to range of thought at *Iliad*, 16.758 and Sophocles' *Oedipus Tyrannus*, 1078; the simple verb has the same force at *Iliad*, 17.23. Φρόνησις means "purpose" at Sophocles' *Oedipus Tyrannus*, 664, "attitude" at *Philoctetes*, 1078, and "pride" at Euripides' *Suppliants*, 216. Φρόνημα means "pride" or "will" at Aeschylus' *Prometheus Bound*, 209, "will" or "sentiments" at Sophocles' *Antigone*, 169, and "spirit" or "resolution" at Herodotus, 8.144.1. Cf. Böhme, *Die Seele*, pp. 37 ff.; Pearson, *Popular Ethics*, pp. 52 ff.; von Fritz, *CP*, 40 (1945), 229.

47. Pindar has εὐσεβεῖ γνώμᾳ at *Olymp.* 3.41, and Herodotus has φιλίας γνώμας at 9.4.2.

48. See Snell, *Die Ausdrücke*, pp. 33 ff., for a detailed discussion and further examples. Friedrich Zucker discusses γνώμη and some of its cognates in "Verbundenheit von Erkenntnis und Wille im Griechischen Sprachbewusstsein beleuchtet durch Erscheinungen aus der Bedeutungsentwicklung von ἄγνοια, ἀγνοεῖν, ἀγνόημα," *Studies D. M. Robinson*, II, (St. Louis, 1953), 1063-71.

We must conclude that many Greek words for faculties and activities of soul, as they are used before Plato, defy classification according to our categories. The intellect, the will, the character, and the emotions seem to have no clear boundaries for the early Greeks. Most striking of all is the fact that words which we think of as primarily expressive of intellect, like νοῦς, "the mind," φρόνησις, "wisdom," and γνώμη, "the judgment," along with their cognates, are used with great frequency to denote temperament, purpose, attitude, passion, or moral character. Did every Greek therefore absorb from infancy the habit of regarding character, decision, and emotion as the expressions of knowledge or ignorance? To some the conclusion seems inevitable. If quirks of speech can express individual character, one ought to be able to trace in the idioms of a language a whole nation's habits of thought. When the nation is Greece, long identified with rationalism in art, ethics, and politics, it is not hard to see in phrases like οἶδε ἄγρια and φρένες ἐναίσιμοι clues to a national frame of mind. E. R. Dodds calls it "habitual 'intellectualism'." Recent critics have found in this kind of speculation a new aetiology for the intellectualist bias of Platonic ethics.[49]

49. Dodds, *The Greeks and the Irrational*, p. 26, n. 105. "Von da aus findet das Problem des sokratisch-platonisch-stoischen 'Tugendwissens' eine überzeugende Lösung" (Zucker, *Studies Robinson*, II, 1064). Cf. Nestle, "Intellektualismus," *Neue Jahrb.*, 49 (1922), 137-38.

The primacy of intellect is sometimes explained by supposing an historical development rather than a primeval identification of intellect, will, and emotion. Von Fritz, for example, claims that all the meanings of νοῦς and νοεῖν "can be derived from one original and fundamental concept, which may be defined as the realization of a situation." He adds, however, that "the terms νόος and νοεῖν can acquire the meaning of 'plan' or 'planning'. With this derivative meaning of the words, a volitional element enters into the concepts of νόος and νοεῖν, which originally designate a purely intellectual function" (*CP*, 38 [1943], 91; *CP*, 40 [1945], 224). As opposed to ἰδεῖν (see), he argues, or γιγνώσκειν (distinguish), νοεῖν means to realize the nature or implications of something. It is therefore perception of a special kind, one that contains the germ of an attitude or a decision. He breaks down the development logically as (1) the realization of a situation, (2) the realization of its future implications, and (3) the plan (*CP*, 38 [1943], 86-88). E. L. Harrison, "Notes on Homeric Psychology," *Phoenix*, 14 (1960), follows von Fritz here (65, 74).

Böhme, *Die Seele*, p. 52, is somewhat narrower in defining the scope of νοῦς than is von Fritz. "Das Wort νόος ist eine Bezeichnung des intellektuellen Lebens wie φρένες und ist sogar—anders als φρένες—auf das intellektuelle Leben beschränkt." Even when the word expresses purpose, "alle durch den νόος erstrebten Ziele sind vernünftig" (p. 53). Snell, *Discovery of the Mind*, p. 13,

Attractive though the theory is, it provokes some serious objections. It applies to nonphilosophical Greek, and in particular to early poetic Greek, rigid definitions and categories which are appropriate only to later Greek, or only to prose, or only to philosophical prose. The explanation of οἶδα in Homer is a good example. The word means "to know," "to feel," "to be of a certain character," or "to have a certain intention." The simplest explanation of this variety is not that all other meanings derive from the first, but that the word in Homer transcends the distinctions we put upon it. The evolution of these distinctions in the Greek mind coincided with the restriction of οἶδα to a part of its former extension. So language adapts itself to culture. If we persist in deriving the other meanings of οἶδα from "know," and interpret οἶδε φίλα, for example, as

---

defines νόος as "the mind as a recipient of clear images, or, more briefly, the organ of clear images." He finds that the line between noos and thymos cannot be drawn with any precision, but "noos may be said generally to be in charge of intellectual matters, and thymos of things emotional" (p. 12).

Snell's discussion of γνώμη in his earlier book, Die Ausdrücke, seems also to imply a development from perception-intellection to volition. Γνώμη is the ability to recognize or the result of recognition; but it is found at times to denote a moral attitude, "und so ist γνώμη oft geradezu der Wille." The extension of meaning is explained in this way: "Die Meinung, die sich in die Praxis umsetzt, kann die eigenen Verhältnisse angehen,—dann wird sie zum Plan oder zum Entschluss." The meanings "counsel," "vote," "resolution," and "verdict" are similarly derived (pp. 33-35).

In the same spirit, Nestle, in explaining the genesis of phrases like οἶδε θέμιστα, in which the verb denotes a moral disposition, derives them from certain other phrases in which the verb means genuinely "to know." Telemachus' new-found maturity, for example, is expressed in the statement, "He knows good and evil" (Odyssey, 18.228-29). Halitherses, an experienced elder, "knows numerous and ancient things" (2.188). Odysseus "knows much" and cannot be outwitted by the Cyclops (9.281). The Sirens promise that those who come to them leave "knowing more" (12.188). Nestle maintains that the key to the use of οἶδα in a sense that goes beyond the intellectual is found in phrases of this type, in which the sum of experience is taken as an earnest of a man's worth or character. The result is intellectualism: moral virtue is intelligence, and wickedness is stupidity (Vom Mythos, p. 34). Buchholz, Die Homerischen Realien, 3.200-201, had anticipated the main points of Nestle's argument here.

This sort of speculation about the historical and logical connection between the different meanings of these words is discountenanced by Zucker, Studies Robinson, II, 1063, at least as regards γνώμη. This word, he insists, joined from the very beginning the two conceptions of knowledge and of choice; so neither is prior to the other. Schottländer, Hermes 64 (1929), 234, would reject for the word νοῦς the kind of development that Zucker rejects for γνώμη. Instead, he suggests, the original scope of νοῦς was at once perceptual, cognitive, and purposive.

"He knows the reasons for friendship," then we must explain οἶδε
ἄγρια (*Iliad* 24.41) as "He does not know the reasons for gentleness." The first is a conceivable abbreviation, but the second is not.
Wundt, who among advocates of the theory seems to be alone in
seeing this difficulty, explains the latter phrase lamely as a formation by analogy, in which the verb's original meaning is changed.[50]
But to call "know" the "original meaning" is pure assumption. No
one applies this kind of tortured analysis to εἶδον and ἰδών, those
parts of the same verb denoting action of the eyes. These can
mean either "see" or "look at with a certain emotion or intention."
Hence phrases like δεινὰ δ' ὑπόδρα ἰδών (*Iliad* 15.13). The emotion
here is not the result of the perception: not "seeing her, and therefore feeling hostility," but simply, "looking fiercely at her." As the
Greek language developed, the note of perception in εἶδον-ἰδών
came to exclude that of attitude or emotion. The same kind of development took place in οἶδα. By the late fifth century, Euripides
can use it to denote knowledge rendered ineffectual by emotion.[51]
But οἶδε φίλα in Homer means simply, "His feelings and intentions
are friendly."[52]

50. Wundt, *Der Intellektualismus*, p. 10.
51. Euripides, frag. 841 (Nauck).
52. According to Fraenkel, *Dichtung und Philosophie*, p. 116, "Die homerischen Menschen 'wissen' Freundliches, Mildes . . . oder Wildes, Arges" etc.
He insists that οἶδα in these phrases really means "know" and tries to deal
with possible objections by saying that one ought not to suppose that the
word "know" now and then simply changes its meaning to "be disposed." He
quotes *Odyssey*, 19.329, ὃς μὲν ἀπηνὴς αὐτὸς ἔῃ καὶ ἀπηνέα εἰδῇ, to show that
the author conceived harshness of character and knowledge of harshness as
two different things, and used οἶδα for the latter. There are two objections to
this: (1) there need be no question of a *change* in the normal meaning of
οἶδα, once we decline to regard knowledge as the "original" meaning; (2) the
lines quoted from the *Odyssey* need only imply a contrast between a man's
overt behavior and his inner feelings or character.
    Richard B. Onians, *The Origins of European Thought about the Body, the
Mind, the Soul, the World, Time, and Fate* (Cambridge, 1954), pp. 15-16,
has a good discussion of this question. He explains the idioms in question by
"the primal unity of mind, in which perception or cognition is associated with
or immediately followed by an emotion and a tendency to action" (p. 16). He
points out that the same comprehensiveness of meaning is found in verbs like
δαῆναι, λανθάνεσθαι, μιμνήσκεσθαι, μνᾶσθαι. Homeric heroes "remember" and
"forget" their valor, their joy in battle, their fear, their wrath, and their as-
tonishment (*Iliad*, 6.112, 15.322, 4.222, 11.71, 16.771; *Odyssey*, 11.554,
24.394). The meaning "is not merely that the emotion or activity is per-
ceived or lost as an object of thought, but that it is recovered in itself, felt,

The interpretation of νοῦς, φρένες, γνώμη, and their cognates and derivatives demands similar precautions. The common assumption that the intellectual note is primary in all of them is based partly on statistics and partly on etymology and history of usage. Only the latter criterion holds any promise of answering whether the intellectual—or cognitive-perceptual—note is historically and logically first. But the evidence here is doubtful. For example, no scholar who has tried to establish the earliest meaning of νοῦς has got beyond intelligent conjecture.[53] The history of usage fails to clear the matter up, since intellectual and nonintellectual meanings can both be found in the *Iliad*. The other causes of this uncertainty as it pertains to νοῦς have been well explained by Schwyzer. They are: (1) that a number of different original forms of the word are equally possible; (2) that the sense "mind" is probably not original, but instead derives from an unknown physical meaning.[54] Since the latter was obsolete in Homer's time, it can be reached only by learned guesses. Hence the judgment of Boisacq's *Dictionnaire Étymologique*, "Étym. obscure."

Even if the etymological evidence were clear, we should not overestimate its value for interpreting the Greek mind. Once a word's original meaning had been extended or superseded, no unlearned speaker would have any basis for recognizing it as original.

and perhaps visibly expressed, or (λάθοντο etc.) that the consciousness thereof, the emotion and the tendency to action, cease together" (p. 19).

53. Νοῦς is tentatively derived by Schwyzer and von Fritz from a root that means to sniff or have a keen sense of smell. This would make it perceptual in origin. See Ed. Schwyzer, "Beiträge zur griechischen Wortforschung," in *Festschrift Paul Kretschmer* (Wien, Leipzig, New York, 1926), pp. 244-51; and von Fritz, *CP*, 38 (1943), 92-93. Schwyzer won the agreement of Ulrich von Wilamowitz-Moellendorff, *Die Heimkehr des Odysseus* (Berlin, 1927), p. 191, n. 2; but his view was rejected by Wolfgang Krause in a review in *Deutsche Literaturzeitung*, N.S. 4, O.S. 48 (1927), 1049. Cf. P. Justesen, *Principes Psychologiques d'Homère* (Copenhagen, 1928), pp. 35 ff., who thinks νοῦς was originally the nose. Others connect νοῦς with νεύω or νέω, and Pearson, who is one of them, suggests that it "might be described as meaning originally 'a mental movement or inclination towards or away from a person or thing'" (*Popular Ethics*, p. 228). If he is right, there was a germ of volition in the word from the start. W. Prellwitz, *Etymologisches Wörterbuch der Griechischen Sprache* (Göttingen, 1892), p. 214, connects it with νεύω. Joachim Böhme, *Die Seele*, p. 27, sees no sure solution to the problem of etymology; nor does E. Boisacq, *Dictionnaire Étymologique de la Langue Grecque* (4th ed.; Heidelberg, 1950), p. 672.

54. Schwyzer, *Festschrift Kretschmer*, pp. 248-49.

Is a "gentleman" originally someone with good manners or the member of a privileged family? Mere common sense, unlike etymology, will work either way here. An example of another kind is "ignore," which has lost all connection with knowledge for Latin-less speakers and is just a synonym for "disregard" or "snub." Even if νοῦς was originally cognitive-perceptual, Homer was doubtless unaware that this meaning had any priority over the others. The keenest egalitarians call each other gentlemen.

The primary meaning of φρένες is also in doubt, and etymology lends no support to the notion that it is basically intellectual.[55] Yet even Pearson, who is sensitive to the variety of meaning in Greek words for psychic activity, cites the Homeric use of φρένες to support his generalization that "throughout Greek literature a man's moral worth is estimated largely in terms of his intelligence."[56]

55. Boisacq records a hypothesis that would connect φρήν with πορφύρω, among other words, "φρήν ayant signifié '*le trésaillement, das Auf- und Abzucken,' puis l'endroit du corps humain où il se produit (c.-à-d. 'le diaphragme') et les diverses émotions" (Dict. Étym., p. 1037). This is close to the view of Joachim Böhme, Die Seele, p. 7 ff., who holds that the earliest meaning of φρήν preceded distinctions of body and soul, physical and psychic. There is disagreement about what part of the body Homer had in mind when he used the word in its physical sense. It is usually thought he meant the diaphragm, but Justesen, Principes, pp. 4 ff., and Onians, Origins, pp. 23-39, think he meant the lungs. That issue, however, is not important here.

56. Pearson, Popular Ethics, p. 52. He does not, to be sure, claim a reference to intelligence in all occurrences of φρένες and φρονεῖν. He finds a "certain vagueness" in Homer's usage and points out that at Odyssey, 1.42-43 ἀγαθὰ φρονέων means "with kind intent." But as examples of intellectualism he cites Iliad, 6.162 (ἀγαθὰ φρονέοντα), Odyssey, 3.266 (φρεσὶ . . . κέχρητ' ἀγαθῇσιν), Odyssey, 24.194 (ἀγαθαὶ φρένες), and Iliad, 4.104 (τῷ δὲ φρένας ἄφρονι πεῖθεν) (pp. 52-54). Now, apart from the last example, a reference to intelligence does not seem even probable in any of these passages. "Good φρένες" are comparable to "just φρένες" (Iliad, 24.40) or "placable φρένες" (Iliad, 15.203). What Bellerophon, the young Clytemnestra, and Penelope had in common was not high intelligence but a good heart or a noble character. Even in Agamemnon's tribute to Penelope (Odyssey, 24.194), where a reference to her intelligence might have been appropriate as a reaction to the story of the great web (24.128 ff.), it is more likely, to judge from lines 195 and 199, that he was thinking of her loyal heart.

Pearson, p. 225, n. 24, refers the reader to Böhme's detailed analysis of the word and its cognates as they appear in Homer. Böhme, too, confines himself to a cautious generalization, that the word φρένες is predominantly intellectual in meaning (Die Seele, pp. 42, 50). Yet he leaps to the conclusion, "Die ἄτη ist . . . Störung der φρένες, also intellektuelle Störung" (ibid., p. 47, in reference to Iliad, 19.137). This is not the only statement in which he tacitly equates φρένες

If φρονέω and φρένες often refer to character, intent, or disposition, then ἄφρων and ἀφροσύνη may originally denote more than lack of intelligence. Neither etymology nor the evidence of context can justify limiting the extension of the words in Homer to a failure of judgment. They refer rather to a deficiency in the φρένες, that part of a man which controls his judgments, emotions, and character. Hence ἄφρων might correspond, in different contexts, to any of several English privatives, such as "senseless," "heartless," or "without character." To judge from form alone, δύσφρων is a synonym and εὔφρων or σώφρων antonyms. It is true that usage has established distinctive preferred meanings for each word. For example, εὔφρων and δύσφρων normally refer to emotion or to attitude, and mean respectively "merry" or "kindly" and "sorrowful" or "malevolent." But both words show traces in their usage of the original breadth of their root component, since in some contexts they must refer to judgment or moral character.[57] Σώφρων has al-

---

with intelligence. Cf. his treatment of *Iliad*, 24.40, *Odyssey*, 14.82, and 15.421 (pp. 47-48). Hermann Fraenkel is another who finds implied in Homer's use of φρένες the primacy of the intellectual (*Dichtung und Philosophie*, p. 110). Von Fritz's statement of his case is more carefully qualified: "Even more than νόος, [φρήν] can refer to emotional, volitional, and intellectual elements in the attitude of a person." He adds, "The intellectual element is always present" (*CP*, 40 [1945], 229).

57. The word δυσφρόνων at Sophocles' *Antigone*, 1261, is moral or intellectual or—better still—both. Its import is re-expressed in δυσβουλίαις a few lines later. Cf. Aeschylus' *Seven Against Thebes*, 875, and *Persians*, 552. At *Agamemnon*, 351, εὔφρονος is a compliment to Clytemnestra's wisdom or piety or both. Moral and intellectual connotations seem bound up in εὔφρων at *Agamemnon*, 849, *Suppliants*, 378, *Persians*, 772, and *Choephoroe*, 88. Such a range of meaning brings intractable problems for the translator. Diels, in *Fragmente der Vorsokratiker*, translated εὔφρονας at Xenophanes 21 B 1.13 as "verständige"; but Kranz has made this "wohlgesinnten." Liddell-Scott-Jones translates it "of sound mind, reasonable." Kathleen Freeman, *Ancilla to the Pre-Socratic Philosophers* (Oxford, 1948), p. 20, makes it "men who are enjoying themselves." Cf. E. Fraenkel (ed.), *Aeschylus, Agamemnon* (Oxford, 1950), 2.366-67 ("cheerful").

The perennial difficulty of translating the corresponding Homeric participle, εὐφρονέων (sometimes written as two words), is traceable to the same lack of a commensurate English term. Liddell-Scott-Jones' definition is simply a statement of the problem: "*with kind* (or *prudent*) *mind*." Since the formulaic line in which the word occurs regularly introduces the remarks of a wise counsellor and often follows an explicit reference to his sound sense or former good advice, the connotation of prudence seems to be foremost. Such an explicit reference occurs at *Iliad*, 1.73, 7.326, 7.367, 9.95, 15.285, 18.253, and at *Odyssey*, 2.160, 7.158, 24.53, 24.453. There is an implication of wisdom in most, if not all, of the other passages where εὐφρονέων occurs (*Iliad*, 1.253, 2.78, 2.283;

ready been discussed. It refers, from the time of Homer on, either to "sound sense" or to "sound character," and so prolongs the original ambiguity of its root. In the Homeric view of life the two meanings are never in conflict, but in the fifth century a new sophistication enabled men to distinguish "intelligence" from the traditional virtue of σωφροσύνη, whose name meant "sound φρένες," and which was normally thought of in Athens as a habit of self-restraint. It then became possible for the same man to praise or damn σωφροσύνη, according to the meaning he gave it.[58]

'Αφροσύνη did not suffer this split in meaning. It came to mean simply "foolishness" and to denote a failure of judgment, and so it served as an antonym to σοφία and φρόνησις, in the sense of "wisdom." But a review of Homer's use of ἄφρων and ἀφροσύνη makes it doubtful that the words were originally limited to their fifth-century meaning. The usage of ἀφραίνω and ἀφρονέω corroborates that impression. When Hera complains to Zeus about the activity of Ares on the battlefield, she calls him ἄφρων (Iliad 5.761), and Ares himself applies the same word to Athena (5.875). Nothing in either context suggests that this means "foolish" or "ignorant."[59] Liddell-Scott-Jones' translation "crazed" is more nearly satisfactory, because it implies an affliction of emotion, character, and judgment all at once. When Zeus decides to entrust Priam to the mercies of Achilles in the last book of the Iliad (24.157), one of his reasons is that Achilles is not ἄφρων. Since the context does not suggest a compliment to the hero's intelligence, it is most natural to take it to mean that he does not lack the proper sensibilities. Penelope's rebuke to Eurycleia for telling what seems a wildly fanciful story about Odysseus' return, includes the word ἄφρονα (Odyssey 23.12). But it is hardly an accusation of stupidity so much as one of madness, which attacks the sense of shame and the affections as well

---

Odyssey, 2.228, 16.399). Yet, in our terms, these are all good men as well as wise, and we cannot exclude secondary implications of uprightness and benevolence. In the hands of Aristophanes the ambiguity of the root is material for a play on the words εὐφραίνω and εὖ φρονέων at Clouds, 561-62.

58. See n. 9.

59. To argue so from the explanatory phrase, ὃς οὔ τινα οἶδε θέμιστα (Iliad, 5.761), would be to make a presupposition about ἄφρων depend on a misconception of οἶδα (see text above).

as the intelligence.[60] Very often, even in Homer, the words in this group refer to a failure of judgment, and in this respect Homeric usage presages their eventual limitation to that meaning.[61] But the epic use of ἄφρων in contexts where we would have written "insensible" or "shameless" does not prove intellectualism; it only shows that the φρένες include the hero's sense of shame and respect as well as his judgment.

The word γνώμη does not occur in Homer, but γιγνώσκω, which occurs frequently, always refers to knowledge or perception.[62] If the meanings "judge," "determine," "decree" are secondary developments, as they seem to be, then we have a genuine example of a root which originally meant "to know" and later acquired a note of volition.[63] Before any conclusions can be drawn from this about the Greek mentality, it must be seen in the light of two qualifying facts: there is a parallel development in English and Latin verbs of knowing, and there is a converse development in the Greek verb κρίνω, to "separate" or "choose." But treatment of these facts may be postponed for a moment, since they come in train with a large number of others.

We are brought to the important supposition that the traits of language in question are distinctively Greek. They are not. I do not refer only to the fact that we need not speak Greek to call a lawbreaker, who risks imprisonment and social ostracism, a fool. It is on more fundamental grounds than this, viz. on the use of common words denoting psychic activity, that the Greeks are al-

60. Cf. μάργην (line 11) and τίπτε με λωβεύεις; (line 15). Likewise, when Telemachus calls himself ἄφρονα at 21.102, he means he has lost control of his emotions, just as Theoclymenus earlier appeared to Eurymachus to have lost control of his perceptions (ἀφραίνει ξεῖνος, 20.360).

61. Intelligence is in question at Iliad, 15.104, 4.104, 16.842, 7.109-110, and Odyssey, 17.586. At times the context gives the translator small help or none, as in the formula found at Odyssey, 6.187 and 20.227. At Odyssey, 8.209, ἄφρων may mean "foolish" in anticipation of line 211; and ἀφροσυνάων at 24.457 is perhaps "short-sightedness," in the light of line 460. At Odyssey, 16.278, ἀφροσυνάων may mean blindness to imminent doom (see line 280), but it may mean only "their wicked ways."

62. The same is true of all the compounds of γιγνώσκω that I have found in Homer. Zucker, Studies Robinson, II, 1065, sees volition implied in the use of ἠγνοίησεν at Iliad, 2.807. But the line makes equally good sense without that assumption. At Iliad, 23.240 (διαγιγνώσκοντες) there may be an incipient note of decision, a meaning which that word develops in later authors.

63. Snell has described how this might have taken place. See n. 49.

leged to be different from us and from the Romans. The argument seems plausible because those who use it habitually contrast Greek words like νοῦς, φρένες, and γνώμη with modern words like "intellect," "cognition," "volition," "emotion," and "disposition." But it should come as no surprise that common or poetic speech lacks the precision of technical language.[64] If we want to contrast Homeric usage fairly with, say, English usage, in order to measure the degree of latent intellectualism in each, we ought to use the plain man's English. We will find that some of the basic English words referring to intellect show the same encroachment upon the will and the emotions that has been observed in Greek. Moreover, there are parallels in Latin.

"Think" means to exercise the intellect. But it also means "to conceive, feel (some emotion): as . . . *to think wonder . . . to think scorn . . . to think shame.*" Or it can mean "to bethink oneself of something in the way of a plan or purpose . . . to contrive, devise, plan, plot," or "intend, purpose, design." "Mind," the word for intellect in common speech, also means "purpose," "intention," or "desire" in phrases like "make up one's mind," "know one's mind," "change one's mind," "have a mind." Or it can mean "inclination, tendency, or way of thinking and feeling, in regard to moral and social qualities: moral disposition; a spirit or temper of a specified character." So Shakespeare speaks of "an honourable mind." The word can mean as well "state of thought and feeling in respect to dejection or cheerfulness, fortitude or fearlessness, firmness or irresoluteness, and the like." The privative "thoughtless," like ἄφρων, is equally versatile, and means "unreflecting," "careless," "free from anxiety," "inconsiderate," or "stupid." So too "mindless" can mean "unintelligent," "insane," or "careless." The authority for these definitions is the *Oxford English Dictionary*.[65] Latin provides a

---

64. The word "will," an apparent exception, leads two lives. The common man and the poet, happily blurring the boundary line of emotion and volition, use it to mean "desire, wish, longing," or even "carnal appetite" (*Oxford English Dictionary* [Oxford, 1933], "Will," I.1 and † 2). But as the philosopher's "faculty of choice" it is also a learned word.

65. Hereafter called *OED*. Some of these meanings are rare, archaic, obsolete, or dialectical, and therefore unfamiliar. See especially "Think," B.I.1.c, and B.II.7,8; and "Mind," II.11, 12, 13, and 15. According to the *OED*,

parallel in the word *mens*, which means not only the intellect but also "disposition," "feelings," "sentiments," "plan," "purpose," and "courage."[66]

If "think," "mind," and *mens* are comparable in range and versatility to φρονέω or νοῦς, another group of English and Latin words parallels γιγνώσκω by showing a history of development from the cognitive-perceptual to the volitional. The obsolete verb "acknow," meaning "come to know, recognize," also means to "acknowledge, confess." "Acknowledge" itself, though derived from "know," always denotes a choice. "Understand" has two usages, now obsolete, in which it means "to give heed to, attend to," and "to plan, devise." The Latin words *nosco, cognosco, recognosco, ignosco, agnosco,* and *ignoro* all show, in varying ways, the same kind of encroachment of knowledge upon choice. *Nosco* can mean "acknowledge, allow, admit of a reason or excuse." *Cognitus* can mean "approved." *Recognosco* can mean "certify, authenticate." (Cf. the English "recognize," which refers both to reacquaintance and to approval.) *Ignosco*, a compound of *(g)nosco* and a prefix of doubtful nature, means "pardon." *Agnosco* is to "acknowledge." Finally, *ignoro*, "not to know," comes to mean, in addition, "to ignore."[67]

None of this means that there is an inveterate tendency to intellectualism in English, Latin, or Greek. One fact would suffice to disprove that: words that normally or originally refer to emotion or will often extend their meanings to refer to intellect. Witness θυμός. Plato was to make this the second principle in the tripartite soul, the natural ally of reason but in no way to be confounded with it. Yet before Plato it had been used at times to mean "mind, soul, as the seat of thought." Its etymology, however, and its actual usage show that it always meant primarily strong feeling or

---

"mind" is connected with μένος ("rage"), μέμονα ("I yearn"), and Latin *memini* ("I remember"). See also Boisacq, *Dict. Étym.* under μέμονα (pp. 625-26). The root embraces a variety of psychic functions.

66. See Lewis and Short, which gives examples of each meaning.

67. See the *OED* and Lewis and Short. See also Alois Walde, J. B. Hofmann, *Lateinisches Etymologisches Wörterbuch* (3rd ed., 2 vols.; Heidelberg, 1938-54), 1.677-78, under *ignosco*. For *cognitus* see *Corpus Inscriptionum Latinarum*, 11.1104 and 13.3735.

passion and only secondarily reason.[68] The verb κρίνω means originally to "separate," "choose out," and then "decide a dispute." At
first the note of will or choice is primary and not that of intellectual
judgment.[69] The phrase σκολιὰς κρίνωσι θέμιστας, for example, at
*Iliad* 16.387, expresses a wilfully "crooked" decision, taken in defiance of the gods, not a misperception of right and wrong. This
meaning survives, and the word even comes to denote, at times,
"choose a course of action or a way of life."[70] On the other hand,
out of the original notion of separation-selection developed that of
intellectual judgment. Hence Thucydides can use κρίνω when he
wants to say that men always "judge" the current war to be the
greatest, or that the interval after the treaty of Nicias ought not
to be "judged" a peace at all.[71] In contexts like these to "choose
well" is to "be intelligent." Once more, English and Latin provide
numerous parallels.[72]

Enough evidence has been cited to allow us fairly to draw a
conclusion. It is no longer possible to maintain that the Greek language is unique in the scope it allows to words for knowledge, or to
see in their free use any implied primacy of intellect. All the phe-

68. Under "mind, soul, as the seat of thought," Liddell-Scott-Jones lists
*Iliad*, 2.409, 16.646, Sophocles' *Electra*, 1347, and other passages. Boisacq,
*Dict. Étym.*, p. 356, gives the origin of θυμός as "i.-e. *dhū-mó-s* 'soulèvement
ondogeant, ébullition, fumée'."
69. I base this conclusion on an examination of all occurrences listed in
G. L. Prendergast, *A Complete Concordance to the Iliad of Homer*, rev. B.
Marzullo (Hildesheim, 1962); in H. Dunbar, *A Complete Concordance to the
Odyssey and Hymns of Homer*, rev. B. Marzullo (Hildesheim, 1962); and in
A. Gehring, *Index Homericus* (Leipzig, 1891).
70. Aeschylus has κρίνω δ' ἄφθονον ὄλβον (*Agam.*, 471), and κρῖνε σέβας τὸ
πρὸς θεῶν (*Suppliants*, 396).
71. Thucydides, 1.21.2, 5.26.2. Cf. 1.138.3, 2.34.5, 2.43.4, 2.53.4, 3.65.3,
4.60.1, 4.108.4, 5.113, 8.2.2.
72. The Latin *intellego*, etymologically "to choose from among," means
"understand." See Walde and Hofmann, *Latein. Etym. Wörterbuch*, 1.352.
*Animus* embraces the meanings "reason, intellect," "opinion, judgment,"
"imagination, fancy," "power of feeling, sensibility, heart, disposition, passions," "character," "courage," "power of willing, will, inclination, desire, intention" (See Lewis and Short). *Sentire*, originally denoting physical sensation, can also mean "to think, deem, judge, opine," as well as "to give one's
opinion . . . to vote, declare, decide" (*ibid.*). In English, "heart," primarily
a physical organ, and then the seat of the emotions, the will, and courage, can
also mean "the seat of the mental or intellectual faculties" (*OED*, "Heart,"
12). "Feel," originally denoting physical sensation, can also mean "entertain
(a conviction)" (*OED*, "Feel," II.9).

nomena mentioned reveal only a haziness of boundary-lines between psychic functions. This inexactitude characterizes the pre-philosophical author like Homer, the poet in a philosophical age, like Sophocles,[73] and the common man of every age, who is innocent of philosophical distinctions. In fact, unless erudition has ruined his feeling for common idiom, it even characterizes the philosopher at leisure.[74] The supposed intellectualist bias of the Greek mind, which is thought to have smoothed the way for the Socratic ethical paradoxes, indeed to have been their very fount and origin, does not exist.

This is not to say that Socratic ethics sprang from an utterly inhospitable soil. There were certain doctrines and beliefs known before Socrates which presaged his intellectualism. But none was universal, habitual, or more "genuinely Greek" than its opposite.[75] The Delphic maxim "Know thyself" is one; another is the new prom-

73. At *Electra*, 913, Sophocles uses νοῦς to mean "inclination" or "character." But at line 1347 of the same play, θυμός means the seat of knowledge.

74. One occasionally finds a scholar who tries systematically to force the language of literature into the rigid categories of philosophy. Victor Magnien has made the attempt in "Quelques Mots du Vocabulaire Grec exprimant des Opérations ou des États de l'Âme," *REG*, 40 (1927), 117-41. He finds the doctrine of a tripartite soul in philosophers, medical writers, and poets alike, from Homer on. The three parts are νοῦς, θυμός, and φρένες or φρήν (ἐπιθυμία in prose). Each has a distinct function which corresponds roughly to that of the respective part of the Platonic soul. Most scholars avoid such extreme perversity, knowing that these distinctions developed only with time. "One may properly ask," says Pearson, "whether the distinction between 'intellectual' and 'emotional' is really applicable to Homer" (*Popular Ethics*, p. 226, n. 31). Cf. Snell, *Die Ausdrücke*, p. 31; Harrison, "Notes on Homeric Psychology," pp. 63, 67; T. B. L. Webster, "Some Psychological Terms in Greek Tragedy," *JHS*, 77, Part I (1957), 149, 154; and Eric A. Havelock, *Preface to Plato* (Cambridge, Mass., 1963), p. 212, n. 17 (discussion of φρονεῖν, φρόνησις, and φρόνιμος).

E. R. Dodds, who observes justly that the Greeks lacked the formal concept of will (*The Greeks and the Irrational*, p. 26, n. 105), implies, by calling Homer's way of explaining behavior "intellectualist," that he possessed the formal concept of intellect. It is, presumably, the intellect of Achilles which, in his eyes, is "merciless" at *Iliad*, 16.35, and which "knows ferocity" at 24.41. As Dodds puts it, "character is knowledge" (p. 17). But if the concept of will is absent, so too is that of intellect, if by the latter we mean a faculty distinct from the will. The translator may in some contexts render νοῦς as "intellect" as the most nearly accurate English equivalent; but, whereas intellect excludes will, νοῦς does not. In most authors it does not even exclude character and emotion. This fact, and the similar wide range of meaning in οἶδα and φρένες, in no way implies that "character is knowledge." The logic which produced that statement and five minutes with a concordance open at the entry "Mind" would prove Shakespeare an intellectualist.

75. Nestle's phrase (see note 3, above).

inence in the fifth century of the conception of τέχνη. The influence
of these on Socrates and Plato will be discussed in the next chapter.
Even apart from these, Greeks normally regarded the good man as
a wise man and the criminal as a fool. They seem usually to have
meant by this that virtue is a form of self-interest. But virtue at
times seemed unprofitable, and when it did few Greeks had doctrinaire scruples about calling a villain wise or a good man a fool.[76]

In the earliest period of their literature, the Greeks often failed
to distinguish knowledge from emotion, character, or purpose. To
us, who habitually make these distinctions, such terms as φρένες,
νοῦς, and Homeric οἶδα seem hopelessly ambiguous. Yet the distinctions were not beyond the powers of the Greek mind or the
Greek language. When the development of culture and thought demanded their expression, they were expressed, and around them
grew philosophical issues and literary themes. The contrast between wisdom and goodness, for example, was known to the authors
of the *Philoctetes* and the *Orestes*. Long before either of these
plays, Medea, in 431 B.C., had announced to an Athenian audience,

> I know what ills I am about to do,
> But my rage is stronger than my resolutions
> 
> (*Medea*, 1078-79).

A few years later Phaedra complained,

> We know and recognize the good
> But do not carry it out
> 
> (*Hippolytus*, 380-81).

The disjunction between knowledge of the good and right action
became a favorite theme of Euripides, undoubtedly commoner than
the few extant plays and fragments allow us to infer. Laius, in the
*Chrysippus*, complained of it twice, and the *Antiope* mentions it
again as one of mankind's principal afflictions.[77]

It was in the face of the common-sense view that knowledge
was often ineffective that Socrates expounded his paradoxes. Per-

---

76. So little is Greek thought hobbled by linguistic usage that a Greek can
deny that knowledge determines action while using the very idioms that are
supposed to prove his intellectualism. Euripides has Phaedra do this at *Hippolytus*, 380 ff. (cf. γνώμη at 391 and ἄνοια at 398).

77. Euripides' fragments 840, 841, 220 (Nauck).

haps his unusual doctrine provoked his critics to the first clear statement of their own views. Unfortunately, such controversies are lost
to us.[78] But the lines cited from Euripides show that, for a Greek,
the conception "knowledge of the good" did not of itself imply right
action. No alert Greek, therefore, need have accepted the Socratic
paradoxes as analytically true. In fact, as Plato's own dialogues
confirm, they went against the grain. According to *Protagoras*
352bc, the ordinary Greek believed that even if a man had knowledge it could be frustrated by his emotions. Protagoras, who is one
step ahead of the common man in his respect for the power of
knowledge (352cd), still believes that a man can be just, for example, and not wise (329e). We have seen that he shares this belief with Sophocles' Neoptolemus.[79]

Protagoras, Neoptolemus, Medea, and Phaedra represent widely
different types of the Greek character. None believes that virtue
is knowledge or that wrongdoing is invariably unintentional. They
are fair proof, in their variety, that no easy reception awaited the
Socratic paradoxes. When compared with the moderate intellectualism of a Protagoras, or with the psychological realism of Euripides' and Sophocles' character studies, those paradoxes must have
seemed to most Athenians, as they do at first to us, untrue to the
complexities of the human heart.

78. Bruno Snell, "Das frühste Zeugnis über Sokrates," *Philologus,* 97
(1948), 125-34, sees in the *Medea* and *Hippolytus* passages evidence of an
open disagreement between Euripides and Socrates. He has reiterated this
theory in *Scenes from Greek Drama* (Berkeley and Los Angeles, 1964), 47-69.
My criticism of his views can be found in a review in *AJP,* 87 (1966), 236.
Cf. the review by Hugh Lloyd-Jones in *Gnomon,* 38 (1966), 12-17, esp. 15.
79. Among other dialogues, the *Hippias Minor* implies throughout that it
is common Greek opinion that a man can do wrong on purpose. Hippias assumes so without question, and when Socrates finally raises the possibility that
it may not be true, it is only because the elenchus has impressed upon him
the anomalies of the normal view (see Chapt. 3). When young Charmides is
asked to define σωφροσύνη, in the dialogue named for him, he first says simply
that it is modesty or shame (160e); and the plain man Laches, asked to define courage, says "doggedness of soul," and mentions intelligence only after
some prodding from Socrates (*Laches* 192bc).

# 2 . SOCRATES

## AND THE FIFTH CENTURY

One of the few things about Socrates of which we can be certain is that he plunged with enthusiasm into the intellectual life of his times. Whatever mysticism he may have had was balanced by an intense interest in his contemporaries. For most of his life he talked and listened to them, and it was the attraction of their company which made him a confirmed city-dweller. As he says in the *Phaedrus*, "I love to learn. But the land and trees will not teach me anything, and men in the city will" (230d). This is ironic, but only half so. Athens taught him much, and even his ethical doctrines show it. These, in the form they take in Plato,[1] were so phrased as to surprise and shock Greek common sense. But a Greek could also have seen in them the development of certain ideas and beliefs that were well known in the fifth century. This chapter deals with what I regard as the three main sources of the ethical intellectualism of Socrates and Plato. These are (1) the

1. The problem of establishing the exact Socratic form of these doctrines is discussed at the end of this chapter.

ethic of self-interest, whose form before Socrates was discussed in the last chapter, (2) the conception of politics and virtue as an art (τέχνη), and (3) the Delphic "Know thyself."

In the second book of the *Republic*, Adeimantus speaks as if Greek morality had no other foundation than self-interest. Quoting Homer, Hesiod, and Musaeus to show the antiquity of this bias, he says, "No one has ever censured injustice or praised justice on other grounds than the reputation, the honors, and the gifts which come from them."[2] But he does not suggest abandoning the canon of advantage. He merely challenges Socrates to prove that justice itself, severed from the extrinsic advantages and the divine favor that so often attend it, is *inherently* good for a man. When the long argument is over, they conclude that it is indeed: αὐτὸ δικαιοσύνην αὐτῇ ψυχῇ ἄριστον ηὕρομεν (612b). There is no denial of self-interest in this, no demand for self-abnegation in the face of a higher duty. Instead, the absolute good shelters the soul's private advantage as a corollary principle. The canniest partisan of personal advantage proves to be, not Euripides' Menelaus, but Socrates. This paradox makes Plato the heir of Hesiodic and Thucydidean intellectualism.[3]

One can find the motive of self-interest in the moral speculations of any age, but in their adoption of τέχνη as an ethical conception Socrates and Plato seized on a theme which Athens in the fifth century had made its own. Politics, according to a well-attested and common belief, was an art. The evidence for this will appear below. Since public office was best discharged by men of personal excellence, the latter, by natural extension, was called an art too. Indeed, in Athens mere citizenship was an art, since all had a palpable share in community life, and a good citizen was a virtuous

---

2. *Rep.* 366e. Cf. 358a, 362e ff.

3. Note the reference to "prizes" in the last, climactic sentence of the *Republic*, and at *Phaedo* 114c. Add to this the punishments of the wicked in Platonic myths of the after-life (e.g., *Rep.* 615a ff.). The just enjoy earthly (612c ff.) and heavenly (615bc) rewards. But these are all ancillary. The essential logic of Plato's position is that virtue is the care of the soul (*Apol.* 30b), and the soul is the true self (*Phaedo* 114c, 115c ff.). The *Meno* at one point simply assumes that to wish the good for oneself is to wish it absolutely (see Chapter 3, n. 4). Moreover, both the *Gorgias* (470d-478e) and the *Symposium* (204e-205a) present happiness as the natural goal of human activity. For a fuller discussion of the role of self-interest in Plato's ethics, see Chapter 3.

and able individual. Socrates in the *Apology* speaks of virtue as ἀνθρωπίνη τε καὶ πολιτική, knowing that the junction of ideas will be familiar.[4] In Plato's *Republic*, where a description of the state serves as a description of the soul writ large and where the most virtuous govern, the union of political and individual excellence finds its classic expression.

The way in which Socrates and Plato use the word τέχνη implies that virtue and politics are ways in which men intelligently control their lives. Virtue, in a way, is knowledge. In the early dialogues this use of τέχνη is treated as a source of fruitful discussion rather than as a fixed doctrine,[5] but its presence in the allegory of the ship of state at *Republic* 488 shows that, in spite of difficulties, it is meant to be accepted. The analogy was already well known by the late fifth century, and Greek readers would have found it far less strange than we do. This had not always been so. Socrates' willingness to put civic rule and personal virtue in a class with carpentry and soldiery was the result of a long development and a new prominence of the conception of τέχνη. By the late fifth century the word summed up for many Greeks the belief that man could in large measure control his own life.

This had not been the earliest Greek view, nor did it ever become universal. Mastery of an art is in Homer evidence of divine favor and inspiration, especially that of Hephaestus and Athena. With the development of a historical sense, the divine role became one of discovery and teaching. Hermes invented the seven-stringed lyre. Pallas Athena discovered the art of flute-playing, taught craftsmen how to build war chariots, showed maidens the household crafts, and brought the olive to Athens. Demeter engaged Triptolemus in the task of spreading cereal culture over the earth, and Dionysus gave men pleasure and consolation when he discovered the grape. These myths are found in Homer, the Homeric Hymns,

4. *Apol.* 20b. Cf. the fragment of Simonides quoted in the *Protagoras*, esp. the lines at 346c (= frag. 5, Bergk).

5. *Gorgias* 509d-510a; *Laches* 192e-193c, 195b-d; *Hippias Minor* 366d-368e; *Rep.* 332c-334b; *Protag.* 319a, 327a ff., 350a. In Xenophon's *Memorabilia*, Socrates refers to politics as "the kingly art" at 2.1.17 and 4.2.11. Cf. 4.2.2., 4.2.5 ff.

Pindar, Sophocles, and Euripides.[6] The best-known legend of this type is found in the *Prometheus Bound* of Aeschylus. In this play, a god gives to mankind not one art but culture as a whole, represented by all the major arts and epitomized in the gift of fire.[7] A similar catalogue of divine gifts, which in their sum comprise the means of civilized life, is attributed to an unnamed god at Euripides' *Suppliants* 201 ff.; and in the brief *Hymn to Hephaestus*, of uncertain date, that god shares with Athena the credit for civilizing mankind.

The belief in divine beneficence took a more generalized form in the doctrine of providence. This appears at Herodotus 3.108 as τοῦ θείου ἡ προνοίη. It is explained at great length in two passages of Xenophon's *Memorabilia*, where the word πρόνοια appears again and is applied especially to the gods' care of mankind. In these passages, god, not man, is the great artisan, who by his devices makes human life good and to whom man owes, among other things, fire, the use of domestic animals, and reason itself.[8]

Not all took the pious view that humanity's unique accomplishments were the result of divine favor. In the eyes of some, man could thank himself for what the race had achieved in its command of the environment and its organization of society. This took both a mythical and a philosophical form, and the origins of both can be traced at least to the sixth century.[9] A fragment of Stesi-

6. *Odyssey*, 6.232 ff.; *Hymn to Hermes*, 39-54; Pindar, *Pythian*, 12.6 ff.; *Hymn to Aphrodite*, 12-15; Euripides' *Troiades*, 801 ff., *Ion*, 1433-34; Sophocles' *Triptolemus*, cited by Dion. Halic., *Roman Antiq.*, 1.12 (Nauck, *sub* frag. 541); Euripides' *Bacchae*, 272 ff.

7. "All arts have come to mortals from Prometheus" (line 506). The statement comes at the end of a catalogue (447 ff.) that includes astronomy, numbers, writing, animal domestication, seamanship, medicine, divination, and mining. But Prometheus is pre-eminently the giver of fire (612), which is the symbol of the arts and is sometimes spoken of as the key to them (lines 7, 109 ff., 254).

8. Xenophon's *Memorabilia*, 1.4 and 4.3. Note especially 1.4.6 (πρόνοια), 1.4.7 and 1.4.9 (god as δημιουργός), 4.3.7, and 4.3.10-11.

9. In the *Phoronis*, an epic dated to about 600 B.C., the Idaioi are said to have "first discovered the craft of Hephaestus" (G. Kinkel, *Epicorum Graecorum Fragmenta* I [Leipzig, 1877], 209-12, frag. 2). If this is meant as a human accomplishment, the terms used are still rather ambiguous. The *Phoronis* may have provided, in the person of Phoroneus, a culture-hero who was neither a god nor a mere passive recipient of divine favors. Certain it is that he had this status in later legend. According to Pausanias (2.15.5), he introduced

chorus,[10] recording the invention of letters by Palamedes, is the first trace of the greatest of these myths. Palamedes, the victim of Odysseus' vindictiveness in the *Cypria*, became for the fifth century the paragon of human inventiveness and skill and the mythical reflection of the waxing confidence that man by wit could control his world. Aeschylus, Sophocles, and Euripides all wrote plays entitled *Palamedes*, as did Astydamas the younger. The *Nauplius* of Sophocles dealt with his legend, and so probably did the plays of the same name written by Lycophron and Philocles.[11] A fragment of Sophocles' *Nauplius* provides us with the longest catalogue of Palamedes' inventions.[12] His ingenuity became proverbial. "A Palamedic discovery" is a phrase of Eupolis. In the *Frogs* of Aristophanes, Dionysus offers Euripides the compliment, "Well done, O Palamedes, O nature most wise!" Pindar called Palamedes wiser than Odysseus, and to Euripides he was πάνσοφος.[13] But the most famous tribute to his accomplishments, amid the wreckage of the large poetic literature devoted to him, is the speech of defense written by Gorgias the sophist.[14] In it Palamedes is the resourceful τεχνίτης (25), each of whose inventions has a social value (30). In

men to communal life and even, according to the Argives, discovered fire (2.19.5). The epic (Kinkel, frag. 1) called him the father of the human race. F. Stoessl, in his article "Phoronis 2" in *R.-E.*, argues that the claims recorded in Pausanias may well go back to the epic. "So erschien also Phoroneus in der P[horonis] als der erste Schöpfer der Kultur" (Halbband 39, cols. 647-48). But these later stories may also reflect the influence of the Prometheus and Palamedes legends.

10. Stesichorus, frag. 34 (Bergk).

11. The fragments, where they exist, are found in Nauck, *Tragicorum Graecorum Fragmenta*. The existence of plays by the three minor dramatists is attested by Suidas under the authors' names.

12. Sophocles, frag. 399 (Nauck). Among the devices and discoveries listed are the Greek wall at Troy, weights, numbers, measures, military formations, astronomy, and fire-signals. Euripides' *Palamedes*, frag. 578 (Nauck), adds sleeping drugs and writing. Plato, *Republic* 522d, refers to Palamedes' claim in tragedy to have discovered number and military formations. He may have in mind the context of the unassigned fragment 470 (Nauck), where Palamedes is very likely the speaker. For other references to his inventions, see Aeschylus' *Palamedes*, frag. 182 (Nauck); Sophocles' *Palamedes*, frag. 438 (Nauck); Sophocles' *Nauplius*, frag. 396 (Nauck).

13. Eupolis, frag 351 (Edmonds); Aristophanes' *Frogs*, 1451; Pindar, frag. 260 (Schroeder) = 275 (Bowra); Euripides' *Palamedes*, frag. 588 (Nauck). The reference to Palamedes in this last fragment, though only implicit, is almost certain.

14. Printed as 82 B 11a by Diels-Kranz.

short, he plays the role of benefactor of the human race, which in the more pious tradition was shared by Athena, Hephaestus, and other gods of limited cultural scope, or assumed in its entirety by Prometheus.

The attribution to Palamedes of inventions and qualities elsewhere attributed to the gods is the expression in myth of a contemporary interest in man the resourceful.[15] The *Prometheus Bound* itself shows this interest in an indirect way, since the model for the god Prometheus is the clever man, the σοφιστής. By grafting the latter conception to the Hesiodic prototype of the wily Prometheus, Aeschylus has produced in his inventor-god a new variation on the old myth of divine beneficence.[16] There is even some evidence that in the lifetime of Socrates Prometheus had already become for some the symbol of man's inventive mind.[17] This is an

15. Authorship of a Palamedes play does not, of course, imply the *poet's* intent to exalt human prestige at the expense of the gods. *Oedipus Tyrannus*, which is also evidence of intense current interest in the human intellect, still leaves man subordinate to god (see this chapter below). Aeschylus wrote a *Palamedes* and a *Prometheus*, but no religious conversion need have intervened. On the other hand, Palamedes' manhood in the fifth century is not affected by his possible status as a god in preliterary myth. For the latter see L. Preller, C. Robert, *Griechische Mythologie*, II, *Griechische Heldensage*, 3.2.1 (4th ed.; Berlin, 1923), 1127 ff.

The Athenians honored a certain Bouzyges as the first man to plough with yoked oxen. A vase painting in which he demonstrates his invention to Athena and Cecrops is dated to c. 430. See David M. Robinson, "Bouzyges and the First Plough on a Krater, by the Painter of the Naples Hephaistos," *AJA*, 35 (1931), 152-60, which also cites the literary references for the story.

16. See Hesiod, *Works and Days*, 48, 54, and *Theogony*, 510-11, 521, 535-65, 616. I find it unlikely that the Aeschylean Prometheus, who is five times called a god (14, 29, 37, 92, 119), is "a symbol of man himself" (Eric A. Havelock, *The Liberal Temper in Greek Politics* [New Haven and London, 1957], p. 64). As divine benefactor and teacher of the arts he plays a role which differs only in scope from that of Athena or Dionysus. No Athenian, therefore, would have felt the need to attribute to Aeschylus an intent to glorify mankind in symbol. Plato merely follows the Aeschylean interpretation when he puts Prometheus in the company of other beneficent gods at *Politicus* 274c. It is true that Prometheus is addressed in the play as σοφιστής (62, 944), and that his "discoveries" and "contrivances" are expressed in language suitable for a human inventor (469, 477). But this shows only that the conception of σοφιστής had become familiar enough for Aeschylus to exploit poetically. His inventor-god, in other words, is characterized anthropomorphically. But so is Zeus, the "tyrant" (224, 312, 736, 942).

17. His name, "Foresight," played on by Pindar (*Olymp.* 7.44; cf. Ἐπιμαθέος at *Pyth.* 5.27), Aristophanes (*Birds*, 1511), and Aeschylus (*Prom. Bound*, 86) and dramatized by his juxtaposition with Κράτος and Βία in the latter play, gives him immediate symbolic value. But this does not take him

beyond such divine figures as Metis and Themis. Not until the late fifth century is there evidence of his treatment as a symbol of human ingenuity. In his play *The Sophists*, Plato Comicus has the line Προμηθεύς γάρ ἐστιν ἀνθρώποις ὁ νοῦς. This is frag. 136 (from Schol. Aesch. *Prom.*, 114), with the emendation Καὶ γὰρ Προμηθεύς, in Kock. Other readings and emendations cited by Kock are either excluded by the context (Dindorf's προμηθία, after Syncellus' Προμήθεια) or do not affect the symbolism (Meineke's ὁ γὰρ Προμηθεύς.) The latter is also true of Edmonds' Προμήθιος (vol. 1, p. 532). Paul Geissler, *Chronologie der Altattischen Komödie*, Philologische Untersuchungen, no. 30 (Berlin, 1925), p. 56, dates the play to about 411. Edmonds, vol. 1, p. 533, note a, prefers 403. In looking for what lies behind this detached fragment of Attic comedy, we find our principal evidence in the myth in Plato's *Protagoras*, where Prometheus plays a leading role. This seems to attest his place in sophistic thought. But is it firm evidence or Platonic mirage?

Some think that the myth stands self-condemned, as an example of Plato's unscrupulous way with his opponents. Th. Gomperz, *Griechische Denker* (2nd ed.; Leipzig, 1903-1909), 2.249, judged the whole speech, myth and *logos*, to be a caricature, a jumble of contradictory ideas composed with satirical intent. Gomperz's arguments, however, have been disproved by G. B. Kerferd, in "Protagoras' Doctrine of Justice and Virtue in the 'Protagoras' of Plato,"*JHS*, 73 (1953), 42-45. Since then, Havelock, *Liberal Temper*, pp. 87 ff., has called the myth a twisted version of Protagoras' views. He objects especially to the divine apparatus, since Protagoras was an agnostic (Diels-Kranz 80 B 4). But agnostics can indulge a literary flair (on this point see G. Vlastos' introd. to M. Ostwald's trans. of the *Protagoras* [New York, 1956], xi). Protagoras would not have been the only sophist to have used a mythical setting for his teaching; cf. Prodicus' Choice of Heracles (Diels-Kranz 84 B 2). Kerferd, moreover, in the article just mentioned, has demonstrated the correspondence between myth and *logos* in the dialogue, and this amounts to showing that Protagoras rationalizes the myth immediately. It has, therefore, no independent value as doctrine. Kerferd's argument here is directed specifically against those who regard αἰδώς and δίκη, Zeus' gifts, as a natural receptivity to virtue. For if the divine gifts of αἰδώς and δίκη were a mere capacity for the art of virtue, rather than the poetic equivalent of the art itself, we would be left with an indigestible kernel of theology. Actually, the two qualities in question are referred to in terms almost identical to those used of political virtue, in adjacent passages that are meant to be mutually explanatory (cf. 322d2-5, linked by οὕτω δή . . . καὶ διὰ ταῦτα with 323a3 and 323c1-2). Hence αἰδώς and δίκη, conferred—mythically speaking—by Zeus, *are* political virtue; and, in plain prosaic terms, this is a product of instruction in suitable natures. When the *logos* comes, the two gifts of Zeus are replaced by νόμοι, εὑρήματα of good lawmakers of old (326d), and the gods are dropped as casually as are the poetic phrases which accompanied them (σμικρότητι ἤμπισχεν 320e3, ἀϊστωθείη 321a2, and others. All are embedded in a flow of "altionionische Erzählungsstils": cf. Ed. Norden, *Agnostos Theos* [Leipzig, Berlin, 1913], pp. 368 ff.). When Protagoras offered his hearers a choice between myth and *logos*, and then elected myth because it was χαριέστερον (320c), he was parading his sophistic versatility rather than any religious belief.

It is true that the *logos* contains no rationalization of the gifts of fire and the arts. But the real subject of the conversation is the political art, and Protagoras, to make his point that virtue is taught, need explain only that aspect of his myth. His explanation of the divine gift of justice as the result of society's conditioning of its members (326d) suggests that he would have explained Prometheus' gift as a poetic version of human technical progress. This conclusion is urged by Wilhelm Nestle, *Vom Mythos zum Logos* (2nd ed.; Stuttgart, 1942), p. 286. The very phrase συγγένεια τοῦ θεοῦ (322a), found so objectionable in an agnostic, is best read as a poetic exaltation of man's powers as an artisan.

In short, the Prometheus myth as told in the *Protagoras* is consistent with the theory of politics and education unfolded in the *logos*. Plato's sophist is a cultivated agnostic for whom religious myth retains a poetic and symbolic value. There is, then, no impediment to our believing that the myth is based on an actual work of the sophist. Some scholars have even seen positive evidence of this in one of the titles in the list of works attributed to him. Protagoras is said to have written a piece called περὶ τῆς ἐν ἀρχῇ καταστάσεως (Diog. Laert., 9.55 = Diels-Kranz 80 B 8b), i.e. "The State of Things at the Beginning." The phrase suggests the condition of primitive man and the development of the arts, which this chapter shows to have been a widely attested concern of the fifth century. Admittedly, the title is ambiguous. On κατάστασις see Liddell-Scott-Jones and Ed. Norden, *Agnostos Theos*, p. 372, n. 1. Eduard Zeller, *Die Philosophie der Griechen*, 1. Teil, 2. Hälfte, (5th ed.; Leipzig, 1892), p. 1120 = 1001, n. 4, prefers to make it the title of a lost political work. So does H. Gomperz, *Sophistik und Rhetorik* (Leipzig, Berlin, 1912), p. 178, n. 363. Paul Shorey, *What Plato Said* (Chicago, 1933), pp. 124, 497, is sceptical and noncommittal. But similar phrases occur elsewhere with a cultural reference. W. Nestle, "Bemerkungen zu den Vorsokratikern und Sophisten," *Philologus*, 67, N.F. 21 (1908), 552, cites Democritus 68 B 278 (Diels-Kranz). Cf. Moschion, frag. 6, line 2 (Nauck), which deals with mankind's emergence from barbarism. But one cannot entirely exclude Diels' suggestion that the title actually refers to the Platonic myth (Diels-Kranz, 80 B 8b, note).

On the whole, however, it seems more than likely that Prometheus was already used in the late fifth century as a symbol of man's inventive intelligence. (L. Eckhart, "Prometheus," *R.-E.*, Halbband 45, col. 682, is sure of it.) The antithesis Foresight-Hindsight, found in Democritus (Diels-Kranz, 68 B 66), had its natural mythical expression in the legend of Prometheus and Epimetheus; the fragment from the *Sophists* of Plato Comicus makes the connection explicit; the use of Prometheus by Antisthenes as the antagonist of Heracles in dialogue, and the Cynic attack on him as an arch-sophist, suggest that he already had an established place in sophistic thought (see the fragment of Antisthenes reported in F. Bücheler, J. Gildemeister, "Themistios περὶ ἀρετῆς," *Rhein. Mus.*, N.F. 27 [1872], 450, n. 1; also Dion of Prusa, 7.33). The *Protagoras* myth, in which ancient legend is adapted to sophistic ideas, provides the missing evidence in the form in which we should have expected it.

To admit Prometheus as a patron of the fifth-century cult of intelligence will throw a new light on Plato's skill in converting that god to his own purposes. At the end of the *Protagoras*, Socrates accepts Prometheus as his own model and puns on his name (προμηθούμενος 361d). This completes his capture of a motif that Protagoras earlier had made his own, not only in the myth, but in his first rather too solemn speech, which begins ὀρθῶς προμηθῇ (316c). Before the dialogue is over he will be forced to admit that courage itself is a kind of foresight (351b-360e), which is more than he had bargained for. This is wit made integral to meaning, such as we find elsewhere in the *Hippias Minor* and the *Laches* (see Chapters 3 and 4). It probably depends in the *Protagoras*, as it does in the other two dialogues, on the use of known idiosyncrasies or real doctrines.

advance beyond Aeschylus, to whom he is still a god with anthro-
pomorphic attributes; and it foreshadows his role in Stoic exegesis.[18]

The fascination with man's technical achievements which characterized the fifth century took forms other than myth. Xenophanes
had denied, in straightforward terms, that these achievements were
owed to the gods when he said: "The gods did not reveal all things
to men from the beginning; instead, by seeking, men discover what
is better in time." How far he concerned himself with details is not
known.[19] But the historians of the fifth century are alert to any
evidence about the origins of the arts, and the answers they give
often depart widely from any legendary version. They are, moreover, usually couched in terms that leave no place for divine agency.
Herodotus, whose interest ranged over all phases of culture and all
countries of the world, claimed to have found the origin of more
than one Greek art in the imitation of foreign practice. From
Egypt came the shield and the helmet, from Phoenicia the al-
phabet. Geometry is owed not to the benevolence of Prometheus
or the brilliance of Palamedes, but to the Egyptian need for accurate land measurement. From there it came to Greece.[20]

Hand in hand with the substitution of men for gods as creators
of the arts came the need to postulate motives and occasions of
invention to replace divine benevolence. An obvious motive was
necessity. It is found in Herodotus' explanation of the origin of
geometry, and it evidently had a place in Democritus' theory of the

18. See Cornutus, *Theologiae Graecae Compendium*, 18, ed. C. Lang
(Leipzig, 1881); and Cicero, *Tusculans*, 5.3.8.

19. Xenophanes 21 B 18 (Diels-Kranz). His interest in technical advances
may be shown by his observation that the Lydians first struck coinage (Diels-
Kranz, 21 B 4). According to Anaxagoras, man, by experience, memory, wisdom, and art, overcomes the natural advantages held by the animals (Diels-
Kranz, 59 B 21b). The view is reflected in Euripides, frag. 27 (Nauck),
Antiphon the tragedian, frag. 4 (Nauck), and the *Protagoras* myth (320c8-
322d5).

20. Herodotus, 4.180.4, 5.58, 2.109.3. Other inventions are mentioned at
1.25.2, 1.94, 1.23, 1.103.1, 2.109.3. Among other historians of the fifth century, Hellanicus speculated about the discovery of fire and of armor, both
of which he assigned to Lemnos; the invention of iron armor he attributed to
Saneunus the Scythian. See frags. 71b, 71c, 189 in F. Jacoby, *Fragmente d.
Griech. Historiker*, 1. Teil (reprinted) A (Leiden, 1957). The subject of
invention in the arts is treated at length in Adolf Kleingünther's book,
ΠΡΩΤΟΣ ΕΥΡΕΤΗΣ, *Untersuch. zur Geschichte einer Fragestellung, Philologus*
Supplementband 26, Heft 1 (Leipzig, 1933).

arts.[21] Democritus thought too that men had been pupils of the animals in these matters. From the spider they learned weaving and mending; from the swallow, house-building; from the swan and nightingale, singing.[22] But for a fully developed theory of τέχνη, we must turn from this fragmentary evidence to a contemporary medical treatise which by good luck has been preserved. This is the work *On Ancient Medicine*. In it the source of progress is again necessity. Necessity drove primitive man to develop a milder diet than that available to the animals. When it further drove him to create a special diet for the sick, the art of medicine was born. All this required time and the cumulative efforts of successive generations of physicians, each building on the discoveries of his predecessors. The notion of a single invention of an art is here replaced by that of an ἀρχή and a ὁδός. The result is a τέχνη in which rational procedure and human control are given full credit for all progress, and no limitations are envisioned. Given proper method and able workers, the author adds, "What remains to be discovered will be."[23]

21. That necessity is the mother of arts seems to be the implication of Democritus 68 B 144 (Diels-Kranz), where music is said to be an exception. The main text cited for Democritus' theory of the arts, however, has usually been Diodorus 1.7-8. This contains a cosmogony and an anthropology which Karl Reinhardt argued was Democritean, in "Hekataios von Abdera und Demokrit," *Hermes*, 47 (1912), 492-513, and which Diels-Kranz prints among the testimonia to Democritus (*sub* 68 B 5). In the passage, primitive man, driven by the need to survive, develops the arts through experience, intelligence, and the use of his hands. Until recently, the few opponents of Reinhardt's identification have at least not questioned the pre-Socratic origin of the passage (see, e.g., Havelock, *Liberal Temper*, p. 406), although Gregory Vlastos has urged discretion in using it as a source ("On the Pre-History in Diodorus," *AJP*, 67 [1946], 59). But Walter Spoerri, in his recent book *Späthellenistische Berichte über Welt, Kultur, und Götter*, Schweiz. Beiträge z. Altertumswiss., Heft 9 (Basel, 1959), has listed a large number of possible late Hellenistic sources for the doctrines mentioned. It now appears that they may be an amalgam of the first century B.C., though perhaps still ultimately dependent on fifth-century ideas. Until further research clarifies that question, it seems inadvisable to use Diodorus 1.7-8 as evidence for pre-Socratic views. O. Gigon, otherwise critical of Spoerri, agrees on this point, in his review in *Gnomon*, 33 (1961), 771-76. Cf. A. D. Nock's review in *CR*, 12 (1962), 50-51. For the large bibliography on this issue, see pp. 1-6 and 247-74 of Spoerri's book, and his more recent article, "Zu Diodor von Sizilien 1, 7/8," *Mus. Helv.*, 18 (1961), 82, n. 87.

22. Democritus 68 B 154 (Diels-Kranz). He also said that accident taught men the generation of mules, and they have made it regular practice (68 A 151 = Diels-Kranz, II, p. 125, line 15 ff.).

23. *On Ancient Medicine*, IV.3, III.1-10, II.1-11, II.1-2. (These and subse-

Medicine is only one of a legion of arts which received attention in the fifth century from those who wished to improve them
or reduce them to systematic form. Among the others were rhetoric,
sculpture, diet, painting, cookery, horsemanship, city-planning,
scene-painting, and music.[24]

quent references to "Hippocrates" are based on the chapter divisions in W.
H. S. Jones' Loeb ed. [London, New York, 1923]. *On Anc. Med.* is found in
vol. 1.) The scientific and cultural implications of this treatise have been
examined in articles by Harold W. Miller: *"On Ancient Medicine* and the
Origin of Medicine," *TAPA*, 80 (1949), 187-202; and *"Techné* and Discovery
in *On Ancient Medicine," TAPA*, 86 (1955), 51-62. The customary dating
of the work to the period before or around 400 B.C. (e.g. by W. H. S. Jones,
*Philosophy and Medicine in Ancient Greece*, with an ed. of περὶ ἀρχαίης
ἰητρικῆς, Suppl. Bull. Hist. of Medicine, No. 8 [Baltimore, 1946], 47; and
A.-J. Festugière (ed.), *Hippocrate, l'Ancienne Médecine* [Paris, 1948], ix)
has been challenged by Hans Diller, in "Hippokratische Medizin und Attische
Philosophie," *Hermes*, 80 (1952), 385-409. He dates it to the late Platonic
period. His arguments, though numerous, are weak, and have been analyzed
and rejected by Josef-Hans Kühn, *System- und Methodenprobleme im Corpus
Hippocraticum* [Wiesbaden, 1956], pp. 46-56, and by Felix Heinimann, "Eine
Vorplatonische Theorie der Τέχνη," *Mus. Helv.*, 18 (1961), 112-13, n. 32.
Diller is not the first to make the work post-Platonic (see Harold Cherniss,
"Plato 1950-1957," *Lustrum*, 4 [1959], 140, n. 2). There has been a recent
attempt to date it to c. 450, by James Longrigg, "Philosophy and Medicine,
Some Early Interactions," *HSCP*, 67 (1963), 162-67.

   Bruno Snell, *Die Ausdrücke für den Begriff des Wissens in der vorplatonischen Philosophie*, Philologische Untersuchungen, no. 29 (Berlin, 1924), 16,
84, has pointed out the special prestige enjoyed by the word τέχνη in fifth
century medical literature. But his belief, following M. Pohlenz, "Das Zwan-
zigste Kapitel von Hippokrates De Prisca Medicina," *Hermes*, 53 (1918), 410,
that Plato owes the explicit distinction τέχνη-ἐμπειρία (*Gorgias* 465a) to medical writers, was shown to be an overstatement by W. Capelle, "Zur Hippok-
ratischen Frage," *Hermes*, 57 (1922), 262-65. Cf. E. R. Dodds' ed. of the
*Gorgias ad. loc.*, and Festugière's ed., *l'Ancienne Médecine*, p. 31, which follow
Capelle.

   24. Corax and Tisias wrote on the art of rhetoric (*Phaedrus* 273a; Cicero,
*Brutus*, 46; Aristotle, *Soph. El.*, 183b; see W. Rhys Roberts, "The New Rhe-
torical Fragment [Oxyrhyncus Papyri, Part III, pp. 27-30] in Relation to the
Sicilian Rhetoric of Corax and Tisias," *CR*, 18 [1904], 18-21). Others who
dealt with the same subject include Thrasymachus (Suidas, Diels-Kranz 85
A 1; cf. Schol. Aristophanes' *Birds*, 880, Diels-Kranz 85 B 3), Gorgias (Diog.
Laert., 8.58-59, Diels-Kranz 82 A 3), and Protagoras (τέχνη ἐριστικῶν: Diog.
Laert., 9.55, Diels-Kranz 80 A 1). Polyclitus wrote a treatise on sculpture
(Diels-Kranz 40 A 3). Mithaecus wrote on cookery (*Gorgias* 518b), Simon on
horsemanship (Xenophon, *On Horsemanship*, 1.1; cf. Aristophanes' *Knights*,
242), and several men wrote on scene-painting (Vitruvius 7, praef. 11, Diels-
Kranz 59 A 39). Herodicus of Selymbria, mentioned by Plato at *Protag.* 316e,
*Rep.* 406a, and *Phaedrus* 227d, wrote on diet. For his written doctrine, re-
ported on a papyrus, see F. G. Kenyon, "A Medical Papyrus in the British
Museum," *CR*, 6 (1892), 238; and H. Diels, "Ueber die Excerpte von Menons
Iatrika," *Hermes*, 28 (1893), 421-22. Democritus' voluminous writings in-

The spreading net of man's technical skill could not but enclose
the most important human concern of all, the city-state. That human society itself depended on an art of living together, which
mankind had discovered as it had discovered medicine and arithmetic, was in the late fifth century a familiar idea. Democritus refers to it when he calls politics the greatest art.[25] The conception
had many forms. One of these was the belief that the laws and
customs of society, even the most sacred, are man-made. In the
Clouds of Aristophanes, produced in 423 B.C., young Pheidippides
invents a law that sons may beat fathers; he justifies it by saying
that the old law, that fathers may beat sons, was just such an invention (1420 ff.). The same theory, expounded in a more serious
vein, appears in a fragment from the Sisyphus of Critias. In it the
speaker attributes the origin of law and religion to the deliberate
attempt of primitive men to create an orderly society by invoking
the fear of human and divine punishment. The process is described
in terms that are elsewhere used to explain the origin of the arts:
intelligent men discover a technique to make human life better
and so raise man above the animals.[26] The late fifth-century

cluded works on medicine and painting (Diels-Kranz 68 B 26b, c, d, and
28a). In fact, so versatile was Democritus that Thrasyllus dubbed him the
"all-round athlete of philosophy" (Diog. Laert. 9.37, Diels-Kranz 68 A 1).
The medical literature of the century includes the well-known anonymous
work On the Art. Other personages of the age who developed technical spe-
cialties were Damon, who had a theory of music (Rep. 400bc); Hippodamus
of Miletus, who invented the science of city-planning (Aristotle, Pol. 1267b22
ff.); and Hippias, who taught and considered himself an expert in a great
number of arts (Protag. 318de, Hippias Minor 368b).

25. Diels-Kranz 68 B 157, reading Reiske's emendation πολιτικήν. The
context of Plutarch's Adversus Colotem, 1126a, where the fragment appears, requires this change from πολεμικήν of the MSS., in spite of Quintino Catau-
della's attempt to defend the latter, in "Democrito fr. 157 D," Maia, 2 (1949),
268-73. Robert Philippson, "Zu Demokrits fr. 157 D," Philologische Wochen-
schrift, 46 (1926), 1100-1101, also upholds the MSS., but he argues partly on
the basis of 68 B 28b and 28c, both of which are perhaps spurious (see Diels-
Kranz, note ad loc.) and in any case are inconclusive. Both Diels-Kranz and
the latest Teubner ed. of Plutarch's Moralia, VI, 2, 2nd ed., M. Pohlenz and
R. Westman edd. (Leipzig, 1959), read πολιτικήν. The fragment, moreover,
finds a parallel in Democritus 68 B 252 (Diels-Kranz). Cf. Xenophon, Memorabilia, 4.2.2, 4.2.11.

26. The Sisyphus passage is frag. 1 (Nauck) and Diels-Kranz 88 B 25.
Its use of ἐξευρεῖν (13) for the discovery of a political technique is parallel to
the use of this verb and its cognates in passages of a more strictly technical
reference. Cf. On Anc. Med., II.1-5; Gorgias, Palamedes, 30 (Diels-Kranz

author who is designated Anonymus Iamblichi also explains the
origin of society in terms which imply that politics began and developed like the arts. Men's present way of life, he says, was an
invention to meet a need. Men cannot live without justice, and
this necessity has led them to accept the rule of law simply because it makes life better.[27]

The student of Plato who reads these fragmentary reports of
fifth-century political theory will know that there are echoes of
them in Plato's *Protagoras*. The resemblance, in particular, of the
doctrine of Anonymus Iamblichi to the *Protagoras* myth was pointed
out long ago.[28] In the myth too, men are unable to survive without
justice, and therefore they receive it as a divine gift along with
reverence. These "gifts," however, are simply the mythical expression of mankind's development of the art of politics.[29] Protagoras'
real view of society, divested of the conventions of myth, is suggested by his remark that laws are the inventions ( εὑρήματα ) of
great men of old. It is intimated further in the speech which Plato
attributes to him in the *Theaetetus*, where he compares the political

82 B 11a); Herodotus, 1.25; Euripides' *Palamedes*, frag. 578 (Nauck); and
Aeschylus, *Prom. Bound*, 460-75 (4 occurrences). Other examples are cited
by Bernard M. W. Knox, *Oedipus at Thebes* (New Haven, London, 1957),
pp. 128 ff., and throughout Kleingünther's book, ΠΡΩΤΟΣ ΕΥΡΕΤΗΣ. A disorderly or beastlike existence, of the kind Critias mentions at lines 1-2, is the
prelude to the first divine gifts at *Prom. Bound*, 450, and Euripides' *Suppliants*,
201-202. There is a fourth-century echo in Moschion, frag. 6 (Nauck). The
Ἄγριοι of Pherecrates, produced in 420, may have reflected the current interest in this theme (*Protag.* 327d; Athenaeus, 5.218d).

27. See especially 6.1 and 7 (Diels-Kranz 89). There is a warning, however, at 2.7 that the τέχνη analogy can be misleading, at least with regard to
individual virtue. The identity of this author has been a matter of dispute ever
since he was discovered by F. Blass in the *Protrepticus* of Iamblichus. See
Blass, *De Antiphonte Soph. Iamblichi Auctore* (Kieler Univ. Progr., 1889).
There is a general consensus only about his approximate date. Bibliography
can be found in M. Untersteiner, *I Sofisti, Testimonianze e Frammenti*, III
(Florence, 1954), pp. 110-12, and more recently in Andrew T. Cole, Jr., "The
Anonymus Iamblichi and His Place in Greek Political Theory," *HSCP*, 65
(1961), 127-63.

28. By Karl Bitterauf, "Die Bruchstücke des Anonymus Iamblichi," *Philologus* 68, N.F. 22 (1909), 508. Cf. Diels-Kranz, II, p. 402, line 24, note. H.
Gomperz, *Sophistik und Rhetorik* (Leipzig, Berlin, 1912), pp. 81-89, points
out this and other coincidences with Protagorean doctrine. He concludes that
the treatise is largely, though not exclusively, a product of Protagorean influence (p. 89).

29. *Protag.* 322b; Anon. Iambl., 6.1, 7.13 (Diels-Kranz 89). See above,
n. 17. Cf. Democritus 68 B 248 (Diels-Kranz).

leader to a physician and a farmer, i.e. to a craftsman.[30] If he wrote laws for the people of Thurii, as he is said to have done,[31] then he practiced the art which he taught. This would have given a sharper edge to Aristophanes' jokes about modern lawmakers.

At Athens, Protagoras seems to have been willing to work within the existing Athenian law, and he is therefore unlike Plato, for whom the political art involved a complete reorganization of society. Plato's radical method had been anticipated in the fifth century by Hippodamus of Miletus, whose success with city-planning evidently helped persuade him that society too could be reduced to exact principles. His theory of the tripartite ideal state, described by Aristotle, with its implied elevation of theory over tradition, is in the full sense an art of politics.[32]

In Thucydides, the century's most adept student of the uses of power, the analogy of politics and art is for the most part only implied. But it is made explicit at least once. When the Corinthians reproach the Spartans for their sluggish and old-fashioned style of statesmanship, they tell them instead to view it as a τέχνη; times of crisis, they add, require not tradition, but artful innovation (ἐπιτέχνησις 1.71.2-3). The historian's own respect for this point of view is shown in the high honor he gives to men of practical intellect. His ideal statesman is Pericles, a man with the intelligence to comprehend needs, the foresight to gauge consequences, and the ability to win public support.[33] The same bias can be discerned

30. *Protag.* 326d, *Theaet.* 167bc. Since Plato does not bind himself to doctrinal accuracy in his portrayal of Socrates (see above, Introduction), one might reasonably doubt the historical value of what he says about Protagoras. (This question is discussed as it affects the myth in n. 17 above.) However, the theory of the Platonic Protagoras that the art of politics is the result of men's contrivance in the face of necessity not only agrees with his known agnosticism about the gods (Diels-Kranz 80 B 4), but is otherwise well-attested as a late fifth-century conception, as this chapter shows. In short, the most likely reason why Plato should have attributed the theory to him is that he really taught it.

31. Diog. Laert., 9.50 = Diels-Kranz 80 A 1.

32. Aristotle, *Pol.* 1267b22 ff. Hippodamus even provided rewards for those who in the future might make discoveries advantageous to the state, thus encouraging technical, and perhaps political, innovation (*ibid.*, 1268a7).

33. Pericles' estimate of himself, made in a public speech, is found at 2.60.5. It mentions, besides intelligence, patriotism and superiority to bribes. But when Thucydides repeats the latter in his own summary, his phrasing makes it clear that it is mentioned mainly for its bearing on his political ef-

in the descriptions of other statesmen. Themistocles, for example, was distinguished by a capacity to judge what had to be done, a grasp of probabilities, and skill at improvisation (1.138.3). The command of politics shown by such men is not explicitly called a τέχνη, but it has the elements needed to make that word appropriate. Based on creative intelligence rather than custom,[34] it is found in its highest form in energetic and foresighted leaders who know how to stamp their wills on the public mind.

The exaltation of man's controlling intelligence, which marks the whole work of Thucydides, had always been latent in Greek thought. A clever man was normally a match for a strong one, and the phrase πολύμητις 'Οδυσσεύς crystallizes in a formula the early Greek admiration for resourcefulness. In one passage of the Iliad, this takes the form of praise for the technical skill of woodcutter, helmsman, and charioteer.[35] Not until the fifth century, however, did Man the Artisan seriously threaten divine prerogative in human affairs. He did so principally in law and politics, where divine injunction became human arrangement, but also by engendering a certain optimism which seemed to religious minds hybristic. The author of the work On Ancient Medicine, who envisages no limits to medical progress, given talent and proper procedure, finds an echo— or a model—in much more sweeping statements of Democritus. Chance, Democritus says, offers only slight opposition to intelligence; for the most part, a shrewd sharp-sightedness suffices to guide a man straight.[36] It is obvious that respect for intelligence and advice not to blame chance for blunders need not constitute intellectual arrogance. Yet there is evidence that in the latter part of the fifth century those who honored man's intellect often caused offense to the pious. To others they caused annoyance or amusement. There are passing references to mankind's technical prowess in Euripides, who allows his characters to treat it with pious re-

fectiveness (2.65.8). The stress on Pericles' intelligence is apparent in the repeated references to it: γνούς (2.60.6), ξύνεσις . . . γνώμη . . . πρόνοια (2.62.5), προγνούς (2.65.5), γνώμη (2.65.8), προέγνω (2.65.13).

34. As the Corinthian puts it, ἀνάγκη δὲ ὥσπερ τέχνης ἀεὶ τὰ ἐπιγιγνόμενα κρατεῖν (1.71.3).

35. Iliad, 23.313 ff. What they all exemplify is called μῆτις.

36. Democritus 68 B 119 (Diels-Kranz). Cf. 68 B 172 and 173.

proof, exasperation, or witty parody. At *Suppliants* 216-218, Theseus, having attributed man's emergence from barbarism to divine beneficence rather than to human ingenuity, attacks the arrogance of those who would be "wiser than the gods." At *Hippolytus* 916 ff., the same character alludes to men's myriad arts, devices, and inventions; yet, he adds bitterly, they cannot teach good sense to those who lack it. Finally, *Suppliants* 902 ff. is a panegyric about heroism in war which parodies the current language of intellectual prowess.[37] There exist other scattered indications, from the same period, of what a modern thinker, if offended, would call anti-intellectualism but the author of the medical treatise *On the Art* calls a depreciation of the arts. He complains of some who ascribe the cures of medical science to chance and of others who "have made an art of denigrating the arts." Evidence of this same distrust of intellect is found in Plato's *Laches*, where the Athenian general for whom the dialogue is named parodies the language of intellectuals and mocks the prowess of those who reduced fighting to an art. As the literature cited above shows, Laches is no isolated eccentric, but the spokesman of an attitude common in the late fifth century.[38]

The most brilliant challenge to Man the Artisan was made on a far higher level by Sophocles, in *Oedipus Tyrannus*. One of that play's principal themes is the uncertainty and inefficacy of man's knowledge. Its hero relies above all else on his intellect; he has saved Thebes once by power of wit and hopes to save her again (380, 396-98). Appropriately, he thinks of the kingship he exercises as a τέχνη. In the long sentence with which he begins his tirade against Teiresias, that word expresses what he is proudest of and what he scorns to find absent in the old prophet. In the words of

37. Note the phrases δεινὸς σοφιστής, πολλὰ δ᾽ ἐξευρεῖν σοφά, διὰ τέχνης δορός, εὑρὼν ἀκριβῆ μουσικὴν ἐν ἀσπίδι. Parody of another kind is found in Eupolis, frag. 351 (Edmonds), where Alcibiades, a Palamedes in debauchery, claims to have "invented," among other things, the practice of drinking wine in the morning.

38. *On the Art*, I.1, I.18, IV.7-8. See *Laches* 182d5-e4, 183b ff., and Chapt. 4 below. Chrysogonus the flute-player said in a poem, οὐ γὰρ ἄνθρωπος τέχναν τιν᾽ εὗρεν, ὁ δὲ θεὸς τοπάν. This Chrysogonus is a contemporary of Alcibiades (Plutarch, *Alcib.*, 32.2, and Athenaeus, 12.535d), and the poem is the *Politeia*, falsely attributed to Epicharmus (Athenaeus, 14.648d), and quoted by Clement, *Strom.*, 5.119 (Diels-Kranz, 23 B 57).

that speech, his own art is τέχνη τέχνης ὑπερφέρουσα, while Teiresias is τὴν τέχνην . . . τυφλός (380-89). Again, at lines 357 and 562, the word τέχνη, applied by a normal Greek usage to the prophet's art, nevertheless conveys scorn: Oedipus thinks his own claim to the word is real and the prophet's claim is false.[39] The sharp edge of the king's confidence is this belief that he is master of his own craft. He personifies the sense of intelligent control over brute nature and random circumstance which was the fifth century's form of humanism, and which Sophocles had already made poetry in his phrase from the *Antigone*, οὐδὲν ἀνθρώπου δεινότερον πέλει.[40] When he finds defeat out of all proportion to his faults and in senseless mockery of his great powers, the explanation is "chance" (τύχη). Chance has intervened throughout his life to thwart and misdirect him, and when he proclaims at line 1080 that he is its child he is ironically telling the truth. The mystery of Oedipus' fall is never really explained, but it is assimilated to the conventional wisdom that art controls some things and chance others. Around that well-worn

39. Τέχνη at 380 might mean only "skill at interpreting riddles." But the rhetorical contrast with the prophet's art and the existence in the late fifth century of the conception of ruling as the highest art make a reference here to the kingly art probable. R. C. Jebb (ed.), *Oedipus Tyrannus* (2nd ed.; Cambridge, 1887), p. 62, cites *Philoctetes*, 138 and Xenophon's *Memorabilia*, 4.2.11 as parallels. Cf. Democritus 68 B 157 (Diels-Kranz). It is suitable, therefore, that the metaphors of the play should identify the king successively with helmsman, doctor, mathematician, farmer, and hunter, i.e. with men who practice the great arts of civilization. Bernard Knox has treated this aspect of the play's imagery in great detail, in *Oedipus at Thebes*, pp. 107-58. See, for example, lines 108-9, 354, 475-76 (hunting); 103-4, 694-96, 922-23, 420 ff., 1207-10 (navigation); 1210-12, 1256-57, 1485, 1497-98 (farming); 68, 101, 218, 256, 1075, 1293 (medicine); 73, 84, 461, 1019 (mathematics).

40. *Antigone*, 332. The same thought is behind the passage in *On Ancient Medicine* which bids us θαυμάζειν τὰ ἐξευρημένα (XII.15). Sophocles' ode, it is true, qualifies its encomium of man's technical achievements with a warning and a moral lesson (366-75), but tragedy absorbs current themes only to transform them. This remains a typical fifth-century poem, which returns again and again, in different phrases, to the single theme of man's resourceful mind. Note περιφραδής (347), μηχαναῖς (348), ἐδιδάξατο (356), παντοπόρος· ἄπορος ἐπ' οὐδέν (360), σοφόν τι τὸ μαχανόεν τέχνας (365-66). One need only contrast Hesiod's *Works and Days*, where success is evidence of justice and hard work rather than of intelligence (289, 303 ff., 397, 411 ff.). A good, balanced analysis of the *Antigone* ode, whose many problems of interpretation cannot be discussed here, is found in Victor Ehrenberg, *Sophocles and Pericles* (Oxford, 1954), pp. 61 ff. The language of *Oedipus Tyrannus*, which purposefully reflects the usage of fifth-century intellectual circles, is analyzed by Knox, *Oedipus at Thebes*, pp. 116-38.

antithesis Sophocles develops an elaborate play of allusion, and what came into his hands as moral commonplace is thereby enlarged to high tragedy.[41]

In spite of the play's undoubted universality of appeal, it remains rooted in the language and thought of the fifth century B.C. It was seen by the same generation of Greeks who heard Democritus say, "Chance opposes wisdom only slightly."[42] In *Oedipus Tyrannus* unknown agencies conspire to demonstrate in Oedipus the limits of practical intellect, even as it exerts its full powers of discovery. The result is ruin. Yet the play, for all that, is not an attack on intelligence; it is a revelation of a deeper wisdom, that man's art and knowledge are nothing compared to the god's. This is implicit in the angry confrontation of king and prophet, the one confident of his intellectual powers (396-98; cf. 509) and later willing to dismiss even the Delphic oracle as worthless (964-72), the other against all likelihood asserting the king's guilt and ignorance (413). The result of this measuring of man's knowledge against god's is first summed up in the ode at 1186 ff., but irony has prefigured that judgment all through the play (e.g. at 264 and 1008).

Sophocles' setting is a mythical past where kings still rule, and

41. See lines 263, 680, 773, 776, 1036. The theme is brought to the fore by Jocasta at 977 and again by Oedipus at 1080. The importance of τύχη in the play is noted by Knox, *Oedipus at Thebes*, pp. 165 ff., 176 ff. The antithesis τέχνη-τύχη is a common one in the fifth century. See Euripides' *Alcestis*, 785-86, *Iphigeneia in Tauris*, 89; Agathon, frags. 6 and 8 (Nauck); *On Anc. Med.*, I; *On the Art*, IV.7-8. Though assonance favors the form τέχνη-τύχη, equivalent antitheses often occur, as at Thucydides, 1.140.1 (λόγος-τύχη), and Aeschylus, frag. 389 (Nauck, γνώμη-τύχη). Cf. Herodotus, 1.68.1; Ion of Chios 36 B 3 (Diels-Kranz); Anaxagoras 59 B 21b (Diels-Kranz); Anon. Iambl., 1.2 (Diels-Kranz 89); Democritus 68 A 151 (Diels-Kranz, II, p. 125, line 16), B 119, B 197, B 210; Gorgias, *Helen*, 19 (Diels-Kranz 82 B 11); Eupolis, frag. 205 (Edmonds). See next note for other examples from Thucydides. That the antithesis remained common after 400 B.C. is shown by the many examples from that period collected in Theodor Gomperz, *Die Apologie der Heilkunst*, Sitzungsberichte Kaiserl. Akad. Wien, Philos.-Hist. Classe, 120, 1889, pp. 118-19.

42. Democritus 68 B 119 (Diels-Kranz). In spite of Thucydides' respect for intellect, the speakers in his history avoid this kind of optimism and recognize the power of chance to thwart men's best-laid plans (1.140.1, 4.64.1-2, 6.23.3, 1.78.1-2). On the other hand, one should not trust chance and so neglect good judgment (1.144.4, 5.104.1, 5.112.2, 5.113, 7.67.4). This is the flaw of false hope (ἐλπίς), which brings the Melians to ruin (5.113; cf. 2.62.4-5, 3.45.5), and which any Athenian would have recognized in Oedipus' penultimate mood of elation.

Thucydides, though he writes of contemporary events, deals mainly with patterns of behavior that transcend differences of constitutional form. But there was one contemporary political issue which gave special relevance to the conception of politics as an art. This was the question of the merits of democracy. If politics is a field for experts, like music or shoemaking, how can one defend a government in which every fool has his say and his vote? The question re-echoes through comedy, tragedy, history and polemic of the late fifth century. One of the jokes in Aristophanes' *Knights* is that a candidate for political leadership in Athens must be stupid. In the third book of Herodotus, where a conclave of Persian revolutionaries indulges in what amounts to a Greek political discussion, one of the charges against democracy is that it puts the ignorant in power. In a set political debate in the *Suppliants* of Euripides, the Theban herald heaps scorn on the inexpert mob, and a fragment of the *Antiope* repeats this in different words. Finally, in the so-called *Old Oligarch*, an antidemocratic tirade, the author assumes the stupidity of the mob and the wisdom of their betters.[43]

The alternative to Athenian democracy was to put government into the hands of the wise and the otherwise deserving. Criticism of the common man's ignorance was equally suitable for oligarchs and for those, like Thucydides, who remembered with regret the Periclean Age, when Athens was in name a democracy but in fact a monarchy (2.65.9-10). But the argument was especially apt for those, like Plato, who envisaged an aristocracy on new principles. In conventional party recriminations, ignorance was only one shortcoming of the Demos and the demagogues, who were attacked as well for uncouthness, wickedness, and low birth.[44] But, in the eyes of Socrates, who had seized on the notion that politics was an art and had concluded that this required the guidance of experts and not a consensus of the ignorant, ignorance became the pre-eminent flaw of democracy. Politics demanded, above all else, wisdom.[45]

43. Aristophanes' *Knights*, 188-93; Herodotus, 3.81; Euripides' *Suppliants*, 417-22, and *Antiope*, frag. 200 (Nauck); pseudo-Xenophon's *Constitution of the Athenians*, 1.5, 1.7.
44. For example, at Aristophanes' *Knights*, 184 ff.
45. The selection of Athenian officials by lot, said Socrates, was a procedure

The debate on the merits of democracy was by no means one-sided, and the rule of the people found some of its strongest defenders among those who valued intellect. Democritus, for one, evidently thought that the democratic system was compatible with the philosophic ideal of government by the wise.[46] So did Pericles, whose encomium of Athenian life and political custom is found in the Funeral Oration as reported by Thucydides. Democracy is defended there as the rule of intelligence, free of deadening custom and unhampered by prejudice against poverty and low birth (2.37). In the same speech, Pericles claims that Athens recognized, more than did other cities, that prudent action requires previous discussion (2.40.2). This remark tends to justify, on a very broad general principle, the procedure of the Athenian Assembly, in which freedom of comment took the form of a political institution. But the obvious objection remained that only expert comment was worth listening to in politics as in all other matters. Democrats could reply with an argument which Protagoras uses in the Platonic dialogue named for him: all men share in the political art, and therefore in matters of politics all are experts in some degree (323a). In this Protagorean theory, the weapon which the anti-democrats had found in the conception of τέχνη is turned with great dexterity back upon them.[47]

---

that no one would think of using to choose a helmsman, a flute-player, or a carpenter (Xenophon's *Memorabilia*, 1.2.9). He makes the same point in a slightly different way at *Mem.*, 3.9.10. Cf. his references to amateurism in politics, at *Protag.* 319a ff., and in education, at *Apol.* 25a. Aristotle alludes to his comparisons of politics and the arts at *Rhetoric* 1393b4 ff.

46. Democritus 68 B 75 and B 251 (Diels-Kranz).

47. The notion of an art in which all men share was not otherwise strange to the fifth century. It is broached in quite a different context, though with some hesitation, by the author of *On Ancient Medicine*, III.49-IV.10. Havelock tries hard to reconstruct fifth-century democratic theory in *The Liberal Temper*, Chaps. 6–9.

The familiar Socratic argument against election by lot is duplicated in the *Dissoi Logoi* (Diels-Kranz 90.7), with differences that imply a democratic point of view. This compendium in Doric of arguments on various topics was probably written shortly before or shortly after the year 400: the inspiration for the antithetic form is late fifth century (cf. Euripides, frag. 189, Nauck), and specifically Protagorean (Diog. Laert., 9.51, Diels-Kranz 80 B 6a, A 20); the Peloponnesian War has recently ended (1.8); the philosophical groups mentioned are sophists, Anaxagoreans, Pythagoreans (6.7-8); the arguments themselves show affinities with the ideas and procedures of Socrates and several sophists. See the extensive bibliographical notes

The conception of virtue and politics as a τέχνη affected not only theology and politics but education as well. The teaching activity of the sophists made this inescapable. Could virtue be taught at all? If it could, how did one go about it? The problem is most familiar to us from Plato's dialogues, but he did not originate it.[48] If virtue is really a τέχνη, it ought to be teachable, since the crafts survive by teaching. But the analogy tended to mislead, because τέχνη at times meant mere knowledge of method rather than practical command of an art. Protagoras implied this when he said that τέχνη without practice and practice without τέχνη come to nothing. His statement is also an implicit distinction between τέχνη and ἀρετή.[49] In the age of the sophists, it was easy to be overimpressed by the spectacular results of instruction, particularly in rhetoric. The *Clouds* ridicules this naive admiration of a rapidly acquired

---

on this last question provided by A. J. Levi, "On Twofold Statements," *AJP*, 61 (1940), 292-306, an article in which the author's own reasoning is not always cogent. But the relation between the *Dissoi Logoi* and Plato's earliest dialogues, or between its author and Socrates, must remain conjectural. H. Gomperz argues in detail against the supposition of Socratic influence, in *Sophistik und Rhetorik*, pp. 151-79. Yet W. Kranz has come to the conclusion that its author knew Socrates, in "Vorsokratisches IV: Die Sogenannten Δισσοὶ Λόγοι," *Hermes*, 72 (1937), 227. E. S. Ramage, in "An Early Trace of Socratic Dialogue," *AJP*, 82 (1961), 418-24, inclines to agree. K. Freeman goes further and, straining chronology to the utmost, finds the influence of five Platonic dialogues in it, including the late *Phaedrus* (*The Presocratic Philosophers* [Oxford, 1946], p. 417, note a1). Our inability to date exactly either the *Dissoi Logoi* or Plato's earliest dialogues makes the question obscure. But one should not overlook the familiarity of the late fifth century with issues and terms which Plato later made his own. This chapter provides many examples of these. For a discussion of the problems of dating the *Dissoi Logoi*, see C. Trieber, "Die Διαλέξεις," *Hermes*, 27 (1892), 210-48. Bibliography can be found in Diels-Kranz, II, p. 405, and in Kranz's *Nachtrag*; in W. Schmid and O. Stählin, *Geschichte der Griechischen Literatur*, 1. Teil, 3. Band (Munich, 1940), pp. 204-6; and in M. Untersteiner, *Sofisti: Testimonianze e Frammenti*, III, pp. ix-xvi. Add most recently Ramage's article, mentioned above.

48. Paul Friedländer, *Platon*, II, *Schriften der Ersten Periode* (2nd ed.; Berlin, 1957), p. 7, calls it "eine—vielleicht die—Lebensfrage der Zeit." Euripides, *Suppliants*, 911 ff., refers to it. At *Apology* 20b, Socrates reports that Evenus the Parian offers to teach virtue for a price of five minae. Gorgias is said at *Meno* 95c to be unique among the sophists in not claiming to make his pupils virtuous, but only δεινοί. He is thereby contrasted with Protagoras (*Protag.* 319a) and Hippias (*Hippias Major* 283c). One of the topics of the *Dissoi Logoi* is, "Whether wisdom and virtue can be taught." In support of the answer yes is the argument that this is precisely what the sophists, the Anaxagoreans, and the Pythagoreans teach (6.7-8; see previous note).

49. Protagoras 80 B 10 (Diels-Kranz).

technique.[50] An argument of the Anonymus Iamblichi, moreover, reads like a rebuke to those who overvalued τέχνη in this sense of the word. One can acquire the art of speaking, he says, quickly and by instruction, but virtue depends on hard work, practice, and time. He has said earlier that it depends as well on chance, i.e. inborn talent.[51] This introduces the familiar antithesis Art-Chance into the discussion under the form Art-Nature, and the emphasis on time and work undermines any possible sophistic claim that brief instruction can open a short cut to virtue. Yet it does not really exclude the possibility that virtue can be taught; it simply adds the qualifications of work, time, practice, and nature. Protagoras himself acknowledged that instruction, to be effective, needs the support of each of the last three. In the dialogue *Protagoras*, moreover, Plato has him derive courage from "nature and good nurture of souls" and not from τέχνη at all.[52]

It would be wrong, therefore, to assume that all the sophists pressed the analogy of virtue and art to unreasonable lengths. Protagoras, the foremost technician of the new art, seems to have stressed his agreement with the traditional views and methods of Athens. His own instruction, he said, was merely a supplement to the education that Athens already gave her citizens.[53] Plato, though he stressed his differences with Athenian educational theory, drew heavily on it. Not only his discussions, but even his solutions, are in large measure framed in terms inherited from his predecessors. This does not impugn his originality. It means only that he introduced his philosophy to Greek readers as a development from ideas that they had already met. More will be said about this in later chapters.[54]

Our survey has shown that around the word τέχνη there flour-

50. Aristophanes' *Clouds*, 112-18.
51. Anon. Iamblichi, 89.2.7, 89.1.2 (Diels-Kranz).
52. Protagoras 80 B 3, B 10 (Diels-Kranz); *Protag.* 351b1-2. See below, Chapt. 4. Another sophist, Prodicus, makes virtue the result of natural endowment, hard work, and practice. He includes knowledge too, but gives it a subordinate and restricted place. See Prodicus 84 B 2 (Diels-Kranz), especially the phrases τὴν φύσιν (27), πόνου καὶ ἐπιμελείας (28), τὰς πολεμικὰς τέχνας (28), παῖ τοκέων ἀγαθῶν (33), διαπονησαμένῳ (33).
53. *Protagoras* 326e6-328c2.
54. See in particular Chapter 4, note 27.

ished in the fifth century questions of theology, politics, and education. The questions were not entirely new, but the way of framing
them was. A growing respect for man's power to discover and control the means to improve his own life found its apt expression in
Sophocles' symbol of Man the Artisan.[55] In that symbol the thoughtful Greek could see profound implications for his view of the gods,
the city, and himself. The more credit he gave to human ingenuity
for the invention of the arts, the less dependent he seemed on divine benevolence and the less subject to natural catastrophe. In
high-spirited, self-made men this bred an optimism of the kind
represented by Oedipus; and it prompted in Sophocles the conclusion that τέχνη is an insufficient paradigm for wisdom. The greater
wisdom is in knowing the limitations to man's artful control of his
destiny. The lesson which teaches this to Oedipus comes, aptly,
from Delphi, where wisdom was honored not as technique but as
self-knowledge. On the other hand, the conception of politics as
an art brought new force to the demand for intelligent statesmen,
and to many it no longer seemed tolerable to rely on the counsels
of the ignorant or on custom for custom's sake. Finally, what the
fifth century discovered in education was a new sense of man's
power to form or reform his own personality. Plato makes drama
of this in the excitement of the young Hippocrates, who has just
heard that Protagoras is in town (*Protagoras* 310b). The cause of
the high expectations engendered by the sophists was their apparent discovery of an art of virtue. In this art they were the master
craftsmen, and they offered to the ambitious who could afford their
instruction some hope of surmounting the shortcomings of φύσις
and of abridging the discouraging requirements of πόνος, χρόνος,
and ἐπιμέλεια. No art could dispense with these, as Protagoras
pointed out; but efficiency in instruction could make the most of
what nature had given and effort earned.

All these influences came to Plato through the mediation of
Socrates. The analogy of virtue with the arts Socrates had made
his own. Critias complained that he was eternally talking about
cobblers, carpenters, and blacksmiths. Hippias, meeting him after

55. See above, notes 39, 40.

a long absence from Athens, remarked that the comparison of justice to the arts of the cobbler, carpenter, blacksmith, and horseman was "the same old thing I heard from you long ago."[56] Intimately connected with the analogy of the arts is the Socratic use of ἐπιστήμη. Bruno Snell has shown how peculiarly well-suited the word is to Socratic ethical theory, since it denotes the knowledge of facts as well as the craftsman's skill.[57] Its use by Socrates shows the essential role in his thought of the analogy of virtue and the crafts, but ἐπιστήμη also unites more readily than would τέχνη the two ideas of skill and the knowledge of truth. It is, in Socratic arguments, the natural bridge between the shoemaker and the philosopher.[58]

None of this would have made of Socrates an extraordinary figure in the decades that preceded 400 B.C. What immediately distinguished him from the sophists was his insistence that he did not profess the art of wisdom and that he taught no one. The only wisdom he claimed to have was a sense of his own ignorance, what he calls in the Apology ἀνθρωπίνη σοφία (20d). That he possessed it and others did not was certified by the Delphic oracle and proved by his interrogation of leading Athenians. This constant question-

56. Xenophon, Mem., 1.2.37, 4.4.5-6.
57. Contrast, for example, Iliad, 21.320 (ἐπιστήσονται), or Euripides' frag. 522, line 3 (Nauck), with Sophocles' Trachiniae, 338. See Bruno Snell, Die Ausdrücke, pp. 81-96.
58. Snell's point is well taken, even though Socrates is in no way bound to ἐπιστήμη as a technical term. Substitutes abound. The cobbler is φρόνιμος at his trade (Alcib. I 125a). The fact that swimmers, horsemen, and soldiers are ἐπιστάμενοι in what they do, and thereby are daring, leads, by some intermediate premises, to the tentative conclusion that courage is σοφία (Protag. 350a-c). At Laches 192e, φρόνιμος refers to the technical skill of a physician. At Meno 88b, ἐπιστήμη, φρόνησις, and νοῦς are used interchangeably, and so are οἶδα and ἐπίσταμαι at Xenophon, Mem., 4.6.10-11. All this is partly an exploitation of the full connotations of these words: σοφός can refer to an able craftsman, and οἶδα can mean "know how to" (Euripides' Alcestis, 348; Iliad, 7.238-41; and Snell, Die Ausdrücke, pp. 7-8, 83), though in fifth-century Attic prose such usages were exceptional (Snell, Die Ausdrücke, pp. 13-15, 83). But it is also partly a straining of language to express a conception of wisdom which no single Greek word of that time evoked. How far the Socratic conception of wisdom went it is impossible to say, but in the mature Platonic system it embraces mastery of the technique of living joined with contemplation of the Ideas and the Good (see Chapter 5 below).
John Gould, in his book The Development of Plato's Ethics (Cambridge, 1955), has made Socrates' use of ἐπιστήμη the basis of a theory which is discussed below, in Chapter 7, n. 2.

ing, which tested pretended wisdom, was designed to reveal the faults in contemporary education and the ignorance of those who ruled (*Apology* 21c). In a sense, it was a tool of political action and educational reform. But Socrates also describes it in unmistakable terms as a religious act, in his words, a service to the god Apollo (30a, 23b). It was, in fact, nothing less than an attack on the pretensions of Man the Artisan.[59] The lesson it taught to all who endured it was "Know thyself," the motto engraved at Delphi. The Socratic irony, so often turned to humorous play or conversational tactic, is also the formalized expression of obeisance to the Delphic rule. To know oneself is to know one's limitations.[60] In this conviction Socrates is one with the Sophocles of *Oedipus Tyrannus*.

Socrates' way of life was shaped by this rule of self-knowledge, and through him it has left a stamp on the whole range of the Platonic dialogues, beginning with the *Apology*. There, Socrates claims to be wiser than the next man only in not thinking he knows what he does not know (21d). Human wisdom, in any case, he adds, is worth little in comparison to the wisdom of the god (23a). Such as it is, it begins with self-knowledge, a difficult, prolonged, and all-absorbing task. The theme recurs again and again in Plato, among other places at *Theaetetus* 157c, at *Phaedrus* 229e, and at *Protagoras* 343b, where it is a serious note in a humorous passage.[61] The fault of not knowing oneself, of which the most serious form is the false conceit of wisdom, is an evil more than once singled

59. Hence the elenchus is sharpest in Socrates' confrontation of Hippias, technical man personified. In particular, *Hippias Minor* 368b provides an ironic echo of the Sophoclean line οὐδὲν ἀνθρώπου δεινότερον πέλει (*Antigone*, 332). For a detailed discussion of that dialogue, see Chapter 3.

60. Acceptance of one's limitations is one of the common implications of the phrase (see *Prom. Bound*, 309). Besides being engraved at Delphi (*Philebus* 48c, *Protag.* 343b, *Phaedrus* 229e), the saying is attributed to Chilon and Thales (references in Diels-Kranz, I, p. 63, line 25; p. 71, line 19; p. 72, line 21; p. 73, lines 1 and 10). To know oneself is difficult (Thales, Pythagoreans: Diels-Kranz, I, p. 64, line 6; p. 464, line 18), or it is a task of which Zeus alone is capable (Ion, frag. 55, Nauck). It is associated with σωφροσύνη (Heraclitus 22 B 116, Diels-Kranz), or identified with it (*Alcib. I* 133c). Σωφροσύνη itself implies at times the acceptance of one's limitations (see above, Chapter 1, n. 9). The subject is treated by T. G. Tuckey, in *Plato's Charmides* (Cambridge, 1951), pp. 9-10.

61. Cf. *Charmides* 167a, *Alcib. I* 130e ff., Xenophon's *Mem.*, 3.9.6, 3.7.9.

out for special condemnation. Plato does not abandon this theme even in his later period.[62]

The result of this fusion of the ancient ethic of self-interest, the new sense of man's power to control his own life by art, and the Delphic admonition, "Know thyself," was the Socratic doctrine that virtue is knowledge. It is a fusion of opposites. It unites the passion for intelligent control of human life with the belief that man's intelligence is weak and puny compared to the god's. The exact meaning, even the exact form, which Socrates gave to this doctrine cannot be settled. The failure of Burnet and Taylor to prove the value as historical documents of certain early dialogues has taught us to be wary of equating the real with the Platonic Socrates.[63] Aristotle and Xenophon, moreover, throw very little further light on the Socratic form of the doctrine. Aristotle's evidence is hard to evaluate simply because he may be referring at all times to the Socrates of the dialogues.[64] In Xenophon's *Memorabilia*, Socrates sometimes defines the virtues as knowledge in an unqualified way, but he also teaches that nature and practice are essential to their existence.[65] A bridge between these two apparently contradictory statements appears in his remark that self-control, strengthened by practice (4.5.1), is a prerequisite of wisdom (4.5.6, 4.5.11). This corresponds to Platonic doctrine, as it will be explained below in Chapter 5. Whether it was also Socratic doctrine, however, is

---

62. *Sophist* 229c, *Philebus* 48c ff. According to Plutarch, *Adversus Colotem*, 20, Aristotle said that the Delphic maxim gave the first impulse to Socrates' investigations (frag. 1, V. Rose [ed.], *Aristotelis qui ferebantur librorum fragmenta* [Leipzig, 1881]).

63. See above, Introduction.

64. Of passages that may derive from the *Protagoras* alone we have *Eth. Nic.* 1116b3 ff., 1144b26 ff., 1145b22 ff., 1147b15 ff., *Eth. Eud.* 1229a12 ff., 1230a4 ff., 1216b3 ff., 1246b33 ff. Cf. *Protag.* 349-50, 352bc, 360d, 361b. The clearest correspondence is between *Protag.* 352bc and *Eth. Nic.* 1145b22 ff., 1147b15 ff. The comments at *Eth. Nic.* 1144b18 ff. may refer to *Meno* 88d, 89a, 98d, and *Phaedo* 69a. The references in the *Magna Moralia* (1182a15 ff., 1183b8-9, 1190b28 ff., 1198a10 ff., 1200b25 ff.) simply duplicate those in the *Nicomachean* and the *Eudemian Ethics*. The possible exception, *M.M.* 1187a5-13, may well be based on *Gorgias* 475e, *Meno* 78b, and *Protag.* 360a. All references are collected in Th. Deman, *Le Témoignage d'Aristote sur Socrate* (Paris, 1942), pp. 82 ff. Cf. V. de Magalhães-Vilhena, *Le Problème de Socrate* (Paris, 1952), pp. 267 ff., 293 ff.

65. Contrast *Memorabilia*, 4.6.6, 4.6.4, 4.6.10-11, and 3.9.4-5 with 1.2.19, 2.1.1-2, 2.1.6, 3.9.1-3.

much harder to say, since modern conventions of biographical accuracy bound Xenophon no more strictly than they did Plato.

In spite of these large uncertainties, it is clear enough that Socrates believed that the good life depended above all else on knowledge. This conclusion rests on a few features of his life and teaching which are certainly not fiction: that he questioned his contemporaries and convicted them of ignorance, that he set great store
by the maxim "Know thyself," that he constantly used the arts and
crafts as analogies. Anecdotes referring to his talk about cobblers
and builders, of the sort found at *Memorabilia* 1.2.37 and 4.4.5,
depend, whether true or not, on the relish of a known idiosyncrasy.
The latter, moreover, became an integral part of the anti-Socratic
polemic (as reported at *Memorabilia* 1.2.9), and no mere literary
invention could have provoked this. Socrates, however, still remains a partly mysterious figure, whose full contribution to Greek
thought it is impossible to separate from Platonism on the one hand
and from the intellectual ferment of the late fifth century on the
other.[66] What detaches itself is a personality and a tone, and a few
doctrines that are so much a part of both that if they are not Socratic we know nothing that is. Among these are the adherence to
the Delphic maxim, with the irony that is its formal expression, the
comparison of virtue with the arts and crafts, and the injunction
to forget all else and care for one's soul. All three elements of Socratic intellectualism are implicit here.[67]

66. J. S. Morrison has recently claimed, on the evidence of *Laches* 197d,
that "Plato does . . . definitely attribute to Damon a belief in the identity of
courage and wisdom" ("The Origins of Plato's Philosopher-Statesman," *CQ*,
N.S. 8 [1958], 205). This, if true, would be an interesting anticipation by
Damon of the Socratic paradoxes. But the "wisdom" which Nicias is said to
have acquired from Damon in this passage is clearly not the identity of courage and wisdom, but only the ability to make distinctions such as "courageous"
vs. "daring." Cf. 197a.

67. Prof. Robert Brumbaugh has shown me an index, compiled by one of
his Philosophy seminars, of the more than five hundred references in the dialogues to the arts and crafts. The sheer number is an indication of Plato's
preoccupation with the subject.

# 3. THE EARLY DIALOGUES, I

The intellectualism which Plato inherited from Socrates has left its mark on dialogues of all periods. Since his presentation of it gradually changed as he grew older, the best method of exposition might seem to be to take up the dialogues in the sequence in which they were written. But discussion of the relevant passages in strict order of composition, however desirable in theory, is not feasible, since the criteria available allow only the broadest chronological divisions. The rule followed in this and subsequent chapters, therefore, combines a general respect for chronology with convenience of exposition. This chapter and the next deal with early dialogues, i.e. with those which, on generally accepted criteria of style, can be dated before the *Republic*.[1] On one or two occasions this limitation will be waived, simply because the best

1. Or at least before *Republic* 2-10. Sir David Ross, in his book *Plato's Theory of Ideas* (Oxford, 1951), pp. 2, 10, shows the relative chronology of the dialogues as worked out by six scholars, including himself. There is very large agreement among them as to what should precede *Republic* 2-10, but very little on the relative positions of dialogues *within* this early group.

commentary on one of Plato's abridged arguments is often the fuller discussion found in a later work.

Of the early dialogues treated in Chapters 3 and 4, the *Apology*, *Meno*, *Gorgias*, and *Hippias Minor* are discussed first, since their treatment of the relation of virtue and knowledge is less thorough than that of the *Laches*, *Charmides*, and *Protagoras*. The latter three dialogues are postponed to the next chapter. The arrangement *within* this pair of chapters implies nothing about chronology. Plato's dialogues do not fall into a logical series, and nothing prevented him from treating cursorily what he had already treated more completely elsewhere. All the works mentioned, however, share a concern with one or more of the following questions: whether men do wrong willingly, whether they ever desire evil, whether virtue is knowledge and can be taught, and in what sense it is an art.

We begin with the *Apology*. This early work shows traces of what can fairly be called an intellectualist point of view in its argument that education is an activity for experts and not for everyone (25bc) and in its insistence on the importance of the primary wisdom of knowing one's own limitations (23ab). But it also introduces, in a brief and cryptic argument, the paradoxical notion of the involuntariness of crime and defends it by an appeal to self-interest. The passage begins at 25c, where Meletus, the accuser of Socrates, admits in cross-examination that it is preferable to live with good associates than with bad ones, because the former will benefit, the latter injure, one. Meletus further acknowledges what seems obvious: no one wishes to be injured rather than benefited by his companions. Yet he accuses Socrates of corrupting the youth intentionally. From these admissions and this accusation Socrates forges an argument in his own defense. Do you think, he asks, that I at my age have reached such a pitch of ignorance as not to realize that by making my associates wicked I run the risk of suffering evil at their hands? On the contrary, either I do not corrupt them, or I do it unwillingly. If I do so unwillingly, I need instruction; for if I am instructed, I shall stop doing what I do through inadvertence. But you, Meletus, have brought me here to stand trial where, according to law, one brings those in need of punishment and not instruction.

Socrates wins his point, but his argument is not of a kind that would sit well with a modern juryman. Assuming that Plato has reproduced it fairly, one may doubt that Socrates' judges were much impressed by it either, in spite of the Athenian respect for quick-wittedness and skill in debate. Taken in isolation, the argument is sophistry.[2] But it bears another aspect too, if compared with other Platonic passages where Socrates expends time and patience in exploring the same difficult subject he treats so abruptly here. The brevity of his argument is an expression of disdain for Meletus, that most unworthy of partners in philosophical conversation. Brief as it is, however, the passage allows us to glean from it a few essential points. According to Socrates, any crime he may be guilty of should be remedied by instruction alone; he therefore ironically asks for lessons in ethics. But what he says of himself at his age he need not mean as a general truth. In fact, at 26a6-7 he suggests that some other criminals need punishment rather than instruction. If instruction is for the ignorant, then punishment is for wrongdoers otherwise afflicted. Their affliction is not mentioned, but it may be incontinence.[3] At any rate, the brief passage implies two causes of error, one ignorance and one unnamed. Beyond this, it treats the universal desire to avoid injury and win

2. John Burnet, *Plato's Euthyphro, Apology of Socrates, and Crito* (Oxford, 1924), p. 106, points out rightly that as it stands it is not a serious argument, except as a demonstration that Meletus does not understand his own charge. Paul Shorey, *What Plato Said* (Chicago, 1933), p. 81, calls it "ironically fallacious." But it is interesting that the argument is of the sort that the Platonic Socrates uses elsewhere seriously, and in fact reads like a parody of the other serious passages discussed in the text below. The *Meno, Gorgias,* and *Republic* show that there is a sense in which the argument, which looks like pure verbal sleight of hand at *Apol.* 25c-e, is true. One cannot accuse a man of wrongdoing and intelligence at the same time.

Guido Calogero, "Gorgias and the Socratic Principle *Nemo Sua Sponte Peccat*," *JHS,* 77, Part I (1957), 12-17, has shown the essential identity of *Apol.* 25c-e with the sophistical argument of Gorgias at *Palamedes* 26, which Calogero thinks Socrates borrowed for his own defense. The question as to who borrowed from whom cannot be decided so easily, and Calogero's other parallels between the *Palamedes* and the Platonic *Apology* do not really demonstrate dependence. But it would not be surprising if Plato, who often uses popular and traditional ethical conceptions, could find gold even in current sophistries.

3. Cf. *Sophist* 227d ff.

benefits as the determining motivation in the moral life. This is the ancient appeal to self-interest, which any Greek would have readily understood whether or not he responded to it in his own practice and belief. Socrates does not, to be sure, deny that he had any disinterested motives in behaving decently towards his young friends. But for the moment such motives are ignored.

The *Apology*, in short, embodies all three kinds of intellectualism as these were described in the previous chapter. It praises the fundamental wisdom of self-knowledge; it implies the use of τέχνη as an ethical conception, in the argument that the improvement of the young is the activity of a few experts; and it bases morality squarely upon the desire for one's own good.

In the passage which begins at *Apology* 25c, summarized above, the argument is so abridged that its general principles remain obscure. To find these more satisfactorily explained we must turn to the *Meno* and the *Gorgias*, where morality is once more derived from self-interest; here, however, the derivation is explicit and of universal application. The first passage to consider is *Meno* 77a ff. Unlike the *Apology*, where an extended dialogue with the hostile Meletus on the grounds of virtuous behavior would be out of place, the *Meno* involves a joint search for the meaning of virtue and an attempt to settle the question, "Can it be taught?" In the passage mentioned, Meno, in answer to Socrates' request, has just framed a definition of virtue, calling it the desire for good things combined with the ability to get them (ἐπιθυμοῦντα τῶν καλῶν δυνατὸν εἶναι πορίζεσθαι 77b4-5). Not all men, in his opinion, have this desire; some of them desire what is evil. These are divided into those who desire it thinking it good and those who know it is evil. Of the latter group, some think it is beneficial though evil, others know it is harmful. Socrates argues in reply that it is impossible to think of an evil thing as beneficial. Those who supposedly desire evil things as beneficial are really under the illusion that they are good. On the other hand, a man desiring what is evil, knowing it to be harmful, would wish the injury to himself: he would choose to be wretched and unhappy. But nobody so wishes, and so no man wishes evil (οὐκ ἄρα βούλεται . . . τὰ κακὰ οὐδείς 78a6).

There are certain obvious resemblances between this argument and the one from the *Apology* discussed above. In both dialogues, man's inability to choose evil as evil intentionally is proved by means of the two premises that no man wishes evil to himself and that an evil deed in some way injures the agent. In the *Apology* evil done to associates is said to put the malefactor in danger of his victim's own evil deeds. In the *Meno* the belief is more general. Once agreed that nobody desires evils for himself (ἐπιθυμεῖν τῶν κακῶν), it seems settled that nobody wishes evils absolutely (βούλεσθαι τὰ κακά). The identification of the two phrases is not seen as a problem and is hence not explained. Instead, they are simply used throughout as interchangeable, on the evident assumption, as yet unproved, that all evildoing injures the malefactor.[4]

In the *Gorgias* the doctrine that no man wishes evil is taken up again, and some of the obscurities and silences of the *Meno* are clarified. The passage in question begins at 466b, where Polus asks Socrates whether he does not think that the orators have greatest power in the cities. Socrates answers no, not if we consider power as a good to him who possesses it; for if it is a good, then the orators have the least power of all. Polus, incredulous, asks: Do they not kill whomever they wish, as do tyrants, and take away money and expel from the cities whomever they decide to expel? Socrates sees this as two questions in one and takes up its different parts separately. Orators and tyrants, he answers, have smallest power in the cities, for they do nothing of what they "wish," so to say, although they do whatever to them seems best. Over Polus' protest that to do what one thinks best is indeed great power, Socrates argues that to have great power must be regarded as a good, whereas to give oneself up to a senseless pursuit of what one merely *thinks* best is an evil. But a man who persists in doing what he does not really wish to do is behaving in just this senseless way. Therefore, if Socrates can prove that orators and tyrants do not do what they wish, he will have proved that they lack power. He proves this by arguing, in effect, that the word "wish" (βούλεσθαι) is properly applied only to the ends of action, not the means, and

4. Compare 77b4-5 with 78b3-4. See also 78a6-b2. As R. S. Bluck says in *Plato's Meno* (Cambridge, 1961), p. 257, "Under the guise of a formal argument, Plato is virtually making an assertion—that κακά must be harmful (in *some* way) to *all* concerned, *including the person who does the harm*."

that orators and tyrants unwittingly pursue ends that they would never deliberately choose. The point is made by analogies. When a man undergoes the pain or discomfort of taking drugs from a physician, or when he faces the dangers of a commercial venture at sea, he does each for the sake of some end, the former for health, the latter for riches. What he wishes is not the means, as we would say, but the end. This is a general rule (467d), and Socrates clarifies it further by dividing everything into the good, the bad, and what is neither. Wisdom, health, and riches are good. Sitting, walking, running, talking are neither good nor bad; when men do these they do them for the sake of a good that they may bring. Now executions, banishments, and confiscations are not things desirable in themselves; they are therefore the means, neither good nor bad, with which the tyrant or the orator intends to secure what is good for himself. In the eyes of Polus (468e) the tyrant's license to do all this at will is a good. But Socrates sees that it can be a means to injustice, and injustice is the greatest of evils (469b). Therefore, tyrants and orators have least power of all men; they only have full license to bring misery upon themselves.[5]

Polus sees this as an intolerable paradox, but Socrates continues to maintain it stoutly. Happiness belongs to the man or woman

5. Plato's argument here has been attacked by E. R. Dodds, *Plato, Gorgias* (Oxford, 1959), pp. 235-36, on the ground that its universality is questionable. It seems not to cover cases of psychological conflict, or those actions which are motivated by disinterested love or hatred; nor are many of our actions consciously governed by a general conception of our own good. But though Plato's argument is somewhat oversimplified and dwells only on actions in which the end is consciously present, it can still be defended. An ultimate end may govern actions without being conscious. It is present implicitly if reflection or interrogation would bring it out. Moreover, the argument is tailored to the example of the tyrant or demagogue, who desires the good for himself and yet in removing his enemies and taking their property gains only injustice. It is a fair assumption that when tyrants and demagogues behave in this way they generally do so for their own benefit. If so, the argument suffices to refute Polus. It does not, to be sure, account for the apparently disinterested or capricious action before leaping to its generalization (467d6), and this is a fair objection to it. On the other hand, one should not extract from the passage more than it implies. It is very doubtful, for example, as Dodds claims (p. 236), that "the perilous distinction between ends and means . . . is treated as absolute." It is hard to believe that Plato really thinks riches are an absolute end on a par with wisdom simply because he chooses to illustrate the notions of end and means by contrasting riches with commercial voyages. That some ends, like riches, are also means was surely obvious to Plato, but also hardly to the point in this argument.

who is noble and good, while the unjust and the wicked are wretched (470e). Archelaus, tyrant of Macedonia, who has set new standards of successful villainy, is unhappy—the more so because he escapes punishment. Polus heaps eloquent scorn on this notion but is unable to refute it, and Socrates resumes the questioning in order to prove it. Polus will admit that unjust action is more shameful, though better, than unjust suffering, while the latter is nobler, though more evil, than the former (474cd). But he is unable to sustain this argument. He admits that the noble is either the pleasurable, or the useful, or both, and the useful he willingly identifies as the good (474e-475a). The shameful is therefore defined by pain or evil. Now since doing injustice is not more painful than suffering it, it must simply be more evil, and Polus has to admit that he would never choose the more evil and shameful of two alternatives (475de). It is not difficult after this for Socrates to prove that to suffer punishment for injustice is actually a benefit. Polus is willing to admit that evils of soul are far more shameful than those of property or of body (477c). These evils of soul, viz. injustice and wickedness in general, must, if the previous admissions were correct, entail the worst kind of pain or injury or both. Pain is out of the question, so there remains the unavoidable conclusion that wickedness involves the greatest injury to the wicked (477de). The happiest man is he who avoids it entirely, the next happiest he who pays the just penalty and is cured of it (478de).

These pages from the *Gorgias* clarify and justify the argument in the *Meno*, which had assumed that, since no one wishes evil for himself, no one will wish evil absolutely. Against that argument the objection might have been raised that a man can wish an evil, such as murder, as the means to a good end, such as happiness. But in the *Gorgias* Socrates restricts the scope of the term "wish" to ends and declines to apply it to means at all. This may seem arbitrary. Greek usage in general, and even Plato's usage elsewhere, does not always conform to the meaning alleged here. This temporary narrowing of a common term, however, makes the valid point that we choose some things only because we wish other things which, in our judgment, the former entail. Another philosopher might have coined a new term to express the "desire of ends." Plato prefers the sharp edge of paradox with its undoubted pedagogical advantage. Hence, "No man wishes evil." The typical ends cited by way of example are kinds of personal advantage, viz. wisdom, health, and riches. Later in the argument, these are generalized in the single term εὐδαιμονία, or "happiness." It remains the basic assumption of both Socrates and Polus that all men agree in their desire for this end. In fact, the statement "No man wishes evil" appears in this context to be a way of saying, "All men wish happiness."

Where the argument fails to satisfy us is in its identification of virtue and happiness. Polus, who is only a half-hearted immoralist, and will not deny that injustice is shameful, is led by inexorable logic through the implied conceptions of the injurious and the evil to an admission that he would never choose the shameful. Socrates' victory is easy, but our desire to see the inherent harmfulness of injustice explained remains unsatisfied by this brief lesson in logic administered by a master to an inept pupil. Not until the *Republic* is that problem attacked with descriptive thoroughness. The conjunction of justice and the other virtues with happiness is, in a sense, the subject of that whole dialogue. The problem is crystallized there in the story of the ring of Gyges, first introduced at *Republic* 359d. Plato's solution to the question which that legend raises is finally stated only after a long interval: justice itself, he concludes, is the soul's best possession, and therefore one should always be just, even if one had the ring which makes its owner invisible (612b). This association of virtue with self-interest is one of those central doctrines to which Plato constantly recurs in dialogues of all periods. Originally expressed in the Socratic concern for the care of the soul, then made the occasion, in the second book of the *Republic*, of Socrates' long and eloquent reply to the misgivings of Glaucon and Adeimantus, it reappears with undiminished conviction at the end of his life in his final work. At *Laws* 731 we read again that to do wrong is to admit the worst evil, injustice, into one's most precious possession, the soul.

What all these passages reveal is a set of ethical principles of a kind Thucydides would not have found hard to understand. Every man pursues his own good, and men are ranked in merit by the degree of intelligence which they bring to bear on that activity. The service of self as interpreted in Thucydides may differ vastly from Plato's justice, but the two men share a respect for intellect and an acceptance of man's indomitable will to pursue his own best interest. This will is normally expressed by Plato in the restricted sense he gives to the verb βούλεσθαι. It appears in the *Symposium*, however, in another guise, as ἔρως, "love," which is redefined by Plato as the "desire for the eternal possession of the good" (206a). This is equated in the same passage with the desire for happiness, a purpose described as ultimate in the order of means and ends and common to all mankind (205a).[6]

If all men wish the good and some fail to achieve it, then the wish is not enough. A man needs discernment. In the *Gorgias*, the tyrant and the orator, who commit crimes that lead ultimately to misery, have simply shown lack of sense: ποιοῦσιν ἄνευ νοῦ ἃ δοκεῖ (cf. 467a). What distinguishes a good man from a bad, in short, is his exercise of intelligence. In coming to this conclusion, we have already grasped the essential logic which puts wisdom at the center of Platonic moral philosophy. Men are distinguished not by good will and decent intentions—they all wish the good—but by the good sense of knowing how to achieve the good. What brings this abiding good sense? Plato begins to frame the answer to this question in the *Gorgias*, and he does so in terms already familiar in fifth-century Greek thought. To be virtuous a man needs not only the desire but also the ability (δύναμις); he needs as well a grasp of the rules of virtue, viz. the art (τέχνη). Ability and art are gained by practice (ἄσκησις) and instruction (μάθησις). All this, which can be found at *Gorgias* 509d7 ff., advances by one step the inquiry that stopped at *Meno* 78b. There Socrates, having proved to Meno that men do not differ in their desire to reach the good, remarks that the difference may lie in their ability to reach it. In the *Gorgias* he develops that suggestion. In doing so he vindicates, to a degree, Meno's earliest definition of virtue, at 77b, "to desire good things and be able to get them," but in a sense of which Meno was unaware.

6. The relationship between "love," as defined in the *Symposium*, and the "wish for good," as explained in the *Gorgias*, is discussed below in Chapter 7.

In the suggestion that virtue may require practice as well as instruction there is an echo of the educational theory of the fifth century, discussed above in Chapter 2. In Platonic ethics, to be sure, the
traditional term "practice" has been incorporated into a system
which makes knowledge, in a unique way, central. In spite of this,
it may seem that to emphasize—even to admit—the presence in
Platonic thought of such conventional ideas is to threaten the integrity of the paradoxes and perhaps deny Plato's claim to originality. But Plato was not original to the point of teaching nonsense, though that is often the tacit assumption of those who ad-
here to theories of Platonic development. These assume that in
his later life Plato himself quietly rejected as foolish what had
been most original in his earlier doctrine, viz. the ethical paradoxes.
But such a rejection was never necessary. What separates the paradoxes from nonsense is that, instead of denying common human
experience, they simply reformulate it. As a result, many beliefs
current elsewhere in Greek thought find entrance to Platonism and
sit in peace with doctrines that seem expressly designed to annihi-
late them. The acceptance in the *Gorgias* of the notion of practice
in virtue is only one illustration of this.

The easy assumption that the ethical paradoxes constitute a
sweeping denial of Greek educational experience has found apparent support in another passage of the *Gorgias*. At 460bc of that
dialogue Socrates has been misconstrued as saying that virtue is a
product of instruction alone.[7] No one who accepts the usual view
of Platonic intellectualism has found such a statement surprising;
however foolish on its own merits, it seems to follow from the belief that no man does wrong intentionally. But the passage does
not say what it is alleged to say. A summary of its argument will
show this. Gorgias has said that the rhetorician can, by persuasive-
ness, seem to have knowledge he really lacks. Socrates asks if he
can do this in matters of justice and injustice, of good and evil; if
rhetoricians, in fact, do not know what these are but simply speak
so persuasively about them that they seem to know. Gorgias replies
that this is not true: a pupil of his would actually learn justice and

7. By Theodor Gomperz, *Griechische Denker* (2nd ed.; Leipzig, 1903-09),
2.285-86.

injustice and come to a real knowledge of them. But is it not true, asks Socrates, that one who has learnt carpentry is a carpenter, one who has learnt music is a musician, and one who has learnt medicine is a physician? Yes. Then, by analogy, will not the man who has learnt justice be just? Of course. Will not the just man act justly? Yes. Must not the rhetorician be just, and will not the just man necessarily want to act justly? So it seems. But then the rhetoricians, who are just, will never want to act unjustly. Yet Gorgias had said earlier that one who knew rhetoric could use it unjustly, and this is inconsistent with what he says now.

The argument here should not be strained to yield more than it implies. Both Socrates and Gorgias assume that justice is an art like carpentry, music, and medicine. But it is Gorgias, not Socrates, who assumes that the art of justice can be imparted by instruction alone, since in fact this is how he teaches it. Socrates merely draws out the implications of this belief to show that it is inconsistent with what Gorgias said before. This is the normal procedure of elenchus, in which the questioner himself avoids commitments even while he entraps the other speaker in contradictions.[8] Socrates does assume that the art of justice, once possessed, makes a man a just man. But he does not say here how he thinks the art can be acquired. Only later, at 509c ff., does he intimate his own belief that it needs both instruction and practice.

In some dialogues, the question whether virtue can be taught at all is seen as a vexing problem in its own right. This old issue, which had been familiar in the Athens of Plato's boyhood and had long before occupied the thoughts of Theognis (lines 437-38), was approached by Plato with fresh energy and new arguments. It occupies much of the *Meno*, directs from beginning to end the discussion of the *Protagoras*, and finds in the *Republic* what amounts to a long and detailed affirmative answer.

At the beginning of the *Meno*, the question is abruptly posed by Meno himself in this form: Can virtue be taught, or does it come to men instead by practice or nature or in some other way? Socrates postpones the inquiry, but later in the dialogue, responding to Meno's insistence, he takes it up with reluctance: he would

8. See below, Chapter 4, note 22.

have preferred not to discuss whether virtue is a thing to be taught before inquiring what it is. He proposes to treat it, however, under a hypothesis, as a geometrician might. Meno first agrees that a man can be taught nothing that is not knowledge. Conversely, if virtue is a kind of knowledge (ἐπιστήμη) it will be teachable. These premises granted, Socrates undertakes to prove that virtue and knowledge can in some way be identified. Virtue, he begins, is surely a good, and it is through virtue that men are good; therefore it is beneficial. Examining this category of the beneficial, he finds that it includes, among other things, health, strength, beauty, and wealth. But these can all injure us too; they are beneficial only when we use them rightly. Qualities of soul, such as temperance, justice, courage, ability to learn, memory, magnificence, and the like, are subject to the same rule. All such qualities which cannot be identified with knowledge help us at times and at times injure us. This is particularly evident in courage. A man who is brave without good sense is injured, but sensible bravery benefits him (88b2 ff.). The same is true of temperance and ability to learn. In fact all of the soul's efforts and acts of endurance produce happiness only when knowledge (φρόνησις) guides them; guided by folly (ἀφροσύνη) they bring misery. Therefore, if virtue is a quality of soul and beneficial, it must be knowledge: all other such qualities neither benefit nor injure except as knowledge or folly guides them. The issue of the inquiry seems clear. Do we agree that virtue, either entirely or in part, is knowledge? Meno acquiesces.[9]

Instead of resting in this conclusion, the argument begins to take an unexpected turn. According to the reasoning, the good would not be good by nature. If not by nature, then perhaps they are so by instruction. This inference will depend on its having been shown beyond a doubt that virtue is knowledge (ἐπιστήμη); but Socrates wonders now whether this has been fairly proved. If virtue is teachable, then there ought to be pupils and teachers of it. Yet there seem to be none. Great men, for example, do not teach it to their sons; nor do the sophists actually teach it, whatever their claims. This is good reason to believe that virtue is not teachable

9. *Meno* 89a. By a similar argument in *Euthydemus* 278e-282a Socrates proves that only through wisdom can a man fare well.

after all; in that event, it will not be knowledge either, since those two suppositions have been accepted as entailing each other (98d). As Socrates points out, moreover, he and Meno have overlooked the fact that the beneficial effects of knowledge can be produced by right opinion as well, and a man cannot teach what he possesses only as right opinion. The obvious solution to the anomaly of the statesman who could not teach virtue to his son is that he was guided by right opinion and not by knowledge. Like an oracle or a prophet, he uttered truths by a kind of divine inspiration. The *Meno* concludes with Socrates' statement that if the discussion has been fairly conducted, virtue is neither a natural endowment nor a product of teaching but a divine grace unattended by knowledge. But he quickly adds the qualification, "Unless there be among the statesmen one able to make others into statesmen." If such there exists, he adds, then his place among the living, in respect to virtue, is like that of Homer's Teiresias in Hades: he is a reality among the shadows.

The *Meno* is obviously not meant to settle either of its principal issues: what virtue is, and whether it is teachable. The inverted procedure which Socrates adopted reluctantly, attempting to answer the second question before the first, has prevented him and Meno from attaining τὸ σαφές (100b). The true teacher of virtue has therefore eluded their grasp, his existence unverified, his nature undefined, a Teiresias who has vanished before yielding up his secret. We must not assume that this secret involved a naive intellectualism. On the contrary, the argument of the *Meno*, though inconclusive, produces two important qualifications. At first, it is true, Socrates demonstrates that knowledge makes all things beneficial to man. His property, his qualities of soul and of body are good for him only insofar as he uses them reasonably. But even this preliminary conclusion is qualified: knowledge has an important share in virtue but may not be the whole of it.[10] The last

10. I find this implication in 89a4: "Then do we say that virtue, either entirely or in part, is knowledge?" Bluck, *Meno*, p. 336, maintains, however, that the Greek here means virtue is either knowledge or a species (μέρος) of knowledge. "If φρόνησις is the source of *all* usefulness, and ἀρετή is *one* thing that is useful, one might reasonably conclude that ἀρετή depends upon φρόνησις but is not necessarily co-extensive with it." He candidly points out, however,

part of the *Meno* offers a different kind of reservation. In some men knowledge, which can justify its convictions on rational grounds, is replaced by right opinion. The latter is present when a man believes what happens to be true (97ab) without having reasoned it out for himself. His convictions are therefore insecurely grounded, but his behavior is as virtuous as that of a man who really knows (97b-98a). Of these two reservations, the first implies that knowledge may not be self-sufficient, the second that it is not in any case indispensable. The full implications of each for Plato's intellectualism will not be evident until the *Republic*.

The *Hippias Minor* confirms our admiration for Plato's dialectical virtuosity in his practice of attacking from a number of vantage points the same fundamental issues. The problem once more is: What makes a man virtuous? But this dialogue combines in a new way two related questions which are treated separately elsewhere: whether virtue is knowledge and ability, and whether wrongdoing is ever intentional. Socrates assumes for the argument that both beliefs are true and demonstrates that taken together they lead to an absurd conclusion. If virtue is knowledge and ability, then it is like the proficiency of a craftsman, or the skill of an athlete, or the knowledge of a scientist. The good man will be one who knows the good and the bad and has the ability and the knowledge enabling him to do either. If, furthermore, it is possible to do wrong willingly, there will be offenders who know the good and have it within their power but choose evil instead. The absurd conclusion is that the man who errs willingly is the good man, whereas the bad man can only offend unwillingly. The argument of the dialogue falls into two complementary parts. The first proves that the wisest man is the biggest liar; the second moves

---

his own decision, at 87d6-7, to follow the better manuscript reading τι αὐτοῦ instead of τιν' αὐτό, a choice which tends not to support his translation of 89a4. On the other hand, the phrasing at 87c5, 87d5, and 88d2-3 might argue in his favor. In support of my translation is the fact that at 88b4-5 and at 88c6 νοῦς and φρόνησις respectively are spoken of as accompanying other qualities of soul to produce certain familiar virtues. This implies that virtue is a compound of which knowledge is one part. The issue cannot be decided with absolute certainty since the point of view shifts: virtue is a kind of knowledge (87c5); virtue is knowledge simply (88c4-5); knowledge is part of the common virtues (88c6-d1).

in a parallel way to prove that the same is true of wrongdoing in general, and that the good man is the one who errs on purpose.

The work takes the form of a conversation between Socrates and Hippias, the sophist who was famous for the range of his knowledge and abilities. As the dialogue opens, we learn that Hippias has just finished a speech about Homer. Socrates confides to Eudicus, who is the third and least important participant in the conversation to follow, that the speech has raised in his mind the question whether Achilles or Odysseus was the better man. Socrates is persuaded to put the question to Hippias. The sophist, who finds himself in an expansive and confident mood, replies that Achilles was the best man of those who went to Troy, Nestor the wisest, and Odysseus the most versatile. The word by which he characterizes Odysseus, πολύτροπος, is capable also of being translated "wily" or "shifty," and it is a sense akin to the last that Hippias actually has in mind. He explains, under questioning by Socrates, that what he means is that Odysseus was a liar, whereas Achilles, for instance, was truthful.

What began as a question of literary characterization has now become Socrates' opportunity to explore larger philosophical issues. Does Hippias take the truthful man and the liar to be different? He does, but Socrates is determined to show him that the distinction may be untenable. Through his questions and the responses of Hippias, the argument grows toward that conclusion. In the first place, liars are able, sensible, knowing, and wise in the things about which they lie (365e, 366a). They are, in short, those who are wise enough and capable enough to lie. The class of liars is, in a sense, an exclusive group to which the ignorant and the incapable cannot belong. Hippias, for example, who is most capable and wisest in arithmetic, and therefore best, has the greatest ability to tell the truth in arithmetical questions. Yet by the same token he has the greatest ability to tell lies, since in planning a lie he is the one who best knows what not to say. The same principle applies to geometry, astronomy, and all the other arts. The same man, in fact, is both truthful and false, and what Hippias said earlier about their being different was all amiss. The truthful Achilles is a liar, and the false Odysseus is an honest man (369b).

Hippias, displeased at this inference, refers in his literal-minded way to the text of Homer and claims to have at his command ample evidence that will prove Socrates wrong. Socrates rises to the challenge with a text of his own, from *Iliad* IX, where Achilles seems to tell a lie about going home. Hippias defends his hero, who, he says, lied unwillingly and without deliberation, whereas Odysseus lied willingly and deliberately (370e). The argument seems plausible, but Socrates, with the larger philosophical issues ever in mind, is prepared to nullify it by adducing still more paradoxes. By Hippias' own statement, he argues, Odysseus must be better than Achilles, inasmuch as willing liars are better than unwilling ones.

When Hippias protests against this unusual doctrine, Socrates defers ironically to his great wisdom and avers that only the trend of the discussion makes him suggest that willing liars are better. Sometimes he inclines to think otherwise; at all events, he is confused and conscious of his ignorance (372b ff.). In his state of uncertainty, he decides to resort to analogy to find out whether the willing or the unwilling offender is better. Relevant analogies seem available in a large range of human activities. In sports, for example, a bad runner runs slowly not on purpose but simply because he cannot run faster. But when we see a good runner running slowly we can be sure that he does it on purpose, since he could do better if he wanted to. In a race, to run slowly is bad, to run swiftly good. Hence, in foot racing, the good man does bad things voluntarily, the bad man involuntarily. What is true of speed is true also of strength, of grace, and of singing. The strong, the graceful, and the musically accomplished, when they show weakness or awkwardness or sing off key, do so on purpose, demonstrating that only the good err voluntarily. The general rule is applied to parts of the body, instruments, and animals. In the arts and sciences, the soul that errs on purpose is better. In our slaves we choose one who might do wrong on purpose, as more capable than one who would do wrong by accident. Finally, we will wish to have a soul of our own that errs on purpose.

Hippias will not accept the astonishing conclusion to which Socrates' argument has led them. But Socrates' recapitulation of the main points finds no refutation from him. He assents to each step but declines once more to accept the conclusion. Justice—to follow Socrates' summary—is an ability or knowledge or both. Therefore, the more capable soul, or the wiser soul, or the soul with more of both qualities, is the juster soul. But it is precisely this soul that is more capable of doing ill as well as good, and would do ill willingly. And so "the man who errs and does shameful and unjust things on purpose, Hippias, if there is such a man, is none other than the good man" (376b). Hippias refuses to agree, and Socrates concedes that only the trend of the argument makes him say what he does. The dialogue ends.[11]

11. This little dialogue, the *Hippias Minor*, has produced an extraordinary variety of reactions and interpretations. Many of them are reviewed at the beginning of Oscar Kraus, *Platons Hippias Minor: Versuch Einer Erklärung* (Prague, 1913), and in W. Schneidewin, *Platons Zweite Hippiasdialog* (1931). Although Aristotle's reference to it (*Met.* 1025a6 ff.) proves that it was in existence at least before his death, it was classified as spurious by Schleiermacher and Friedrich Ast, among others. Ast, who called it sophistical and saw in it the seeds of moral indifferentism, could not conceive of it as being Platonic (*Platons Leben und Schriften* [Leipzig, 1816], p. 464). Maurice Croiset, who edited the dialogue for the Budé series (Paris, 1920), does not question its authenticity but thinks it is at best "strange," "paradoxical," and an example of "youthful temerity" (p. 21). Its content is for him an expression of extreme and myopic intellectualism, which ignores the role of appetite and passion in the moral life. This is essentially the same view of the dialogue as that shown by George Grote, *Plato and the Other Companions of Sokrates* (London, 1865), 1.399-400.

Benjamin Jowett's introduction to his translation of the *Hippias Minor*, in *The Dialogues of Plato* (New York, 1871), 4.491, calls attention to Socrates' dialectic skill but does not try to defend his reasoning. The dialogue is "conceived in the spirit of Plato, who is very far from making Socrates always argue on the side of truth." Ulrich von Wilamowitz-Moellendorff, *Platon* (2nd ed.; Berlin, 1920), 1.136-37, does not take the dialogue seriously as a work of philosophy. It is a humorous piece of literature and an impressive example of dialectical skill, but its conclusion is negative.

The least tenable interpretations have been put forward by A. Fouillée and Ernst Horneffer. Fouillée, in his *Platonis Hippias Minor* (Paris, 1872), argued at length that the dialogue was an attack on the doctrine of free will. This was merely an anachronism (see below, Chapter 7), but Horneffer offered in his *Platon gegen Sokrates* (Leipzig, 1904) an interpretation which was in itself a paradox. Plato, he said, wrote the *Hippias Minor* to disprove the Socratic doctrines that virtue is knowledge and that no man errs on purpose. Plato's two obviously absurd conclusions, he points out (369b, 376b), can only be meant to cast doubt on the premises of the argument, and the main premise is that virtue is knowledge. But the argument, of course, has other premises too, e.g., that the truthful man can at times misuse his knowledge, and that the man who errs on purpose exists. Plato rejects the notion that virtue is knowledge only in the sense that it is not knowledge of the facts of arithmetic, astronomy, and geometry. This is a sly hit at Hippias the polymath,

Though it occupies scarcely more than thirteen pages in the Stephanus edition, and has not received a disproportionate amount of scholarly attention, the *Hippias Minor* is a fine example of the mutual dependence in Plato of literary technique and philosophical method. While the discussion advances along a paradoxical course to an inconclusive summation, the personal dialogue of Hippias and Socrates, in humor, allusion, and unspoken inference, leaves the pretensions of the proud sophist in a shambles.

Regarded as a contest of personalities, the *Hippias Minor* is modeled on the Embassy to Achilles in *Iliad* IX, a Homeric passage which also provides, with fine literary economy, the basis for the philosophical discussion. The dialogue begins with a question that is ostensibly scholarly and literary: "Who is the better man, Achilles or Odysseus?" But this problem, whose implications for philosophy seem at first glance remote and uninteresting, is the mask for another issue of more immediate and pressing concern: "Who is the better man, Hippias or Socrates?" Their conversation, regarded as a dramatic confrontation of two men of contrasting character and

---

not at Socrates. Finally, Horneffer's conclusions involve two intolerable anomalies: Plato uses Socrates to attack Socratic doctrine, and the dialogue utterly contradicts Plato's later ethical theory. As to the first, Horneffer can only appeal to Plato's generally free treatment of his teacher (p. 22); the second he merely accepts (p. 28).

By and large, however, the main tenor of the argument of this dialogue has been understood, especially the crucial importance of the condition at 376b5-6. Cf. A. E. Taylor, *Plato, the Man and His Work* (4th ed.; London, 1937), pp. 37-38; Shorey, *What Plato Said*, p. 89; Max Pohlenz, *Aus Platos Werdezeit* (Berlin, 1913), p. 65; John Gould, *The Development of Plato's Ethics* (Cambridge, 1955), pp. 41 ff.; T. Zielinski, "De Hippia Minore," *Eos* (Vratislaviae), 26 (1919), pp. 27-30; Gomperz, *Griechische Denker*, 2.239-40; Robert G. Hoerber, "Plato's *Lesser Hippias*," *Phronesis*, 7 (1962), 128; and Rosamond Kent Sprague, *Plato's Use of Fallacy* (London, 1962), p. 76. This last work presents a detailed logical analysis of the arguments of the *Hippias Minor* (pp. 65-79). Mrs. Sprague shows a clear grasp of Plato's purpose when she concludes that the "chief point" of this dialogue is "to call attention to the distinctive doctrines in the Socratic ethics" (p. 78). Plato achieves this end, she thinks, by a deliberate pedagogic use of fallacies, viz. equivocation in the terms "good" and "voluntary." The meaning of "good," for example, varies between "morally good" and "skilled." But is Socrates' "equivocal" use of "good" really equivocal if we grant the Socratic assumption that virtue is an ability or knowledge (cf. 375d)? In Mrs. Sprague's terms, "the distinctive character of [Socratic] ethics is expressed by means of these particular equivocations" (p. 77). If this is true, rather than conclude that Plato intentionally resorted to equivocation, would it not be more exact to say that he adopted usages which he knew that others, not he, would regard as equivocal?

temperament, who seek wisdom in quite different ways, is
Plato's transposition to late fifth-century Athens of the Homeric
scene in which the candid Achilles faces the subtle Odysseus. Plato,
in suggesting that analogy through echoes and parallels, endows an
apparently jejune question of literary interpretation with philosophic importance.

Hippias, who entertains no doubt that Achilles was the best of
the Achaeans (364c), is equally assured in gratuitously pronounc-
ing himself the best of contemporary Greeks (364a8). He possesses
what Socrates tactfully calls self-confidence in his own wisdom
(364a2). Both of his judgments, about Achilles and about himself,
will come into question in the course of the dialogue. The first
will be challenged explicitly in the formal argument; the second
will fall under the damning implications of Hippias' failure to deal
effectively with that argument, a failure heavily stressed by Socrates' continual ironic deference to his superior wisdom and excellence (369d1, 372b, 376c, 368b).

Achilles, says Hippias, was not only the best of all the Greeks
at Troy, but also the most ingenuous and the most truthful
(364e7-8). He is a natural object for the admiration of the sophist,
whose candor in admitting his own pre-eminence borders on naiveté
(364a8-9) and whose frank self-adulation is represented as habitual (368b). By his own admission and Socrates' ironic agreement,
he is the best in arithmetic (366d4-5) and in various other accomplishments as well (367d6 ff.). In all such matters there is between him and Socrates "no contest," and Socrates' mock deference
to his superiority colors even conventional locutions like ὦ βέλτιστε
Ἱππία (373b6). To recite the long catalogue of things which Hippias does well is itself a challenge to which Socrates is unequal,
and he willingly admits it. Hippias, in reciting such a list, would
have overlooked nothing, since he laid claim to a powerful memory.
Socrates pointedly says he had almost forgotten that (368d). This
is one of many indications that he and Hippias are being measured
against each other by Plato, just as they in turn are measuring
Achilles and Odysseus. Although Socrates disclaims any comparison of his own merits with those of Hippias, the sophist quite frank-

ly regards the conversation as a contest (cf. ἀγωνίζῃ 369c1) and
Socrates as the most recent of many antagonists, all of whom he
has found inferior to himself (cf. 364a7-9). "Match argument with
argument," he says, "to prove that the other hero is better, and
these people will know more clearly which of us argues better"
(369c6-8).

Odysseus, whom Hippias esteems less than Achilles, is wily and
deceitful (365b5). He is, in a way, like the ironical Socrates, whose
tributes to Hippias' wisdom show a notable lack of candor and
whose disruptive tactics in discussion Hippias strongly resents. "I
hate like the gates of Hades the man who holds one thing in his
heart and utters another," says Achilles to Odysseus at *Iliad* IX,
312-313, a remark quoted twice in this dialogue (365a4-b1, 370a4-5).
"Socrates is always creating confusion in discussion and playing the
rascal," says Hippias at 373b4-5, echoing that complaint. Socrates'
pose as a simple-hearted bumbler confronted by a man wiser than
he (372b, 376c), whom he even accuses ironically of deceiving him
(370e10-11), is also reflected in his interpretation of *Iliad* IX.
Achilles, he says, is the clever deceiver, and Odysseus, like himself,
is the simpleton (371d5).

The discussion of the merits of the two Homeric heroes, therefore, involves a kind of protracted *double entendre*. Socrates' argument throughout the dialogue is an overt though ironic attempt
to discredit Achilles and a covert but serious attempt to discredit
Hippias. Achilles, the truthful man, turns out to be no better than
a liar; Hippias, the polymath, who best knows how to tell the truth
about so many subjects, is also proved to be the most expert liar.
Socrates directs the argument *ad hominem* with such mock-re-
spectful insistence (366c5, 367d6, 367e9) that no doubt can remain
that it is meant to undermine Hippias' pretensions. This is clear
not only in small details, like Hippias' failure to use his famous
mnemonic art in following a simple argument (369a7), but in the
far more important revelation that the kind of ability, wisdom, and
excellence which he so proudly claims (368b2 ff., 368e1 ff.) implies
no distinction between the truthful man and the liar, the virtuous

man and the villain. He believes in the distinction, to be sure, but he has no means of defending it.

The upshot of the literary discussion is that Odysseus has a stronger claim to be called the best of the Achaeans than does Achilles. As a discussion of Homeric characterization the dialogue is a mere *tour de force*, and its air of perverse virtuosity has alienated many critics. But the frivolity with which Plato treats Homer's heroes is only the surface gloss which hides a deeper seriousness. The true contest is between Hippias and Socrates. The grotesque honor accorded to Odysseus, the willing liar, is only a paradigm of the honor more seriously tendered to Socrates, who proves himself in the course of the argument a better man than his confident rival. The dialogue, with its play of parallels between the two figures of Socrates and Hippias in the foreground and the two Homeric heroes in the background, is a gem of Platonic wit. It can also claim a place in the vast Ulysses literature, since it offers Odysseus, the willing liar, as an archetype of Socrates, the ironical man.[12]

As well as being an implied attack on Hippias himself, the dialogue is a brilliant *jeu d'esprit* on the fifth-century notion that virtue is a kind of τέχνη. A legion of arts is dragged forward in evidence, but the modern reader is in danger of remaining bewildered, like Hippias, as to what it all means. He may well believe at first that the sly wit of Socrates is urging what modern common sense thinks it knows: that the analogy of virtue and art is a false one and leads to absurd conclusions. To prove this in the presence of Hippias, who by his versatility epitomized the prestige of the arts in Greece,

---

12. Little attention has been given to the *Hippias Minor* as a piece of literature. W. Eckert, *Dialektischer Scherz in den früheren Gesprächen Platons* (Nürnberg, 1911), p. 45, explains it as a kind of protracted jest. Wilamowitz, *Platon*, 1.136-37, sees humor in the fact that Socrates, the better man, is throughout disingenuous and ironic, i.e., a "liar." Cf. Paul Friedländer, *Platon*, II, *Die Platonischen Schriften* (1st ed.; Berlin, 1930), p. 145, and Schneidewin, *Platons Zweite Hippiasdialog*, pp. 24 ff. Pohlenz, *Aus Platos Werdezeit*, pp. 66-67, notices the wit with which Plato has Hippias the polymath admit that the man who knows the most is the best liar. Hoerber discovers in the dialogue what he calls a "dramatic technique of . . . construction in 'doublets'" ("Plato's Lesser Hippias," p. 128), and he maintains that this throws light on the argument. I disagree with his implication that the key to Plato's meaning in the *Hippias Minor* is to be found in an appeal to Aristotle, who is credited with "solving the riddle" (p. 131). In a sense he did, of course, but not in Platonic terms.

would be a clever stroke and worthy of Plato. So easy is it to in-
vert the meaning of the dialogue that this interpretation has been
seriously defended.[13]

To explain the *Hippias Minor* in the way described would be to
indulge modern preconceptions at the expense of Socrates' and
Plato's known acceptance of the τέχνη analogy. But if we read it
instead in the light of other dialogues, the vulnerable premises,
from Plato's point of view, appear elsewhere in the discussion. Two
similar false assumptions are, for purposes of the argument, left
unchallenged by either Socrates or Hippias. First, in 366bc, a man
is said to be capable who does what he wishes when he wishes it.
A page later, in 366e, it is assumed that this implies ability to tell
lies, a practice which is unhesitatingly classified by both Hippias
and Socrates as immoral (365e8-9, 369c4-5, 370e2-3, 371e9-372a5,
372d5). But the definition of the capable man recalls Socrates' remark in *Gorgias* 466 that tyrants and orators may carry out all their
whims but they do nothing of what they wish, for only the good
can be the object of desire. If so, the capable man could never
wish the wrongs that Socrates suggests are in his power in the
*Hippias Minor*. By choosing to do wrong, he would frustrate his
own desire of the good and so prove himself "not capable." The
other, related assumption, found in the second part of the dialogue,
is that there are men who do wrong willingly. Hippias implies this
in 370e when he says that Achilles lies involuntarily but Odysseus
voluntarily. Socrates takes up the discussion on the basis of this
assumption and concludes that the willing malefactor is none other
than the good man. But he lets drop an important qualification:
"If such a man exists." In that clause we glimpse the presence of
Plato's constant teaching, elsewhere frankly avowed and here only
implied, that such a man exists nowhere. Here is the point of junction with recognizable Platonic doctrine and our path of return, offered at the last moment, to philosophical sanity. A man cannot
wish evil nor can he do wrong on purpose. The contrary assumptions are different forms of the same basic misconception,[14] whose

13. By Horneffer. See note 11 above.
14. In *Gorgias* 509e the two assumptions are stated as one.

lingering presence in the arguments of the *Hippias Minor*—through Plato's deliberate artistic intent—leads to *aporia*.

The dialogue, as we saw earlier, deals with two beliefs: (1) virtue is knowledge and ability, and (2) some men wish evil and err willingly. The absurd conclusion with which the discussion ends is meant to discredit only the second. About the first belief we know only that the *kind* of knowledge and ability which Hippias represents cannot be identified with virtue. The belief that virtue is knowledge and ability of some kind is not challenged explicitly or by implication. Plato means to keep it, but he has not yet fully explained it.[15] In accepting it, he makes himself the heir of all the poets and teachers who in the century before had succeeded in rephrasing moral issues in the language of the arts. At the same time, in his biting portrayal of Hippias, the artisan-phi-

15. He will explain it further in the *Republic* (see Chapt. 5, below, throughout), but only after the dialogue with Polemarchus, in a way reminiscent of the *Hippias Minor*, has shown again that an uncritical use of the τέχνη analogy in ethics can lead to anomalies. So, e.g., the just man is an able thief (334a).

The *Hippias Major*, like its shorter namesake, touches on the problem whether ability and wisdom can serve evil purposes. The subject of the dialogue is "the beautiful" or "the noble" (τὸ καλόν), which Socrates provisionally defines at 295c as "the useful." Since usefulness depends on ability, the latter must be καλόν, and lack of it ugly or base. Like wisdom, ability is the fairest and noblest of all things, or so it seems for the moment. Yet a person could not do what he had not the knowledge and the ability to do, and this seems true of his good and his evil actions alike. But if ability and usefulness can serve evil, neither one is καλόν in an absolute sense. The problem is essentially that of the *Hippias Minor*, but in the *Hippias Major* it is much further from solution. Knowledge and ability are good; to have them is virtue. Yet they can serve evil ends; to have them facilitates vice. The *Hippias Major* simply goes on to distinguish between ability for good and ability for evil. The *Hippias Minor* shows that, if a man can wish evil, knowledge and ability for good are also knowledge and ability for evil; but, if a man cannot wish evil, there is a knowledge and ability that never serves evil. This is the knowledge of the ultimate good and the ability to fulfill our inmost wish to do good (the βούλησις of *Gorgias* 467d).

The *Hippias Major*, in which the humor is broader than in its companion dialogue, was called by Ast a "ganz unwurdige Persiflage" (*Platons Leben und Schriften*, p. 458) and was rejected as spurious by him and many others after him. More recently Dorothy Tarrant pronounced it un-Platonic for a variety of reasons in her articles, "On the *Hippias Major*," *JP*, 35 (1920), 319-31, and "The Authorship of the *Hippias Major*," *CQ*, 21 (1927), 82-87. Her objections were successfully met by G. M. A. Grube, "On the Authenticity of the *Hippias Major*," *CQ*, 20 (1926), 134-48, and "The Logic and Language of the *Hippias Major*," *CP*, 24 (1929), 369-75.

losopher, and in his unmistakable preference for paradox, he serves
notice that he will use his predecessors' conceptions with originality.

In the dialogues discussed above, several doctrines are stated
or implied, which, when put epigrammatically, constitute the familiar ethical paradoxes. All men ultimately desire the good for
themselves; they wish to be happy. They also desire the good absolutely, because the pursuit of one coincides with the pursuit of
the other: happiness lies in justice. When they err it is in the choice
of means to the good, and their wickedness is therefore unintentional with respect to its ultimate evil effect. Virtue is what makes
them behave sensibly; sensible behavior consists in choosing the
right means to happiness. Virtue, therefore, is good sense, or knowledge, and the ability to use this knowledge. It is like a craft or
skill, which is also a knowledge and ability. But it differs from a
craft or skill, because a craftsman can sometimes reject the purpose
of his craft, but a man can never reject the good. Hence the paradox
that a mathematician can miscalculate on purpose, but a man cannot do wrong on purpose.

There are questions raised and not answered by the above passages. It is not settled whether virtue can be taught, although Socrates' remark in the *Gorgias* that it requires both instruction and
practice suggests that it might be learned by a combination of
these. If so, by what kind of instruction and by what sort of
practice? The answer to this question is complex, and it will be
taken up in our discussion of the *Protagoras* and the *Republic*.
The hesitations, moreover, and qualifications in Plato's reduction
of virtue to knowledge remain to be explained. At *Meno* 89a,
the tentative conclusion is merely that virtue is wholly or
partly knowledge. At 97a ff. of the same work the doubt is compounded when Socrates realizes that right opinion can, to an extent,
be a surrogate of knowledge. In several dialogues, the term "abil-
ity" ($\delta\acute{\nu}\nu\alpha\mu\iota\varsigma$) and its cognates appear in descriptions of the virtuous
man: indeed at one stage of the *Meno* the "ability to attain the
good" is a tentative definition (78bc). At the end of the *Hippias
Minor* the likelihood that virtue is knowledge and ability of a sort
not yet defined is the one real residue of the inconclusive discus-

sion. But the term "ability" is extremely vague. It can even include the power of intelligence, as it evidently does at *Gorgias* 466b ff. It embraces whatever the virtuous possess which sets them apart from others who merely "wish" the good and cannot achieve it. It begins to find a more precise definition at *Gorgias* 509d7 ff., where it is mentioned along with art as a requirement for just conduct, and both are said to depend on learning and practice. Elsewhere, Plato's employment of the word "ability" has the effect of leaving undecided the issue whether virtue is simply knowledge or involves as well other things. His solution, when it comes in the *Republic,* will incorporate the three ways of attaining moral goodness which Meno implied are mutually exclusive: Does a man, he asked, get virtue by instruction, by practice, or by nature (*Meno,* 70a)? The *Meno* has no answer, but the *Republic* welcomes and reconciles all three alternatives. In doing so, it clarifies finally the source of moral "ability."[16]

16. Robert G. Hoerber, "Plato's *Meno," Phronesis,* 5 (1960), 78-102, is in part an attempt to show that the *Meno* itself teaches the importance of nature, practice, and instruction. But his argument that "the entire dialogue seems to emphasize the three factors necessary to education through its rather obvious threefold construction (p. 84) is far from persuasive. R. S. Bluck offers a detailed and convincing criticism of his conclusions in "Plato's *Meno," Phronesis,* 6 (1961), 94-101. For an explicit recognition of the place of nature, nurture, and παιδεία in education, see *Alcibiades I,* 120d-122b.

# 4. THE EARLY DIALOGUES, II

In reading the *Hippias Minor* we found reason to believe that beneath the Socratic mask of uncertainty there lay a well-thought-out Platonic scheme. The abrupt and inconclusive dénouement, coming at a point in the argument when a casual parenthesis has opened up fertile possibilities of inquiry (376b5-6), is proof that Plato could teach by suggestion and by silence. In the other dialogues which have so far come under discussion, at least in the passages dealt with, there is no such clear indication of what positive thought, if any, lies behind Socrates' diffidence in drawing conclusions. Taken separately, the passages seem as apt to be evidence of scepticism and caution as of artful reserve. They show, nevertheless, a common ethical intellectualism which, though paradoxically expressed, makes use at times of traditional conceptions of morals and education. Read carefully, they demonstrate that at no time did Platonic ethics hold rigidly aloof from these traditions, hoping to favor the truly wise with an apocalyptic vision in which common sense would be confounded. Instead, when Plato taught that no man did wrong intentionally, he meant his words to be acceptable to any intelligent Greek who had the will to put his own thoughts into order. In spite of this, the gap between common Greek opinion and Socratic paradox seemed wide, and the problem of bridging it by dialectic was formidable. In three dialogues Plato made the attempt, by using the technique of suggestion found in the *Hippias Minor*. These are the *Laches* and *Protagoras*, which deal at length with courage, and the *Charmides*, which deals with temperance.

In none of these dialogues does Plato offer a solution to the problem of defining the virtues in question, but there is every indication that in writing them he had a better understanding of the problem than he allowed to any of his characters. These characters offer separately arguments and definitions which are complementary, and there is reason to believe that Plato thought of them as complementary. But instead of advancing the argument to the limits of his understanding of it, he was content to play the dramatist and lead his characters into a conflict without result. This appears to be an adaptation of the Socratic method to the written word. The reader cannot be questioned like the slave in the *Meno*, but he can be asked to watch a discussion in which lines of inquiry are opened and not exhausted. The alert student is expected to pursue the inquiry further. In following it through he will find that he has been prodded into doing philosophy himself instead of merely observing how others do it. This method, by which Plato, as it were, pretends ignorance in order to awaken the mind of the reader, is his own version of Socratic irony. It is also his way of justifying the technique of written dialogue, by avoiding what he elsewhere deplores, viz. the attempt to put knowledge into the reader's soul "like sight into blind eyes."[1]

The three dialogues to be discussed in this chapter, whatever their chronological place, are logically transitional in our discussion. The *Meno, Gorgias,* and *Hippias Minor* have established the unity of virtue in knowledge or right opinion and in the universal desire of the good. The *Laches, Charmides,* and *Protagoras* reiterate this in their own way but have something to say too about diversity

1. *Rep.* 518c.

among the virtues. Their implication, to put it as briefly as possible, is that courage and temperance have two aspects each, a rational and an irrational; each virtue is a junction of wisdom and temperament joined by education. As wisdom, each is one with all the other virtues; as temperament, each is distinct. In these dialogues, to be sure, Plato does not make this conclusion explicit; his method is dialectic and dramatic, and he leaves the reader with various unreconciled points of view. These will not be drawn together until the *Republic*. In the *Republic*, moreover, it will become clear that even this new and balanced formulation of the problem of virtue is not final.[2] It is only a step further in the difficult progress toward perfect knowledge. We will nowhere discover a final "solution" to the nature of virtue written down in any of Plato's works. The reader who has received the impression that I intend to read the dialogues of this chapter as *oeuvres à clef* is therefore only partly right. If we read them with attention we will be able to follow Plato's intent well beyond what he makes explicit. But we will not find in this way a definition with which he would have wanted us to rest content.

We begin with the *Laches*, a dialogue which opens with a practical problem in education. Lysimachus, son of Aristides, and Melesias, son of Thucydides, are the undistinguished offspring of famous fathers. Wishing to school their sons to greater distinction than they themselves have achieved, perhaps by training in arms, they ask the advice of the Athenian generals Laches and Nicias. How does one train one's son to noble deeds (179cd)? Laches defers to Socrates, who is also present and whose valor at Delium has qualified him to give this kind of advice (181ab), but Socrates insists that his elders should speak first. They do, but their advice leads to an inconclusive argument about the merits of theory and practice (181d ff.), and before long the leadership of the conversation has by common consent been given to Socrates.

Socrates begins by steering the discussion to general questions. What they really want to know is how to make the sons of Lysimachus and Melesias virtuous. This would require knowing what virtue is, certainly too broad an issue. Socrates proposes instead

2. *Rep.* 504d.

the narrower question: What is courage (190d)? Laches confidently offers the first definition: the courageous man is one who holds his place in the ranks and does not run away (190e). Against this Socrates gently points out that timely retreat is a recognized part of good military practice; moreover, what he had asked for was a definition of courage, not an example of it. Laches, with a palpably less assured tone, tries again: courage, he now thinks, is perseverance or steadfastness (καρτερία) of soul. But this quality, objects Socrates, might be intelligent or foolish, and when it is the latter it surely cannot be identified with courage, which is a good. Yet if we define courage as intelligent perseverance we seem to be attributing courage to the man who perseveres in spending money because he foresees gain and to the physician who intelligently perseveres in treating a patient. This will not do. Even in war, intelligent steadfastness is not equivalent to courage. It is intelligent to persist in fighting an outnumbered and disadvantageously placed enemy; yet if both sides fight on, the enemy, who is foolish enough not to give way, is accounted the more courageous. When two men fight with equal steadfastness, the one who has less knowledge of the soldier's art is the more courageous, and the inexpert swimmer needs reserves of courage to stay in the water. What all this seems to prove is that courage is foolish perseverance, though a moment ago it was agreed that this was an evil.

The first stage of the argument has ended in their defeat, and it falls to Socrates, good soldier in discussion as in battle, to rally the company. Their deeds, he points out, are not in harmony with their words. They have their share of bravery, but evidently cannot talk about it successfully (193e). Yet the argument itself bids them be steadfast; let not courage mock them for failing to seek her out courageously. Socrates turns to Nicias for help.

What Nicias proposes is that courage is knowledge of the fearful and the safe in war and in all other matters (194e-195a). Laches, with poor grace, calls this definition rubbish and tries to discredit it. Physicians know better than laymen what is fearful and what is not in matters of health, farmers know in farming, and every artisan has that knowledge in his own craft. Does this fact make all doctors, farmers, and artisans brave men? Not at all, says

Nicias; what seems fearful with respect to the limited purpose of a single craft or profession may not be so in broader perspective. A doctor may not know if his patient would be better off alive or dead, and in that sense he does not know which is really fearful. Even the prophet, who can predict suffering, cannot by his prophetic art judge whether it will prove to be good or bad, to be feared or welcomed. Courage is a thing distinct from any art or profession. On the other hand, it is a knowledge, and so one should not attribute it to animals and children, or even to many unreasoning adults. These are bold, or daring, or fearless, but not courageous.

All these fine distinctions exhaust the patience of Laches. Ironically, he lacks steadfastness on the unfamiliar terrain of philosophy, and he announces that he has had enough of questions and answers (196c, 197e). Nicias, with barbed solicitude, tells him not to lose heart: the argument does not reflect on *his* courage (197c). Yet it does, for Socrates begins now to treat Laches like a lagging comrade whom he will not let run away from the fray. They are comrades in battle again, as they were at Delium (*Symposium*, 221ab), and here, as at Delium, Socrates has a clearer grasp of what must be done.

Socrates has his own objection to the definition of Nicias. Courage is presumably only one part of virtue among others like justice and temperance. Nicias has called courage a knowledge of the fearful and the safe, i.e. of future good and evil. This implies that its object lies entirely in the future. Yet, by the definition, courage is a knowledge or science, and the objects of science are independent of time. The science of medicine, for example, deals, within its limited field, with past, present, and future alike. Courage, the knowledge of future good and evil, must also be knowledge of good and evil in general. But then courage, contrary to what they assumed, is the whole of virtue, not a part. The dialogue ends in apparent failure. "Then we have not found out what courage is, Nicias" (199e).

Plato's failure to uncover even a tentative answer to the question he raises in the *Laches* is what has tempted philosophers to abandon the dialogue to the literary critics. They would be wrong to do so. The inconclusiveness of the *Laches* is apparent rather

than real. Not only does the argument contain important implications which are left undeveloped, but the dramatic interplay of
character is itself integral to the meaning.

First the argument. In spite of their perplexity at the end of
the dialogue, the three friends have made some progress towards a
definition of courage. Socrates has discredited the final definition
of Laches and that of Nicias, but it has gone unremarked that the
merit in each corresponds to the fault in the other. Courage is not
"intelligent steadfastness," as Laches proposed, because in some
things the more a man knows the less courageous he is. But this
last point has been made by assuming that "intelligence" means
either technical knowledge, e.g. in warfare or swimming, or the
good sense of fighting on when victory is almost assured. When
Socrates "proves" to Laches that courage is actually foolish steadfastness, he means "foolish" in technical skills or in regard to immediate ends like victory in battle. He does not raise the possibility that other forms of intelligence are consistent with courage,
nor does he challenge the use of the term "steadfastness."

At one point the argument repeats itself in a significant way.
When Nicias has defined courage as the knowledge of what is
fearful and safe, Laches objects that the craftsman has such knowledge within his craft and is not thereby courageous. This is very
like the objection that Socrates raised against "intelligent steadfastness" when he proved that the brave man's courage has nothing
to do with his technical competence and that he often has the bad
sense to put his life in danger. Laches could not answer Socrates,
but the more adept Nicias easily answers Laches. In doing so, he
shows how Laches might have dealt with Socrates' objection to
"intelligent steadfastness." Courage, according to Nicias, is the
knowledge of what is ultimately fearful; it is beyond technical
skill or grasp of immediate ends. But then, asks Socrates, what is
there to distinguish courage from virtue in general?

In trying to determine whether the argument implies any conclusion that is not revealed to the participants, we should not overlook the fact that each definition is only partially discredited. Courage remains a kind of steadfastness—or at least the relevance of
that word is not challenged. On the other hand, since all virtue

involves knowledge of good and evil, so must courage. Laches anticipates Socrates' objection to Nicias' definition (the lack of a distinguishing mark) by calling courage not intelligence alone, but intelligence joined with perseverance; and Nicias answers the objection to Laches' definition by explaining "knowledge of the fearful and safe" as Laches ought to have explained "intelligent." This apparently unrehearsed conversation is planned and guided by an artist, a fact that we are tempted to forget because of the very realism of his description. The definitions of Laches and of Nicias complement each other too well not to suggest Plato's contrivance. It would be overstatement to claim that he has brought us to the brink of a completely satisfactory conception of courage. In Plato's mind this is not accomplished by brief conversations. It is nevertheless clear that when the dialogue is interrupted it is moving towards a conception of courage which joins knowledge of good and evil with a steadfast quality of soul.

This interpretation is confirmed if we turn from the impersonal premises and conclusions of the discussion itself to the play of character in which it is set. The *Laches* is excellent proof of Plato's ability to write a piece that is at once philosophical and dramatic-biographical, or, in his own terms, one which concerns itself with both λόγος and ἔργον.[3] The dialogue is built upon this verbal motif. It begins with a search for the path to noble ἔργα (179cd) and pursues it through a protracted λόγος (187cd). The discussion gradually reveals Laches as the man of action, Nicias as the man of words, and Socrates as qualified in both and aware of the importance of both (193e). By the end of the dialogue, this revelation of character has in turn illuminated the meaning of the argument.

Laches is a practical soldier who has fought with the hoplites at Delium (181ab) and is destined, according to the account of Thucydides (5.74.3), to die fighting at Mantinea. He despises mere theoreticians of war, whom he has seen acquit themselves poorly

3. The pairing of these two words as doublet (word and deed) or as antithesis (claim vs. fact) was an ingrained feature of Greek style in the fifth and fourth centuries. Its frequency can be confirmed by reference to the special lexica of Sophocles, Euripides, Plato, and above all Thucydides. The *locus classicus* is perhaps Thucydides, 2.40.2-3, where the Athenians are praised for their ability to combine thoughtful discussion with decisive action.

ἐν αὐτῷ τῷ ἔργῳ (183c); and his impatience extends to teachers of any sort (185e), sophists (197d6), and Nicias' favorite, Damon (200a). He is out of his depth in intellectual discussion, regards subtleties of argument with suspicion (196b3), and quickly gives in when the discussion goes against him (196c, 197e). He is a man of deeds, not words. He consents, in fact, to participate in Socrates' λόγοι only because the latter's ἔργα, his actions at Delium, recommend him (181b, 188c ff.). Suitably enough, his first definitions of courage contain no reference to intelligence at all (190e, 192b).

Nicias makes an excellent contrast. Since he is the more prominent of the two men, Plato's portrait of him can be checked with other sources. His interest, perhaps excessive, in the musical education of his son (180d) is confirmed by Xenophon and Aristotle.[4] There is more than a touch of parody in Plato's picture of him as the soldier-intellectual, who thinks fighting men should be graceful and intelligent (182cd) and that swordsmanship is an introduction to strategy. The words μάθημα and ἐπιστήμη occur eleven times as noun or verb in this brief speech, a hint of pedantry which Laches parodies with sarcasm in his reply at 182d6 ff.: he repeats the words eight times in the first seven lines. Laches, moreover, in further contrast to Nicias, has no use at all for music; he makes an exception only for the good old Doric harmony of λόγοι and ἔργα (188d).[5]

Nicias is as distinctively a man of words as Laches is of deeds. He is accustomed to having discussions with Socrates (188b), and he is even a bit vain about his skill in argument (200b), and not without reason. Plato's sketch of him conforms very well to the record, which has come down to us in other sources, of the intelligent general without much force of character whose life ended in disastrous failure. No one in the fourth century, reading Nicias' definition of courage as "knowledge of the fearful and the safe," could have failed to see over it the shadow of the disastrous expedition in which Athens sent an enormous fleet to its destruction in an attempt to conquer Syracuse. Nicias had a leading role in that disaster. Ironically, he had understood more clearly than any other Athenian what was "fearful and safe" about the plan before it was

---

4. Xenophon, *Symposium*, 3.5; Aristotle, *Rhetoric*, 1413a.

5. Aristophanes' *Wasps*, 959, seems to corroborate this bit of characterization.

ever voted. His speech in the Assembly and his later proposals for
a large armament or none were models of good strategic sense.
Even Plutarch, who is on the whole not well disposed to him, admits his reputation for intelligence.[6] But this good strategist was
a failure in the field, especially at the end of the campaign. His
vacillation about the decision to retreat, in which superstition over
an eclipse of the moon caused a fatal delay, showed a flaw in his
make-up. Plutarch, who draws on the Sicilian historian Philistus
as well as on Thucydides, calls it cowardice. Thucydides does not
go so far, but he does attest to his extremely cautious nature. That
he had a reputation for timidity and superstition seems to be clear
from Plutarch and from references in Aristophanes and Phrynichus.[7]
Plato himself perhaps refers to Nicias' superstition at Syracuse at
*Laches* 195e and 198e-199a.

The best evidence that Nicias' character (as well as that of
Laches) is important in this dialogue, that his ἔργα and not merely
his λόγοι are relevant, is that he says so himself. Socrates, he points
out, as the discussion of courage begins, is about to submit them
to a test of their whole way of life; the argument will concern, not
the boys, but Laches and Nicias (188ab). This is not surprising.
The *Hippias Minor* was, among other things, a personal scrutiny
of Hippias' way of life. In the *Laches*, neither general succeeds
in defining courage in a way that satisfies the objections of Socrates,
and each one expounds a view of courage that reflects his own
shortcomings. In each man λόγος matches ἔργον. No theoretical
solution of the question, "What is courage?" is reached. The dialogue gives no support either to the extreme intellectualism of
Nicias or to the anti-intellectualism of Laches. It finds, however, a
practical solution in the person of Socrates, who is qualified as an
expert in the subject by his ἔργα (185e11), to which Laches can
bear witness (188e), and whose mastery of λόγοι (to which Nicias
testifies at 187e ff.) enables him at least to reject unsatisfactory
definitions. He, not they, is the one best qualified to teach the

6. Thucydides, 6.9-14, 20-24; Plutarch, *Nicias*, 18.5.
7. See Thucydides, 7.50, 7.48, 7.42-43, 5.16; Plutarch, *Nicias*, 2.4, 14.2,
21.4, 8.1, 4.3, 4.1-2; Aristophanes, *Birds*, 638, and *Knights*, 358; Phrynichus,
frag. 59 (Edmonds). Plutarch's sources are discussed in G. Busolt, "Plutarchs
Nikias und Philistus," *Hermes*, 34 (1899), 280-97.

young men, and both admit it (200cd). He is the truly "musical" man, in Laches' sense of the word (188d): his deeds match his words.

This careful balance of character in the *Laches*, its matching of personality with argument, and its clear construction around the motif of λόγος and ἔργον, familiar ground to any Greek reader, belie the semblance of disorder which it offers to the unwary modern reader. Moreover, as a piece of dramatized biography, it strongly supports the kind of interpretation I have offered of its philosophical content. The definitions of courage offered by Laches and Nicias complement each other and light up each other's defects as clearly as do the characters of those two generals. As Laches lacks knowledge, so Nicias lacks "endurance." The cause and nature of this "endurance" are not specified. It even seems capable of uneven development. Laches, for example, who exemplifies doggedness in battle, lacks that quality in philosophical discussion (196-97). But through his gruff manner we recognize a spirited nature, or what Plato's Greek readers would have recognized as a φύσις disposed to bravery in war. The affectionate portrayal of Laches, Socrates' friend and comrade in battle, makes it extremely likely that Plato means us to judge him a courageous man in some limited sense. This fact supports the philosophical and literary arguments urged above; it proves, as they do, that the conception of courage to which this dialogue tends is not rigidly intellectualist.[8]

8. The scholar confronted by a dialogue as apparently inconclusive as the *Laches* has several paths of interpretation open to him, according to whether he emphasizes λόγος or ἔργον. He may decide, with Wilamowitz, that it was not written to solve the theoretical question of courage at all, but rather to convey a personal tribute to Socrates, brave soldier and good teacher (Ulrich von Wilamowitz-Moellendorff, *Platon* [2nd ed.; Berlin, 1920], 1.186-87). The biographical note is certainly evident (181b, 189b, 200cd). Moreover, at first glance, it seems that "the conversation wanders, as actual talk does, over a wide field of topics," to quote a remark made by A. E. Taylor about the early dialogues as a group (*Plato, the Man and His Work* [4th ed.; London, 1937], p. 25). It is this semblance of spontaneity, even of disorder, which lends plausibility to the notion that the *Laches* should be read merely as drama and biography, or at most, perhaps, as "une simple exposition de méthode" (A Croiset [ed.], *Hippias Majeur, Charmide, Lachès, Lysis* [Paris, 1921], p. 88).

Another, perhaps even more prevalent, way of reading the *Laches* is to find its meaning in the definition of Nicias as revised by Socrates. This at least puts one on the familiar ground of Socratic intellectualism and allows one to

The *Charmides* deals with the virtue which the Greeks called
σωφροσύνη and which speakers of English translate by a variety of

conclude with George Grote that "the perfect condition of the intelligence, is
the sole and all sufficient condition of virtue" (*Plato and the Other Companions of Sokrates* [London, 1865], 1.480). This company also includes
Eduard Zeller, *Die Philosophie der Griechen*, 2. Teil, 1. Abth. (4th ed.; Leipzig, 1889), p. 502; H. Raeder, *Platons Philos. Entwickelung* (Leipzig, 1905),
p. 210; and C. Ritter, *Platon: Sein Leben, Seine Schriften, Seine Lehre* (Munich, 1910-23), 1.295-97.

Ernst Horneffer, *Platon gegen Sokrates* (Leipzig, 1904), pp. 35-48, finds
in the *Laches* an attack on Socratic intellectualism, joined with a tribute to
Socrates' personal courage. He points out that the existence of a real distinction among the virtues is agreed upon without question by Socrates and Nicias
(198a). The tendency of the dialogue must therefore be to cast doubt upon
whatever conflicts with this supposition, i.e. upon the identity of virtue and
knowledge. Horneffer frankly admits that the *Laches*, read in this way, contradicts his own understanding of the *Protagoras* (p. 48). His views have reap-
peared in Hermann Gauss, *Philos. Handkommentar zu den Dialogen Platos*,
1. Teil, 2. Hälfte (Bern, 1954), pp. 91-92. Gauss argues that Plato's sym-
pathies, like the title of the work, belong to Laches rather than to Nicias.

E. Trubetzkoy, "Zur Erklärung des *Laches*," *Hermes*, 40 (1905), 636 ff.,
maintains that the dialogue, under the guise of a criticism of Nicias, actually
attacks the erroneous intellectualism of some contemporary of Plato. The person he suggests is Phaedo, under whose name there existed a dialogue *Nicias*,
according to Diogenes Laertius 2.9, a passage which adds that the ascription
is doubtful. But Trubetzkoy can hardly be said to have proved his case with
this evidence. T. de Laguna, "The Problem of the *Laches*," *Mind*, 43 (1934),
170-80, also finds fourth-century relevance for the dialogue, but admits he
cannot prove which contemporary of Plato is being criticized in the person of
Nicias. Antisthenes, he says, is a possibility (pp. 174-75). The error of Nicias
lies in not realizing that below rational courage is an ordinary "traditional"
level of the virtue, which Laches exemplifies (p. 178). Erazim V. Kohák, "The
Road to Wisdom: Lessons on Education from Plato's *Laches*," *CJ*, 56 (1960),
123-32, interprets the characters in the dialogue as representatives of stages
on the Divided Line of *Rep.* 509d ff. To that hypothesis he adds an existential-
ist interpretation which is frankly speculative (cf. pp. 129, 132).

There is something to be said for most of these views, but none of them
accounts for the whole dialogue. The best explanation was offered by Hermann Bonitz in his article "Zur Erklärung Platonischer Dialoge," *Hermes*, 5
(1871), 413-42. He repeated it in *Platonische Studien* (Berlin, 1886), pp. 216
ff., and also replied to Zeller's criticism. He argues, as I do, that Laches and
Nicias are both partly right, but he confines himself to the merits of the formal
argument. Benjamin Jowett's introduction to his translation of the dialogue
expresses briefly the same view (*The Dialogues of Plato* [New York, 1871],
1.70). My interpretation was first offered in "The Unity of the *Laches*," *Yale
Classical Studies*, 18 (1963), 131-47. Since writing that article I have read
Werner Nagel's valuable analysis of the *Laches* as drama and character-study,
in "Zur Darstellungskunst Platons insbesondere im Dialog 'Laches'," *Serta
Philologica Aenipontana*, ed. R. von Muth, Innsbrücker Beiträge zur Kultur-
wissenschaft 7-8 (Innsbruck, 1962), 119-42. Nagel shows that the contrast between Nicias and Laches is illustrated by speech-patterns, emotional
reactions, and ways of arguing. He maintains, as I do, that much of this
characterization has a demonstrable historical basis.

approximate equivalents, the most common being "temperance." Its pattern of development and its use of character remind one of the *Laches*, though its argument is on the whole more complex. It involves, as does the *Laches*, two main characters apart from Socrates. One is less adept in philosophical discourse but better endowed with a natural capacity for temperance: the other has some facility in argument but is less disposed by nature to that virtue. These are Charmides and Critias respectively, kinsmen of Plato and destined participants in the oligarchical tyranny of the Thirty, in the year 404.

The scene is the palaestra of Taureas, where Socrates appears unexpectedly after an absence from Athens. Here he finds that the center of attention is the modest and handsome young Charmides, whom high birth and beauty have combined to favor above his companions. It is not long before Socrates has engaged the young man in conversation on the subject of temperance, a virtue which Critias claims that Charmides already possesses in the highest degree (157d). Asked to say what he thinks temperance is, Charmides first replies that it is to do everything with propriety and gentleness (159b3) in walking, talking, and every other activity. But Socrates has an objection. Temperance is a noble thing ($\kappa\alpha\lambda\delta\nu$), as Charmides readily admits, and in physical and mental activities alike it is "nobler" or better to be speedy. This is the conclusion to which Charmides agrees after Socrates has appealed to the varied examples of writing, reading, playing the harp, athletics, learning, teaching, memory, and quick-wittedness. Evidently speed and not slowness is more suited to the temperate life. The first definition has failed before the Socratic elenchus.

Charmides' second suggestion is that temperance is shame or modesty (160e4). But once more Socrates objects that temperance must be a good, since temperate men are good men; yet Homer says that modesty is no good to a needy man. If temperance is always a good it cannot be modesty (161a).

The young Charmides lacks the confidence or ability to defend his own ideas beyond this point, and he merely agrees that Socrates has made a valid objection. He has, however, a third suggestion, one that he has heard from Critias, who is at first reluctant

to admit it as his own. Temperance, according to this new definition, would be to do what was proper to oneself (τὸ τὰ ἑαυτοῦ
πράττειν 161b6). Socrates professes to find this enigmatic: it says
one thing but evidently means another. Men, after all, learn to read
and write not only their own names, but the names of friends and
enemies too. Physicians, weavers, and shoemakers all busy themselves with what pertains to others. A state which forbade their
practices as forms of meddling would not be well governed, that
is to say temperately governed; therefore, temperance cannot be
doing what pertains to oneself (162a3 ff.).

The gentle jibes of Socrates and Charmides against the anonymous author of the proposed definition force Critias to come to
its defense, thus confirming Socrates' suspicion that he is its true
source (162c). He defends it by elaborating on the difference in
meaning between "to do" (πράττειν) and "to make" (ποιεῖν), words
which Socrates has been using interchangeably. He also shows aristocratic impatience at any inclusion of the baser crafts in this discussion of something as essentially noble as temperance. Socrates
treats his distinction of terms with some condescension: Critias may
use words in any sense he wishes. It appears, at all events, that
what Critias meant by "what pertains to oneself" was simply "what
is good," and therefore temperance would be the performance or
creation (πρᾶξις ἢ ποίησις) of good things (163e1-2). Against this
new definition Socrates lays the objection that a man sometimes
does good unwittingly; this would make it seem that he could be
temperate and yet ignorant of his own temperance. Did Critias
mean to imply this?

Critias accepts this criticism with a good grace which he will
later abandon (cf. 169cd). At the moment, however, he is so
struck by the flaw thus exposed that he says he is willing virtually
to identify temperance with self-knowledge. This conviction, he
avows, has even influenced his interpretation of the Delphic in-
scription "Know thyself," which he regards as the god's command
to be temperate. Socrates subjects this latest suggestion to a long
and intricate examination. If temperance consists in knowing, then
it is a knowledge or science (ἐπιστήμη) and has an object. Now some
types of knowledge, such as medicine or house-building, are useful

and effect good results (165c8 ff.); others, whose utility is less immediately evident, like arithmetic and weighing, at least have an object distinct from themselves. Critias insists that temperance differs from both types in that it is the knowledge of other forms of knowledge and of itself; it consists in knowing what one knows and does not know (167a6-8). Socrates asks: (1) Is a knowledge of knowledge conceivable? (2) Would it be of any advantage? In the first place, other human activities, like sight, hearing, desire, etc., all have objects distinct from themselves. A knowledge of knowledge is at least a strange and unparalleled conception. In other matters self-relatedness seems impossible: a thing, for example, cannot be larger, greater, heavier, or older than itself. Socrates leaves the matter unsettled (169a6 ff.) and moves to the second question: if there is such a knowledge, of what use is it? It seems to be of little use. Presumably it would allow its possessor to tell whether he or others possessed particular sciences (170b3 ff.). But since the temperate man will not know the details of medicine or music, for example, he will be able to judge only whether a man has those sciences; he will not know what the man actually knows (170d1-3). But then the temperate man will never be able to distinguish a real physician from a pretended one. In fact, the physician and the temperate man can never discuss medicine. The former will know only the healthful and the unhealthful without knowing the science itself, the latter only the science, not its details. If temperance is the knowledge of knowledge, what the temperate man actually knows is hard to say and certainly not of much use (171c4 ff.). None of the conclusions seems tenable. Perhaps, says Socrates, the advantage of a science of sciences is merely to give us an easier and clearer apprehension of everything we know.

The whole attempt, he concludes, to prove temperance, the knowledge of knowledge, useful has been in vain. They have conceded too readily that for men to do what they know is a great good (172d6 ff.). Even in a perfect society, in which all arts were conducted efficiently, it would be clear only that men in it would live according to knowledge ($\dot{\epsilon}\pi\iota\sigma\tau\eta\mu\acute{o}\nu\omega s$). But it is not yet clear that to live according to knowledge is to live well and happily (173d3 ff.). To live by the science of shoe-making or of bronze-work hardly insures happiness. The one science that does is the knowledge of good and evil (174b10). Without it each of the arts and sciences will perform its function as efficiently as before, but the profit and advantage will have left them (174c9 ff.). But if it belongs to the knowledge of good and evil to secure advantage for us, then temperance, the knowledge of knowledge, will have no use at all (175a3 ff.). The discussion seems to have been fruitless.

Actually, as in the *Laches*, the reader is in a position to draw conclusions which evade the characters themselves. In the former dialogue Laches gave expression to the irrational aspect of courage and Nicias to the rational; here Charmides and Critias do the same for temperance. This is admittedly to put the matter in broad and somewhat oversimplified terms. Actually the intricacies and difficulties encountered in Socrates' conversation with Critias exceed anything found in the *Laches*. If, however, we read the *Charmides* with attention to characterization and dramatic action and with a willingness to entertain the possibility that its arguments may complement each other, we will find far more unity and order than it at first presents. In the first place, for reasons to be explained shortly, Charmides' contribution to the discussion must not be dismissed as valueless. Temperance is indeed based on gentleness and modesty of character. But such tendencies are not always appropriate, and virtue is always appropriate. Temperance, then, cannot be defined by these alone; in order to be virtuous they must be ruled by a principle. As in the *Laches*, however, the progress of the discussion leaves discarded definitions to lie forgotten, and therefore the notions of Charmides form no part of the suggestions subsequently analyzed. The meaning of this tactic is easy to misunderstand, and only our attention to significant statements beyond the bare argument can forestall the false inference that Charmides has said nothing worth remembering.

The first definitions of Critias, that temperance is doing what pertains to oneself or simply doing the good, are an advance on those of Charmides, since they imply a rational principle and not merely a temperamental trait. But they do not make the rule of reason a conscious one and so imply that a man can be temperate without knowing it. This fault at least Critias remedies in his new definition of temperance as self-knowledge. But when he explains his definition by supposing a knowledge that has itself and other forms of knowledge as its object, he opens the door to all the difficulties mentioned above. The notion of a knowledge of knowledge, problematic in itself and of doubtful usefulness, is finally laid aside in favor of the knowledge of good and evil, which alone assures good, noble, and beneficial action. But it is never suggested that insofar as temperance is knowledge it may be the knowledge of good and evil. Socrates' earlier insistence that temperance itself is good and noble would have made that suggestion natural, at least as a line of inquiry. To be sure, the objection to it is easy to formulate, with the example of the *Laches* before us, viz. that it would not distinguish temperance from virtue in general. But these final steps are not taken. Instead, we are left with an argument which, in the vivid summary of Socrates (175a9 ff.), lies in complete disarray, a series of disconnected inquiries linked here and there by unjustified concessions and ending in uncertainty.

When we read the *Charmides* as an expression of personality and dramatic action we find considerably more than the formal argument suggests. As in the *Laches*, the key to Plato's own conceptions is Socrates himself, not as the mouthpiece of Platonic ideas but as their exemplar in action. In the most difficult section of the argument, the discussion of the knowledge of knowledge, it is hard not to see an attempt to express in a philosophically satisfactory way the quality which Socrates actually possessed—the awareness of the limits of his own knowledge.[9] This quality, which he attributes to himself at *Apology* 23b, is constantly demonstrated in the dialogues. That it lies at the root of these pages of the *Charmides* is brought home to us by the special emphasis with which Socrates is made to display it in these very passages, at 165b and again at 166cd. That one should know what one knows and does not know remains a paradox, but in a sense as yet unexplained it is true of Socrates. The further paradox, that a man might convict of ignorance a pretended specialist in a subject in which the questioner himself lacked knowledge, is never explained or justi-

9. Others have already noticed this. Cf. T. G. Tuckey, *Plato's Charmides* (Cambridge, 1951), p. 65.

fied (171bc). But when Critias tries to hide his own ignorance on
the subject of virtue (169cd) and is exposed by Socrates, the dialogue itself becomes a demonstration of the paradox. We learn at
least that if the ability to do this is temperance, Socrates is temperate.

It was explained in an earlier chapter that the term σωφροσύνη,
through historical development, acquired meanings which seem at
first sight to have little connection with one another.[10] Modesty,
chastity, caution, and wisdom are all possible translations in different contexts, and even the association with self-knowledge is not
new. The man who knows his limitations in the face of divine
power will act more temperately than one who is deluded. Since
all men are in the same weak and vulnerable position, the Delphic
admonition to know oneself defines a virtue that all can aspire to.
One of its effects is to bridle self-assertiveness and keep a man's
desires well within the limits of his prerogatives. To put it in terms
found elsewhere in this dialogue, it makes a man "do what is proper
to himself." In short, the problem of defining the virtue is approached through familiar conceptions of it. The problem of dramatizing it is solved in the same way. For dramatized it is: the
*Charmides* is a display of temperate and intemperate behavior
in the various common meanings of those words. It is like the
*Laches* in its creation of a dramatic contrast between two men of
diverse character. Charmides, whose notion of temperance is or-
derliness or modesty or gentleness, was apparently well known for
his retiring ways. Xenophon, at *Memorabilia* 3.7, records a conversation in which Socrates urged him to be less shy of taking part in
public affairs. In Plato's dialogue he is not only becomingly modest about his own virtue (158cd) but he shows hesitation in putting
forward his ideas in the presence of his elders (159b). Critias, by
contrast, is φιλότιμος, and that quality is what first induces him to
join the discussion (162c). It later leads him to the dishonest tactic
of concealing his own confusion (169cd). This portrayal finds con-
firmation in Xenophon's report, in the *Memorabilia*, that Critias had
no equal in φιλοτιμία in all Athens, except perhaps Alcibiades (1.2.
14). Xenophon goes on to imply that his outstanding failing was

10. See above, Chapter 1, note 9.

an absence of temperance (1.2.15-18); he was the bloodiest and greediest of the Thirty Tyrants (1.2.12). This eventual degradation of his character, if not fully foreshadowed, is at least hinted at in Plato's picture of a self-assertive man more concerned with honor than with truth. He is convicted of intemperance, moreover, in the terms of the dialogue itself. Not only does he lack the modesty which Charmides thought was essential to temperance, but he fails in the self-knowledge which he offered as his own notion of that virtue. This charge is first introduced as a friendly jibe on the part of Charmides, who says at 162b that his unnamed friend perhaps μηδὲν εἰδέναι ὅτι ἐνόει. Critias takes up the challenge with heat and sets out to prove that he knows his own mind on the subject of temperance (162d). He does not succeed, for Socrates reduces him to confusion. In the terms of his own definition that the temperate man knows what he knows, Socrates is temperate and he is not.

Xenophon, in the passage mentioned above, tries to exculpate Socrates of responsibility for the notorious intemperance of Critias, who had been his companion of earlier years. This plea is implicit in the *Charmides* too. Just as Socrates was the true exemplar of courage in the *Laches*, in the *Charmides* he shows the modesty in discussion which comes from self-knowledge, and on one occasion he reveals the chastity which was commonly thought to be one aspect of temperance (155de). This last incident is reminiscent of the account of Alcibiades in *Symposium* 219bcd and foreshadows the statement at *Republic* 430e that temperance is a "kind of order and a continence of certain pleasures and desires." The apologetic intent is unmistakable: Socrates was a model of virtue and not a corruptor of his associates, their public vices notwithstanding. But there is more in Plato's description of his behavior than apologetics. Socrates exemplifies all the many aspects of the good and the noble which in the discussion are classified tentatively as σωφροσύνη but never find their place in a single satisfactory conception of the virtue. His temperate conduct in the dialogue is too pointed to be overlooked; it is Plato's reminder that the *Charmides* is moral action as well as intellectual inquiry, and that the virtuous man, whom all seek to define, is ever present, hidden behind a veil of irony and self-effacement.

There remains Charmides himself. My contention that not only Critias and Socrates but Charmides too makes a contribution toward the true definition of temperance depends in part upon Plato's portrayal of the boy's character. Charmides, who as yet has no knowledge of what temperance is, is presented as in some rudimentary way temperate. Socrates' desire to see if he has a naturally good soul (154e) is justified by his modest demeanor (158c), by his docility under questioning, and by his final admission that he does need the "charm" which Socrates can apply (176ab). Socrates never accepts Critias' assertions that the boy already has the virtue of temperance, except in polite conditional sentences (175de, 158b), but when Charmides accepts Socrates' tutelage, the implication is that he is already naturally disposed to temperance as many boys his age would not be. Critias says it proves he is already temperate (176b). This is not altogether false; it is merely overstatement. Plato is not prepared to place this much reliance on φύσις. Now when Charmides calls temperance gentleness and then modesty, he is describing qualities that he exemplifies in his own character. Socrates advises him at 160d to "look within himself" before he answers. Charmides' next reply, as comparison of 160e with 158c will show, amounts to a self-description. Since the dialogue clearly presents him as the kind of young man in whom temperance can be made to flower, his contribution to the discussion is valid too. He both describes and typifies those aspects of emotion and temperament which are prerequisites for the full virtue of temperance. He stands in relation to that virtue as Laches does to the virtue of courage, although neither has the knowledge which would make his virtue complete.[11] Charmides is, if anything, too submissive. Modesty, which, as Socrates pointedly remarks (158c), is charming in a boy, must be balanced in the adult

---

11. Tuckey, *Charmides*, quotes the sentence of Schirlitz, "*sophrosyne* is the prudent reserve or modest discretion that depends on moral insight," and says of it, "the dialogue does suggest such a definition" (p. 93). He adds, "Plato could not give the dialogue anything but an indefinite conclusion if he was to remain true to Socrates' undogmatic method" (p. 94).

In Plato's later writings, the importance of temperament and emotion to σωφροσύνη is made more explicit. For example, in the struggle which the soul wages to maintain that virtue in the myth at *Phaedrus* 253c-256a, shame and modesty play a major part.

by qualities of strength. Plato, who knew the boy's later history in association with the more masterful Critias and knew also how the latter had bullied Socrates,[12] may intend an ominous hint of Charmides' ruin in the joking remark he lets drop at 176c: "I shall use violence, since he commands me."

The problems which Plato chose to take up in his early dialogues were intimately connected with the careers and pretensions of the great sophists. It was in deference to the important role which they had played in forming the moral and educational ideas of the late fifth century that Plato wrote the *Protagoras*, a dialogue filled with sophists and admirers of sophists. The work is too large and too varied to analyze here completely. I have selected only the points of highest relevance, and especially those which controversy has obscured. In this work, more than in any other, Plato stamped on the mind of posterity his own view of sophistry. That view is one of fundamental opposition. But there is more wit than passion in the *Protagoras*; Plato paints with humorous rather than angry strokes the scene that introduces the three great schools of sophistry, the ambulatory, the sedentary, and the recumbent (314e3-316a2); and he gives his sense of playfulness full rein in the long intermission (335c-347b). In the argument proper, the Socrates who entangles Protagoras in his own admissions seems at first sight even more perverse than the questioner who spun a web of dialectic around the clumsy Hippias in the *Hippias Minor*. When we penetrate the dazzling surface, however, we find a train of argument as well controlled as that of the shorter dialogue.

The occasion of the *Protagoras* is the decision of young Hippocrates to take advantage of the instruction offered by Protagoras, newly arrived in town. In his eagerness, Hippocrates comes at dawn to ask Socrates to accompany him to the house of Callias. Going there together, they find Protagoras, Hippias, and Prodicus all present. Introductions are made, and Socrates asks what Hippocrates can expect to learn if he accepts Protagoras' tutelage. Protagoras claims that he knows the political art and can teach men to be good citizens (319a4-7). Socrates finds it hard to believe

12. Xenophon, *Memorabilia*, 1.2.33 ff.

that such an art can be taught. The Assembly, he has noted, will listen only to trained experts in matters concerning the other arts, but in politics it accepts anyone's advice. Moreover, Pericles and others like him seemed unable to teach statecraft to their own sons, and this fact is incomprehensible unless what they failed to teach could not be taught (319a-320b).

Protagoras' reply to these objections is long. He argues, in the myth of Prometheus and Epimetheus, that every man shares in the political art, i.e. in virtue, although each of the other arts is restricted to a few men (320c8 ff.).[13] This is why the Athenians will listen to anyone's opinion in affairs of state, and their action implies no disbelief that virtue can be taught. The rearing of children, both at home and at school, proves the contrary: virtue is taught from the cradle. No one assumes that it comes to a man by nature,[14] or by chance, as a man is born handsome, tall, or strong. It is rather a product of diligence, practice, and instruction, and those who lack it are admonished and punished (323c3-324d1). From all this it is clear that when Protagoras says virtue is a διδακτόν he uses the word to mean more than mere instruction. Instruction is only part of his educational scheme, which includes as well both physical and moral pressure and an effort on the learner's part. The question "Can virtue be taught?" is ambiguous, and this helps explain why Socrates and Protagoras will seem to have reversed positions at conversation's end. Protagoras finds that education in virtue starts at home, where the child is warned, beaten, and threatened for the good of his character (325d). It continues at school, where he reads about great men, whom he should emulate, and where he learns music and gymnastic. All human speech and action requires proper rhythm and harmony, and so he reads the works of good poets, which make him gentler and improve the rhythms and harmonies of his own soul. Gymnastic strengthens him, so that his body may serve his soul and not incline it to cowardice (326c1-3). Protagoras' words here foreshadow the much

13. This myth is discussed above in Chapter 2, note 17.
14. *Protag.* 323c5. That is, by nature alone. Protagoras believes that nature has some influence on virtue (327b8, 351b2).

longer passage in the *Republic* where Socrates describes the musical and gymnastic education of the Guardians.[15]

Protagoras can now explain why great statesmen do not have great statesmen for sons. Everybody in the state is always teaching political virtue, because everybody has a share in it. Everybody, therefore, has equal opportunity to learn it too, and so there is no great likelihood that sons of great fathers will learn it much better than others. Protagoras claims only that as a teacher of virtue he is superior to other men and so worth his price (326e6-328c2).

Socrates says that he is charmed by this brilliant exposition, but he has one small question to ask. Protagoras has spoken of justice, temperance, holiness, and other such qualities as if they were all one. Now, however, Socrates wants to define more precisely the relationship among the virtues, and he begins by presenting a series of alternatives. The proposition, "These are all collectively one" (329c5), defines the unity of virtue in the most general way. But this is not enough. (1) Does this one virtue have μόρια (i.e. parts or species; at *Euthyphro* 12c shame is a μόριον of fear, and the odd a μόριον of number), or does it not, having instead only several names? (2) Do the μόρια differ in kind, or not? As Socrates puts it, are they like the μόρια of a face—mouth, nose, eyes, and ears— or like the μόρια of gold? (3) Does the presence of any one virtue in a man imply the presence of all, or can a man possess one and not the others?[16]

Protagoras thinks that virtue is one but has several names, corresponding to several μόρια, which differ in kind, and that the presence of one of these does not entail the presence of any other. Moreover, the power of action which each bestows is not like that of any other, nor is any one virtue itself like any other (330b3 ff.). Taken strictly, this would mean that each shares with any other only the

15. See especially *Rep.* 401d and 411e. In the *Republic*, however, gymnastic has a direct effect on the soul, not merely an indirect one (410cd).

16. The relationship here envisioned between virtues is what modern logicians sometimes call biconditional (If A, then B, and if B, then A). Plato's way of putting it is not less clear (329e4). Elsewhere, he deals with this logical problem by the device of converted predication, with whose use he shows himself well acquainted at 350c7-9. Cf. *Euthyphro* 11e-12c.

name "virtue." As it appears later (331de), however, Protagoras does not take so strict a view of his own phraseology, for he thinks it allows some "small" resemblance between the virtues. But for the moment Socrates has used an excellent technique of revealing, in outline at least, what Protagoras means by the unity of virtue, and of exposing the best line of attack. Degrees of unity are defined which range from a difference only in name to a unity only in name.

Three arguments follow. The third is cut short, but in the first two it is important to notice every indication as to what Socrates thinks he has proved. This is one way of determining what Plato at this stage of his career meant by the unity of virtue. Socrates first attacks the proposition that no virtue is like any other, in an argument which I shall abbreviate as follows. There is such a thing as justice, and it is just rather than unjust. There is such a thing as holiness, and it is holy rather than unholy. Moreover, justice is holy rather than unholy, and holiness is just rather than unjust. Justice is like holiness, and holiness is like justice. This last contradicts Protagoras' earlier assertion that no virtue is like any other. But Protagoras is not ready to concede that justice is holy and holiness just, for there is, he says, some distinction to be made. But, he adds, so be it, if you wish. Socrates wants no concession of that sort, and the argument boils away in a moment of annoyance.

One should not overlook the fact that Socrates has dropped his role of wary questioner, and not only states his own beliefs here but actually runs away with the argument at 331ab. In fact, an imaginary questioner has been brought in at 330c in order to allow Socrates to adopt the role of answerer. "I would answer him that [justice] is just. What would your vote be?" (330c5-6). Socrates casts several other unqualified votes: holiness is holy (330d8-e1); justice is holy and holiness just (331b1 ff.); justice and holiness are either the same thing or very much alike (331b3-6). This last is repeated at 333b5-6 as "Justice and holiness are almost the same thing." Socrates also makes a great point of distinguishing what *he* has admitted from what Protagoras has admitted (330e-331a). This decisiveness should be contrasted with the way he handles the argument at 332a-333b. Though he is decisive, however, his conclusion is vague, and in the face of Protagoras' annoyance (332a) he is unwilling to clarify the point by further questions.[17]

When the next argument begins, at 332a, the imaginary questioner has vanished. Socrates gets Protagoras to assent to the following main propositions. (1) Wisdom is quite the opposite of folly (332a4-5). (2) Those who act wrongly act foolishly and not temperately (332b1-3). (3) Therefore foolish action is the opposite of temperate action (332b3-4). (4) Folly is an opposite of temperance (332e4-5). (5) Everything has only one opposite (332e7). All this would seem to disprove (6), that wisdom is other than temperance (333a3). Socrates' actual conclusion is that one must reject either (5) or (6). He adds, "Then would temperance and wisdom be one thing?" (333b4-5).

The quality of his assent to this last identification must be distinguished from that, for example, at 330c5 and 7, 330d7, 331b2, and later at 352d4. This distinction is commonly not made.[18] But ἐγὼ μὲν γὰρ αὐτὸς ὑπέρ γε ἐμαυτοῦ φαίην ἄν . . . εἶναι (331b1-3) is not the equivalent of οὐκοῦν ἂν εἴη; (333b4). The latter is another version of κατὰ τοῦτον τὸν λόγον ἂν εἴη; (350c4), which concludes an argument in which Socrates uses premises repugnant to him but which he

17. This whole argument provokes some objections. In the first place, Socrates, in the series of questions beginning at 330c, does not state the alternatives fully. They should have the form: "Is justice just or unjust or neither?"—to take only the first example. A modern logician would probably choose the last alternative and say that the proposition "Justice is just" contains a mistake in logic. But that problem is not relevant to this study and involves discussion of the nature of the Ideas. See R. S. Bluck, *Plato's Phaedo* (New York, 1955), pp. 174 ff., and especially p. 180, for a recent treatment of this question. Socrates' failure to state all the alternatives is not due to a general inability to distinguish contrary from contradictory (see 346d, 351d6, and other examples given in note 19 below). The real answer is probably that a fuller statement of alternatives would not affect the direction of the argument, and therefore Plato does not seek exactitude. If the anonymous questioner had suggested at 330d that holiness was neither holy nor unholy, Socrates would still have replied, "Εὐφήμει. How could anything else be holy if not holiness itself?" A detailed discussion of the rights and wrongs of this argument can be found in David Gallop's article "Justice and Holiness in *Protagoras* 330-331," *Phronesis*, 6 (1961), 86-93. See also David Savan, "Self-Predication in *Protagoras* 330-331," *Phronesis*, 9 (1964), 130-35.

18. Cf. J. P. Sullivan, "The Hedonism in Plato's *Protagoras*," *Phronesis*, 6 (1961), 15, "Yet Socrates now assumes that self-control and wisdom are the same, as justice and piety appeared nearly the same." *Protag.* 360d4-5, taken by some as a Socratic commitment, is also a *question*, as 360d7 shows.

thinks Protagoras has accepted. (See below, note 20.) Socrates is quite willing to assert roundly that the virtues are *either* very much like one another *or* the same thing (331b), but to the very end (361bc) he declines to state the latter in an unqualified way.

Socrates' doubts at 333a center on two propositions, one of which he implies must go: (5) Everything has only one opposite; (6) Wisdom is other than temperance. Now it would be a mistake to prejudge this question by assuming as self-evident that everything has only one opposite.[19] In Plato, as in nonphilosophical Greek and English, there are degrees of opposition. Some things are more "opposite" than others to a given thing, and others are equally "opposite" to it. Common usage allows us to say that rap-

19. Gregory Vlastos says that "the undeniably true proposition (true by definition)" is (5), viz. "Everything (which has an opposite) has only one opposite." It is true that this view of contrariety seems already implicit in Aristotle's treatment of contraries (ἐναντία). Cf. *Categ.* 6a17. But Plato is not bound by Aristotelian usage. Vlastos thinks the real "lame duck" is (4): Folly is an opposite of temperance. The latter depends, he says, on the faulty inference from (2) to (3). "The fallacy will be obvious if one compares 'Being triangular implies being not square; therefore, being a triangular figure is the opposite of being a square figure'" (G. Vlastos [ed.], Martin Ostwald [trans.], *Plato's Protagoras* [New York, 1956], p. xxix). This criticism seems justified, unless one can take ἐναντίον to mean "contradictory." But Platonic usage does not encourage our taking it in this sense (see this note below).

Sullivan ("Hedonism," p. 15) doubts (5), as I do, but for reasons that I cannot accept. He says, "Not only is the very term [opposite] extremely vague but Plato elsewhere himself recognizes the distinction between contrary and contradictory, which may both be called opposites (cf. e.g. *Prot.* 346d, 351d, *Meno* 91c, *Symp.* 201e, cp. *Rep.* 584e)." Now it is undeniably true that Plato was not confused by the distinctions involved in, say, beautiful, not beautiful, and ugly (cf. the above passages and *Lysis* 216de, *Gorgias* 467e). His way of making these distinctions, however, is to speak of (a) the beautiful, (b) the ugly, and (c) that which is neither. The first two he calls "opposites" (ἐναντία), and the third is "in between" (μέσον, μεταξύ). He does not, to my knowledge, use the word ἐναντίον to denote (b) and (c) together, i.e. the contradictory. At *Lysis* 215e several contraries are called "opposites," and at 218b that word is by implication restricted to the contraries, in a passage which also mentions the intermediate class. At *Gorgias* 467e evils are the "opposites" of goods, and a class is recognized "between" these. At *Rep.* 583c pain is "opposite" to pleasure, and tranquillity is "between." At *Meno* 91c9 corruption is "opposite" to benefit, and is distinguished from mere nonbenefit. At *Symp.* 201e-202a Plato recognizes a condition "between" good and evil, beauty and ugliness, wisdom and ignorance. At *Protag.* 346d there is a "mean" between black and white, noble and shameful. The man who does no evil is μέσος. Plato is following his normal usage when at *Protag.* 332c he lists as "opposites" the beautiful and the ugly, the good and the bad, the high-pitched and the low-pitched.

ture and contentment are each "opposite" to pain, and that bitter and sour are both "opposites" of sweet. Plato himself, at *Meno* 91c, says that ὠφελία is the opposite of διαφθορά, though one normally expects ὠφελία to be paired with βλάβη (cf. *Rep.* 334b, *Meno* 88a, *Laws* 904b). Thucydides uses the word "opposite" even more freely when he has Diodotus say that two things are most "opposite" to good counsel, haste and anger (3.42.1). There is no compelling reason to think that Plato must have accepted the proposition that everything has only one opposite. Wisdom and temperance need not be the same thing and yet can both be opposites of folly; no more need be implied than that the former have something in common. Therefore the alternative which Socrates offers at 333a does not force him or us to affirm that wisdom = temperance, and the qualified nature of his conclusion confirms this.

The third argument, which begins at 333b7, seems to be an attempt to prove that the possession of temperance entails the possession of justice. This, if pursued, might have led to an identification of those two virtues, or at least to another conclusion of the form, "They are very much alike." Since successive arguments have by now linked holiness with justice, temperance with wisdom, and justice with temperance, none of these four virtues—if we grant the success of the last argument—can be called utterly different from any other. This is precisely the concession which Protagoras makes at 349d, when he sets courage, the fifth virtue, apart. The argument at 333b ff., however, is never concluded, but quickly bogs down amid strained feelings.

After a brief altercation and a long, digressive exercise in the analysis of poetry, during which Socrates makes some serious points through parody, the earlier discussion resumes. Protagoras now is willing to confine his argument to one virtue, courage, which, he claims, stands apart from the rest (349d2-5). Many men, he contends, are unjust, impious, intemperate, and ignorant in the extreme, but, in spite of all this, they are very brave. Courage was the one quality that Socrates omitted in his first attempt to identify the virtues. Its long and separate treatment is understandable. There is in courage, as Protagoras says, something that makes it compatible, in the common way of speaking, with all the worst vices except cowardice.

Are the courageous daring ($\theta a\rho\rho a\lambda\acute{\epsilon}o\iota$)? asks Socrates. Protagoras says yes. Virtue, moreover, they agree, including courage, is noble. Now in every activity the experts are the most daring: the good swimmers, the skilled horsemen, the well-trained soldiers. Some men, of course, are daring though quite ignorant of what they do, and Protagoras suggests that they are mad. They cannot be courageous, then, because this would make courage an ignoble thing. Yet if the brave are the daring (as Protagoras insists) and if those who know are more daring than those who do not, wisdom will be courage (350c4-5).

ᵉProtagoras contends that Socrates has argued from what we would call the fallacy of undistributed middle: the courageous are daring; the wise are daring; therefore, the wise are courageous.[20] With equally bad logic, he says, you could prove that strength ($\mathrm{i}\sigma\chi\acute{\upsilon}s$) is wisdom. Thus: the strong ($\mathrm{i}\sigma\chi\upsilon\rho o\acute{\iota}$) are able ($\delta\upsilon\nu a\tau o\acute{\iota}$); the knowing are more able than those who do not know; therefore, strength is knowledge ($\mathrm{i}\pi\iota\sigma\tau\acute{\eta}\mu\eta$) or wisdom ($\sigma o\phi\acute{\iota}a$). The fact is, continues Protagoras, that not all the able are strong and not all the daring are courageous. Mere ability ($\delta\acute{\upsilon}\nu a\mu\iota s$) comes from knowledge and madness and anger, just as mere daring comes from art ($\tau\acute{\epsilon}\chi\nu\eta$, mastery of technique) and madness and anger. Strength, on the other hand, comes from nature and good training of the body, and courage comes from nature and good training of the soul ($\mathrm{i}\pi\grave{o}$ $\phi\acute{\upsilon}\sigma\epsilon\omega s$ $\kappa a\grave{\iota}$ $\epsilon\mathrm{i}\tau\rho o\phi\acute{\iota}as$ $\tau\mathrm{\hat{\omega}}\nu$ $\psi\upsilon\chi\mathrm{\hat{\omega}}\nu$ 351b2).

20. Actually, Protagoras has not only said that "the courageous are daring" (349e2-3) but in the confusion of the argument has also said that "the courageous are the daring" (350b6-7), i.e. he has made the two classes coextensive. His later protestations show that he is unaware of this slip, but it allows us to acquit Socrates of the fallacy charged to him. I have explained in full my reasons for this interpretation in "The 'Fallacy' in *Protagoras* 349d-350c," *TAPA*, 92 (1962), 408-17, which also contains a summary of the extensive scholarship on this passage. The essential point is that 350b6 contains, in question form, an identity-proposition of the type "The A are the B." This type occurs also at *Gorgias* 489e, *Euthydemus* 277c, *Theaetetus* 205ab, *Protag.* 312c, and *Rep.* 509e. Its occurrence in Greek authors in general was examined by A. Procksch in "Über den gebrauch des artikels, insbesondre beim prädikat," *Philologus*, 40 (1881), 1-47, with results that confirm the above interpretation of *Protag.* 350b6. The article in the predicate, he concludes, always indicates identity or, if the clause is negative, nonidentity (p. 47).

This argument of Protagoras is presented with lucidity and force, and it concludes by offering a conception of courage which Socrates might well have paused to examine. But instead of confronting the argument directly, Socrates chooses to undermine it indirectly by a lengthy and seemingly digressive interrogation. His purpose shortly becomes evident: he will show that Protagoras has not thought out the implications of his opinions about courage. Socrates begins by assuming tentatively that the pleasant is good and the painful evil (351c4-5). He is not followed in this assumption by Protagoras, who agrees rather with the opinion of the common people that there are evil pleasures and good pains. Socrates presses him to answer whether they are not good insofar as they are pleasant, evil insofar as they are painful, but Protagoras remains reluctant to commit himself.

The common people also believe that often when a man has knowledge (ἐπιστήμη), it is not this that rules him but something else, e.g. anger, pleasure, pain, love, or fear (352b5-8). Does Protagoras agree with them in this? No, he believes that knowledge and wisdom rule all a man's actions, and Socrates agrees emphatically. Then what do the common people mean when they say a man is worsted by pleasure or by pain? They mean, it is decided, that he chooses pleasures that he knows are evil, i.e. pleasures that will bring future pain (353cde). In the same way, their judgment that present sufferings are good implies only that they cause future pleasure (354ab). They cannot mean anything else, because they recognize no other standard of good and evil (354d7-e2). The phrase "worsted by pleasures" would then mean "worsted by the good," and one must infer that it is sometimes wrong to be mastered by what is good. To be mastered by the good, i.e. the pleasant, would consist in choosing a course of action in which there is more pain and less pleasure, or, in effect, in making a mistake in the weighing of alternatives. A man naturally overestimates present pleasures and pains and underestimates those in the future, and such mistakes can be avoided only by ability in the art of measuring pleasure and pain. This ability must be an art and a knowledge (357b4). Hence, what the many call being overcome by pleasures is nothing more than ignorance (357d1). Protagoras, Prodicus, and Hippias agree. To be mastered by one's self, then, will be ignorance; and to master one's self, wisdom. In the common Socratic phrase, no one will choose willingly what he thinks evil in place of what he thinks good, or choose a greater evil in place of a lesser (358c6 ff.).

Protagoras had said earlier that courage was unlike the other four virtues, and Socrates will now make him reconsider that judgment. According to the argument, the brave man, who goes into battle to meet dangers which are commonly judged fearful, cannot regard them as really fearful, because no one knowingly chooses what he thinks to be fearful or otherwise evil. By the same token, the coward could not flee battle if he really knew that to fight would be good and honorable. He is a coward, then, because of his inability to estimate the good and evil involved in fighting for one's country, and the brave man is brave because he can estimate them correctly. Cowardice is ignorance, and courage is knowledge. Socrates remarks that the conversation has taken an odd turn. He had started by arguing that virtue cannot be taught; he has ended by trying to show that all virtues are knowledge, and nothing is teachable if not knowledge. Protagoras, on the contrary, had started by arguing that virtue *can* be taught and has ended by arguing that virtue is other than knowledge. And if it is not knowledge, how can it be taught?

The long argument of Socrates, which began at 351b and ends with this surprising conclusion, rests on a foundation of plain hedonism. But we are not justified in accepting that hedonism as an expression of Plato's own thought. Socrates himself shows no satisfaction in the conclusions and says only what he also says at the end of the *Meno*, that before they can answer whether virtue can be taught they must first find out what virtue is. This he regards as still undecided (361c2-6).[21] Moreover, from the begin-

---

21. It is very important to notice Socrates' reservations about the definition of virtue as knowledge. The intellectualist interpreters of the dialogue underestimate their significance (cf. A. E. Taylor, H. Raeder, F. Seidel, and J. S. Mill as cited below, note 23). The notion that all of the virtues are merely knowledge appears at 361b as the conclusion towards which Socrates' recent arguments *tend*. It takes two forms: (1) "Everything is knowledge, justice

and temperance and courage alike," and (2) "Virtue will appear as wholly knowledge." Yet he declines to accept it, and at 361c5 regards the question "What is virtue?" as still open.

The intellectualist interpretation does not, however, rest on this passage alone but calls into evidence two others in which Socrates seems to have no reservations. These are 352a-c and 358cd. Vlastos formulates the two passages as "Knowledge is Virtue," which he interprets to mean "knowledge is . . . the sufficient condition of virtuous action" or "Virtue = Knowledge" (*Plato's Protag.*, xxxviii, n. 47). He says of the formula "Knowledge is Virtue" that "we may use it for the Socratic doctrine that anyone who knows what is the best course of action open to him in any given situation cannot fail to follow it" (*ibid.*). Now the striking thing about the doctrine expressed at 352a-c is that Socrates vouches for its truth, in an interrogation otherwise marked by his constant hedging and irony. "You speak nobly and truly," he says at 352d4, when he has got Protagoras' assent to it. And the second passage, 358c6-d4, apart from Socrates' apparent assent to it at d4, is familiar Socratic doctrine: no one willingly chooses evil rather than good, or the greater of two evils (cf. *Meno* 78a, *Gorgias* 468c). If Socrates understood these passages to mean virtue = knowledge, it is at least very odd that he should back away from that formulation at 361bc. The passages demand a closer look.

*Protagoras* 352a-d is couched in metaphor and simile. The many think knowledge is not strong, capable of ruling, fit for command. They think that it can be present in a man and not rule, that it can yield command to anger, pleasure, etc., and be "dragged around" like a slave. Socrates believes knowledge is a noble thing, fit for rule; that if a man knows the good and the bad, he will not be overcome by anything so as to do other than knowledge directs; that wisdom is able to assist a man. But the majority think that many who know the best do not wish to do it (352d6-7). This last statement shows that we have here an expansion of the dictum "No man wishes evil" or, in its more familiar shape, "No man does wrong on purpose" (cf. 358c). In his later dialogues, Plato found this dictum compatible with a belief that reason could be overcome by passion. See, e.g., *Rep.* 577de and *Tim.* 86c-e, and compare *Laws* 860d1 and 863e2-3 with 863e6 ff. (cf. 731c). In these dialogues the doctrine that no man willingly or knowingly does evil is coupled with (1) the admission that the passions can tyrannize reason, or (2) the doctrine that virtue is not knowledge alone, but knowledge (or right opinion) built on natural endowment and long training (cf. *Rep.* 374de, 376c, 429d ff., 487a, and below, Chapter 5 *passim*).

These last two beliefs are, of course, not stated or implied at *Protag.* 352a-d. But are they excluded? I think not. The passage does not say that reason cannot yield command to passion etc. (as it obviously yields, e.g., at *Tim.* 86cd, *Laws* 863e, and *Rep.* 444b) but that knowledge ($\epsilon\pi\iota\sigma\tau\eta\mu\eta$) cannot. (Vlastos' translation of the word as "reason" [p. liv] could on this account be misleading.) When knowledge is present in a man ($\epsilon\nu\sigma\nu\sigma\eta\varsigma$ 352b5) it cannot be ruled, "dragged about," enslaved, or mastered. This leaves two questions unanswered: (1) Once knowledge is present, can it ever be driven out? (2) Can knowledge be present in a man whose nature and training have not prepared him for it?

Regarding question (1), Vlastos considers the suggestion "to (i) concede 'seduction' by pleasure but contend that (ii) at the moment it occurs one *no longer* knows or believes one is doing wrong" and concludes that "Socrates could not afford this defense for it would trivialize his [argument at 352a-c], conceding to passion to 'master' knowledge after all" (xliii). This objection has some force, in view of the strong metaphorical language in 352a-c. Yet,

ning, Socrates reserves judgment about the opinions that he proposes. He offers them as arguing points (351c4-6, 351e1-3) and not as convictions. The exception is his statement, accepted by Protagoras too, that knowledge rules in a man (352d4). The whole argument is an imaginary conversation with the common people, and Socrates' conclusions are only inferences from the moral presuppositions entertained by them. In concluding that the good life is based on knowledge alone, he is only making explicit the logical basis of hedonism, and he points this out emphatically (354e8-355a5). Protagoras is beaten in the debate because he agrees that self-mastery consists in knowledge alone (358a) and because this is inconsistent with his former statements about courage. Socrates, moreover, wins the agreement of Protagoras and the other sophists without committing himself, and he encourages their assent in a complimentary little speech, full of irony, recommending sophistic education (357e4-8). This is more than an ironical aside in an otherwise straightforward exposition: it is rather a clue that Socrates is not being straightforward at all.[22]

---

if one ceases to know because of passion, does not one's knowledge escape mistreatment, enslavement, and subjection by its absence? At *Rep.* 412e the danger to the young Guardians-in-training is not that they will act against their right opinion but that they will *lose* it through persuasion, pain, pleasure, or fear. To say that a man always does what he thinks good, as Plato evidently did to the end of his life, and then concede that he can do the opposite of what his better judgment dictates, as in *Rep.* 412e, might seem a trivialization too. It seems to many to falsify experience. Yet it is evidently what Plato believed in later years about the role of right opinion. Now right opinion is not knowledge. We cannot, for example, overlook *Meno* 98a, where knowledge, in contrast to right opinion, is said to be "stable" ($\mu\acute{o}\nu\iota\mu os$). But that passage does not mention the passions, and it may only be making the obvious point that right opinion, unlike knowledge, is always vulnerable to false reports. In short, there is no clear answer to question (1). Plato may have thought at the time he wrote the *Protagoras* that knowledge could not be driven out by passion, and this may be the reason for his forceful language at 352a-c. But the opposite view is also possible.

It is more important that *Protag.* 352a-d leaves question (2) entirely open. One can therefore look for the answer elsewhere in the dialogue without prejudice.

22. For contrary arguments see R. Hackforth, "Hedonism in Plato's *Protagoras*," *CQ*, 22 (1928), 39-42, and Vlastos (ed.), *Plato's Protag.*, p. xl. Hackforth believes that the hedonism is seriously urged by Plato, pointing out that it is forced on Protagoras (351d) and forced on the many, who do not at first hold it (351c). Vlastos' main reason for thinking that Hackforth is "much more nearly right" than his critics is that "it is most unlikely that Socrates

would deliberately offer a false proposition [viz. that the pleasant and the good are identical] as a premise for establishing his great proposition" that knowledge is virtue (p. xl).

The most nearly complete answer to these arguments has been given by Sullivan, who maintains (a) that, whereas Protagoras does not at first agree to the hedonistic premise, he is driven to assent to it ("Hedonism," pp. 22-23); (b) that the whole argument, like the elenchus in general (cf. R. Robinson, "Plato's Consciousness of Fallacy," *Mind*, 51 [1942], 101-102), is essentially *ad hominem*, and Platonic rules allow the use of false premises which the answerer holds explicitly or implicitly, if their use will clarify the lines of argument (Sullivan, pp. 25-26); and (c) that "the reader is given sufficient indications to realize . . . that Socrates is being 'ironic' " in his espousal of hedonism (p. 22), especially in the calculated stress on the word τέλος. Can the many point to any other τέλος when talking of good and evil? This repetition (354b, 354de, 355a) would be labored and pointless if it were not meant to imply that another τέλος is conceivable (p. 27). Werner Jaeger saw this too, in *Paideia*, trans. G. Highet (New York, 1939-44), 2.143.

My own explanation of *Protag.* 349d-350c as an argument *ad hominem* (see note 20, above) is an attempt to prove in another context a point which Vlastos rightly insists is crucial here and which he strongly challenges, viz. (b) Socrates' use of a false premise. In that passage the false premise is "The brave are identical with the daring," which allows the conclusion, "Wisdom is courage." Socrates' only justification for this procedure is that Protagoras assents to the premise (350b7). Another example of this method is *Gorgias* 458e-461b, where Socrates argues *ad hominem* to conclude "The orator is just" (460c). This conclusion, reached through premises admitted by Gorgias, contradicts his earlier statement that the orator can use his art unjustly (457bc). This is normal elenchus. The discussion about hedonism in the *Protagoras*, though far longer and more intricate, is still an elenchus; it ends by trapping Protagoras in a contradiction (360de). It is not exact to say, as Vlastos does (p. liv, n. 13), that Protagoras "repudiates" the identification of the good and the pleasant at 351cd. He declares himself tentatively against it, then at 351e4-7 says he is willing to be persuaded of its truth, and by 360a3 he is giving reluctant assent to it.

One of the problems faced by those who regard Socrates' hedonism as seriously meant is its inconsistency with what the Platonic Socrates says elsewhere about pleasure. Vlastos attacks the problem with candor, mentioning among passages where the identification of good with pleasure is rejected *Philebus* 60a and *Gorgias* 495a ff. (One should also mention *Phaedo* 68e-69a, where Socrates scorns those who reject one pleasure only to get another.) Vlastos proposes that in the *Protagoras* "what Socrates most likely meant to assert is . . . (a) that pleasure is *a* good (not the only one), (b) that whatever is best will *in fact* be the most pleasant. (a) and (b) do not add up to hedonism, i.e. to making pleasure *definitive* of good." He says in defense of this that "it would be perfectly possible for Socrates to have failed to understand a matter which no one had as yet explained or even properly investigated, and thus assert [that the pleasant and the good are identical] when all he in fact *intended* to assert was (a) and (b)" (xli). Now this argument fails in the light of certain clear assertions in the *Protagoras*. At 354b several conventional goods are reduced, qua goods, to pleasure and prevention of pain. Between 354b and 355a it is stressed repeatedly that the many have no other τέλος but pleasure and pain, and at 355b the good is taken to be *synonymous* with the pleasant, the bad with the painful (cf. Sul-

The *Protagoras* does not yield its meaning easily, especially when taken by itself,[23] but comparison with the *Laches, Charmides,* and *Republic* strongly suggests one line of interpretation. In the former two dialogues it was seen that suggestions were made separately which, if combined, would have produced a more satisfactory conclusion. This, I argued, was by design. The ideas of *Laches* and *Charmides*, in particular, were not to be disregarded when they argued that courage and temperance respectively involved qualities other than the rational. The *Protagoras*, though longer and more complex, has a similar pattern; here it is Protagoras whose perceptive remarks are most in danger of being overlooked.

---

livan, pp. 18-19). It is hardly possible to interpret all this as implying anything other than pure hedonism.

A great deal has been written about this problem. Bibliography can be found in Sullivan, Vlastos, and P. Friedländer, *Platon*, II, *Die Platonischen Schriften, 1 Periode* (2nd ed.; Berlin, 1957), p. 280. David Gallop has discussed in detail the logic of Socrates' demonstration, in "The Socratic Paradox in the *Protagoras*," *Phronesis*, 9 (1964), 117-29.

23. Wilamowitz says that it is futile to search the *Protagoras* for "ein wissenschaftliches Resultat" (Ulrich von Wilamowitz-Moellendorff, *Sappho und Simonides* [Berlin, 1913], p. 179, n. 2). Plato is in this dialogue not so much a philosopher as a comic poet. The *Protagoras* is not a "Lehrschrift" (*Platon* [2nd ed.; Berlin, 1920], 1.151). "Au point de vue philosophique, le *Protagoras* n'est pas un des dialogues essentiels de Platon," is the opinion of A. Croiset, L. Bodin, eds., *Protagoras* (Paris, 1923), p. 3. The dialogue is developed "selon l'esprit de Socrate, sans aucune intervention des théories proprement platoniciennes." Some others do find Platonic theory in the *Protagoras*. "The aim of Socrates, and of the Dialogue, is to show the unity of virtue," according to Jowett, *Dialogues*, 1.105. Taylor, *Plato*, p. 235, finds that the *Protagoras* teaches "the Socratic thesis that 'all the virtues are one thing—knowledge.'" Its "central purpose" is "to exhibit clearly the ultimate ethical presuppositions of the Socratic morality and the 'sophistic' morality at its best, and to show exactly where they are in irreconcilable opposition" (p. 238). Raeder, *Platons Philos. Entwickelung*, p. 210, finds that in the *Protagoras* "die Tapferkeit . . . als Wissen definiert wurde." So too Fritz Seidel, *Intellektualismus und Voluntarismus in der Platonischen Ethik* (Weida i. Th., 1910), pp. 36-37; and John Stuart Mill, *Four Dialogues of Plato*, ed. R. Borchardt (London, 1946), p. 66.

Alfred Gercke, who approved of Horneffer's way of reading the *Hippias Minor* (see above, Chapter 3, note 11), proposed a similar interpretation of the *Protagoras* in "Eine Niederlage des Sokrates," *Neue Jahrbücher für das Klass. Altertum* 41 (1918), 145-91. Socrates, he maintains, is not here the mouthpiece of Platonic doctrine. On the whole, Protagoras is not only more courteous (pp. 162-63), but he gets the better of the argument. His educational principles are those of Plato in the *Republic* (p. 153). When he insists on the importance of natural endowment in courage, at 351ab, he not only silences Socrates (p. 172), but he expresses Plato's own belief (p. 180).

The dialogue treats two questions, "Can virtue be taught?" and "What is virtue?" in that order. At the end, Socrates remarks that in changing questions he and Protagoras have apparently changed sides. Actually, they have not. Socrates' arguments that virtue cannot be taught are based on analogies with the arts and crafts, and he assumed that virtue would be taught as one teaches carpentry, shipbuilding, or flute-playing, i.e. by instruction. Since such instruction is not given with any success by statesmen to their sons and is not required in the Assembly, he concludes that virtue cannot be taught. Protagoras, on the other hand, means by "teaching virtue" something quite different. His notion of it comprehends punishment, emulation, music, and gymnastics, the training of character as well as of mind. Hence his argument that the virtues, particularly courage (349a6 ff.), cannot be reduced to knowledge, does not contradict his earlier statement that virtue can be taught, for he does not understand "teaching" to mean "instruction," as does Socrates. Nor does Socrates contradict himself in anything to which he lends full assent. His proof that courage is a mere technique of measurement, i.e. a kind of knowledge, rests on an assumption to which he does not commit himself—that the pleasant and the good are the same thing. Therefore, it does not impair the validity of his earlier remark that such a technique is in fact nowhere taught.

Laches and Charmides, in their respective dialogues, offered opinions subsequently ignored. So too Protagoras. Courage, he maintains (351b2), comes ἀπὸ φύσεως καὶ εὐτροφίας τῶν ψυχῶν, a phrase whose importance ought not to be overlooked,[24] but one whose meaning has not always been clear. It has been variously translated as: "from nature and the healthy state of the soul," " 'nature' . . . and a 'thriving' or 'well-fed' state of soul," "nature and good acquired habits of mind," and "from the nature and good nurture of the soul." Gercke finds that the phrase in question "die

<hr/>

24. But Paul Shorey, *What Plato Said* (Chicago, 1933), p. 129, merely speaks of Protagoras' "trifling temporary advantage." "Some critics," he adds, "think that Socrates is baffled; others that he disdains to answer so trivial a point. At any rate he goes off abruptly on another line." Grote, *Plato*, 2.60, says that Protagoras draws "a distinction somewhat confused: upon which Sokrates approaches the same argument from a different point." Jowett says that Protagoras here tries to draw "a futile distinction between the courageous and the confident in a fluent speech" (*Dialogues*, 1.102).

Tapferkeit als eine angeborene Charaktereigenschaft ansetzt, sie also aus der Natur und nicht aus der Erziehung herleitet."[25] There is no doubt what φύσις means: some men are born braver. But εὐτροφία does not mean simply "healthy state"; it means good nurture, or the state that it produces, and good nurture of soul must mean good training. Protagoras has already described what he means by good training: the refinement of the soul by good rhythms and modes and the lessening of cowardice by physical exercise. In short, he refers to the acquisition, through practice and punishment, of good habits.

These remarks of Protagoras, once made, are not referred to again. Socrates chooses to confute him indirectly by a new line of argument, and the conversation ends with Socrates victorious but with no clarity as to what has been proved. Therefore, the dialogue is often dismissed as a mere exercise in Socratic method, albeit a brilliant and humorous work of literary art.

The mere fact that Plato allows the clear and well-developed argument of 350-351 to go unchallenged should draw comment. But there is, beyond this, an illuminating passage in the *Republic* which provides, I think, the key to Plato's intention. In *Republic* 428 ff. Socrates discusses the four virtues that make a state good in the full sense of the word: wisdom, courage, temperance, and justice. Wisdom is in the ruling class, and courage is in the soldier-police class. Courage is a preservative of the opinion given by law through education about the identity and nature of fearful things (429c7-8). Courage is like the quality by which wool, when dyed, keeps its color fast. This quality, too, is a preservative, which one gets by first choosing the one right kind of material (μίαν φύσιν), white wool (429d6), by giving it a careful preliminary treatment, and only then by dipping it in the color. The threefold process in-

---

25. The translators are, respectively: Jowett, *Dialogues*, 1.151; Taylor, *Plato*, p. 258; Mill, *Four Dialogues*, p. 60; Ostwald (Vlastos [ed.]), *Plato's Protag.*, p. 55; and Gercke, "Eine Niederlage," p. 156. M. Pohlenz, *Aus Platos Werdezeit* (Berlin, 1913), p. 95, n. 1, says that Protagoras here bases courage exclusively on natural endowment. Raeder, *Platons Philos. Entwickelung*, p. 110, has a similar view. But cf. Hans von Arnim, *Platons Jugenddialoge und die Entstehungszeit des Phaidros* (Leipzig, Berlin, 1914), p. 5: "auf natürlicher Begabung und guter Ausbildung der Seele."

sures the best results, which are lost if either the first or the second step is left out (429e4-5). The three stages of dyeing correspond to the three stages in making the warrior class courageous. First, those of a suitable nature are selected; their characters are disciplined by music and gymnastics; and it is upon this double foundation of natural temperament and proper upbringing (διὰ τὸ τήν τε φύσιν καὶ τὴν τροφὴν ἐπιτηδείαν ἐσχηκέναι 430a4-5) that their convictions, imparted to them by instruction, rest. So chosen and so educated, they will preserve their attachment to the laws of the state, their right opinion, as white wool, well prepared, preserves its dye (430a2-3).

This passage, which summarizes a large part of the *Republic*, is filled with terminology already familiar to the reader of the *Protagoras*. One of these echoes is so extraordinary that the lack of comment on it in the scholarly literature is hard to understand. The phrase διὰ τὸ τήν τε φύσιν καὶ τὴν τροφὴν ἐπιτηδείαν ἐσχηκέναι, in which Socrates sums up the first two parts of his threefold conception of courage, is surely another way of saying ἀπὸ φύσεως καὶ εὐτροφίας τῶν ψυχῶν, the words expressing Protagoras' whole conception of that virtue. It is true, and no less important, that Socrates, in *Republic* 429-430, subordinates φύσις and εὐτροφία to right opinion (which they serve) in a way that Protagoras had not done. But this is only to say that the whole program of education in the *Republic*, and this passage in particular, is an attempt to reconcile the arguments which divided Socrates and Protagoras in the earlier dialogue. This statement requires one important qualification: right opinion, and not knowledge, guides the virtuous soldier in the *Republic*. This is a mark of his inferior rank and limited education, in a society in which knowledge in the proper sense comes only to a few. There are gradations in virtue envisioned in the *Republic* of which the *Protagoras* gives no hint. But this does not affect the essential synthesis in the *Republic* of nature, nurture, and instruction, Plato's three prerequisites for virtue, both ordinary and philosophic. It is my contention that this synthesis, at least in broad outline, was in his mind at the time he composed the *Protagoras*, but that he chose to present the conceptions that make it up antithetically.[26] This implies no haphazard arrangement of ideas, but rather an art that works by omissions and silences as much as by statements. The *Hippias Minor* quite clearly omits one of its main points, that no man does wrong willingly. In the *Laches* and *Charmides* too a resolution is withheld by artistic intention rather than philosophic indecision. In the *Protagoras*, such an intention explains the sudden transition after 351b, which allows Protagoras' strong summary of his position to stand at the end, as it were, of a dramatic act. The very words of that summary, little altered, reappear in *Republic* 429-430, absorbed into the Platonic system and given their proper place. In the *Protagoras*, the great sophist defends and rationalizes traditional Athenian education, while Socrates expresses his own deeper insight that knowledge is central to virtue, but without offering any method of making that insight practical. The educational program of the *Republic* is the fruit of the Socratic doctrine, but it uses, in large measure, traditional forms.

There is, to be sure, more than one way to explain these coincidences of words and doctrine. One could say that Plato, at the time he wrote the *Protagoras*, saw two possible and reasonable theories of virtue, to one of which, the Socratic, he doubtless leaned. One might then argue that he formulated these theories by having recourse to the familiar triad of nature, training, and knowledge.[27]

26. This method of reading a Platonic dialogue as a deliberately incomplete expression of Plato's thought is well known and often practiced. Paul Shorey argues that the early dialogues present in dramatic, antithetical form what the *Republic* presents as systematic exposition, in *The Unity of Plato's Thought* (Chicago, 1903), pp. 14-15. Jaeger says that inconclusiveness in these dialogues is Plato's way of "setting us a riddle . . . the solution [of which] lies within our grasp," in *Paideia*, trans. Highet, 2.91. Gomperz says the *Protagoras* is a kind of riddle, in *Griechische Denker* (2nd. ed.; Leipzig, 1903-09), 2.261. The results reached by these scholars often vary, but this in itself cannot impugn the method if it rests on otherwise good grounds.

27. The revolutionary aspects of Plato's educational program are so often stressed that we are apt to forget the degree to which he relied on traditional conceptions both in the *Republic* and in the *Protagoras*. The categories of nature, practice-nurture, and instruction had thoroughly penetrated the social, political, ethical, educational, and artistic thought of the fifth and early fourth centuries before Plato ever adopted them. They partly determined the form taken by controversy and polemic in these fields, and their presence is felt even in poetry. They appear most often as an antithesis between the natural and the acquired or in the triadic pattern adopted in the *Republic*. Paul Shorey, in "Φύσις, Μελέτη, Ἐπιστήμη" *TAPA*, 40 (1909), 185-201, demon-

strated that these ideas were commonplaces of Greek thought. Some of the examples which follow are his.

Pindar's aristocratic belief in the pre-eminence of nature is well known. It appears at *Olympians*, 2.86 ff., 9.100, 13.13, at *Pythian*, 8.44 ff., and at *Nemean*, 3.40 ff. That standard falls under a shadow, however, in Euripides' *Electra*, a play in which the recurrent theme of hereditary worth only emphasizes how poor a replica Orestes is of his father (lines 206, 338, 368, 880, 941). Thucydides calls Themistocles an outstanding example of excellence of nature (1.138.3), but this judgment is questioned at Xenophon, *Mem.*, 4.2.2, where Themistocles' success is attributed not to nature alone but to teaching as well. The virtues of his great rival Aristides caused similar speculation. A fragment of Eupolis attributes them to nature combined with effort (Edmonds, frag. 111* = 91K). Nature can also explain artistic excellence, as in Democritus' tribute to Homer (Diels-Kranz, 68 B 21). At Euripides' *Hippolytus* 79 ff., Hippolytus praises those who are temperate by nature and not by teaching. The author of the *Dissoi Logoi* acknowledges that a talented nature, with no opportunity for formal sophistic instruction, can match or surpass those who have had systematic teaching but lack talent (Diels-Kranz, 90.6. 10-11). The word φύσις obviously meant different things for different people. The aristocrat saw in it a justification for inherited privilege. But the brilliant child of undistinguished parents and the weak scion of a noble stock showed that natural worth did not always run in predictable patterns. Protagoras' answer to the question, "Why do many sons of good fathers turn out bad?" shows an awareness of this fact (*Protag.* 326e6 ff.). So do Plato's provisions, at *Rep.* 415bc, for the crossing of class lines.

According to Democritus, those naturally predisposed (εὐφυέες) recognize and imitate noble deeds (Diels-Kranz, 68 B 56). Hard work, on the other hand, as well as practice and learning (πόνος, ἄσκησις, μάθησις) also have a role in causing virtue (68 B 179, B 242, B 182), and more men are good from practice than from nature (68 B 242). The latter belief is attributed also to Epicharmus and Critias (Diels-Kranz, 23 B 33, 88 B 9). But time alone, says Democritus, will not teach a man good sense in the absence of ὡραίη τροφή καὶ φύσις (68 B 183), and the constant company of knaves will increase a man's habit of wickedness (68 B 184). What he is taught, moreover, becomes second nature to him (ἡ διδαχή . . . φυσιοποιεῖ 68 B 33).

Art can improve what nature has already given, as at Eupolis, frag. 116A** (Edmonds, = Adesp. 403K); or it can spoil a good nature, as at Euripides, frag. 186 (Nauck); or it can enable a man to overcome naturally superior adversaries, as at Antiphon the Tragedian, frag. 4 (Nauck). Τέχνη without μελέτη, however, is worth nothing, and vice versa, said Protagoras (Diels-Kranz, 80 B 10). According to the same sophist, instruction requires the aid of nature and practice, and men must learn starting from youth (80 B 3, which might be a summary of his speech in Plato's dialogue). The argument of the Corinthians at Thucydides, 1.121, uses the terms ἐπιστήμη, διδαχή, μελέτη, εὐψυχία, and φύσις. At Euripides, *Suppliants*, 911 ff., εὐανδρία is said to be teachable, but the process involves childhood training and practice. The *Hecuba*, 592 ff., discusses the effect of φύσις and τροφαί on character. Isocrates, *Against the Sophists*, 14-15, lists the three requirements for effective speech and action as φύσις, ἐμπειρία, and παίδευσις. In the medical treatise *On the Art*, ability to advance the art by discoveries is said to depend on education and nature (IX, 15-18). At Anonymus Iamblichi, 1.1, virtue is made dependent on nature, enthusiasm, long study, and practice (Diels-Kranz 89); and Antiphon the Sophist emphasizes the importance of instructing the young (Diels-Kranz,

He separated the first two from the last as if irreconcilable, producing a dialogue in which the final *aporia* masked an acceptance of the Socratic arguments, or else represented a real doubt as to where the answer lay. He forsook a technique, practiced in the *Hippias Minor*, *Laches*, and *Charmides*, of suggesting more than the text made explicit, and especially of implying a synthesis of complementary views. Or, if the *Protagoras* was written first, he had not yet learned that technique, though he had learned to make Socrates withhold from Protagoras his real convictions about hedonism. Then, in the *Republic*, he hit upon a solution that satisfied

87 B 60). Aristophanes' prerequisites for the demagogue could almost be predicted: low birth and a minimum of education (*Knights*, 184 ff.).

Xenophon, in the *Memorabilia*, reflects this traditional aetiology of virtue and makes it a part of his record of Socratic teaching. The familiar conceptions appear at 3.9.2 (φύσις, μελέτη, μάθησις), at 4.1.4 (φύσις, παίδευσις, μάθησις), at 3.9.14 (μελέτη, μάθησις), at 1.2.19-20, where the company of good men is called the ἄσκησις of the soul, and elsewhere at 2.1.2, 2.1.6, 2.1.20, and 4.2.7.

The next chapter will illustrate the degree to which the ethical doctrine of the *Republic* is based on the threefold division enunciated at 374de of that dialogue. Here the requirements of the good Guardian appear as ἐπιστήμη or τέχνη, μελέτη or ἐπιμέλεια, and φύσις. They reappear later, at 376c, in the words φύσιν, θρέψονται, and παιδευθήσονται. In the *Phaedrus*, they become the basis of skill in oratory, in the form φύσις, μελέτη, ἐπιστήμη (269d).

The threefold division of terms is in some respects artificial, since ἄσκησις and τροφή, to take one example, express different aspects of the process to which they both refer. Some of the terms used, moreover, are ambiguous and cannot be made to fit neatly into any category. Protagoras seems to express the full range at 323c-324a. He minimizes the importance of φύσις in justice, which depends rather, he says, on διδαχή and μάθησις, ἐπιμέλεια and ἄσκησις. Since the use of punishment, however, is said to prove that Athenians think virtue is a διδακτόν (324c), διδαχή must include punishment and not merely instruction; and Protagoras' views on instruction would not coincide with Plato's. But conventional formulas are always subject to varying interpretations, and meanings can be sharpened when occasion demands. Protagoras does this at 351ab with ἐπιστήμη-τέχνη, εὐτροφία, and φύσις.

The *Protagoras* and the *Republic* build their discussions of education around the familiar three requirements, in which the middle term appears variously as τροφή, μελέτη, ἐπιμέλεια, and εὐτροφία. Here, as elsewhere, Plato does not avoid the common coin of contemporary language. It is an argument in favor of the analysis offered above of the *Protagoras* that it explains the dialogue in those terms which would have struck the eye of an Athenian reader in the fourth century, and in which he would instinctively have sought the nub of the discussion. Some further light is thrown, moreover, on the two dialogues treated earlier in this chapter. Laches and Charmides must have struck Plato's Athenian readers as untutored examples of good φύσις, improved perhaps by τροφή and μελέτη. Laches makes the point partly explicit at 185e when he says that men have sometimes become better at their art without teachers than with them.

him, one which consisted of a modified synthesis of the views of Protagoras and Socrates, and indeed combined, in scarcely altered form, the very three words they had used to formulate their opposition. This theory, though logically flawless, would lack probability, in spite of the fact that it merely assumes that development in Plato which the nineteenth century found so attractive and which analogy with some modern philosophers makes so plausible. In the *Protagoras*, the three aspects of the "later" theory are too sharply defined and clearly contrasted to suggest the early stages of a true development. They have instead the look of a mature theory deliberately fragmented for the purpose of dramatic and stimulating presentation.

Though Plato normally preferred to furnish intellectual challenges to the reader rather than easy solutions, he sometimes found it suitable to present straightforward answers to questions which were in other dialogues left open. This is why we find that the issues which have occupied these two chapters are in a measure solved in the *Republic*. Absent is the hesitant, slow spiraling of a dialectic which never rests in a conclusion, traced out by a teacher who professes to know no answers. Socrates' artful diffidence is transferred in the *Republic* to other problems more profound, many of which, like the nature of the Good, Plato must have thought were genuinely beyond the powers of written exposition. The explanation of the Socratic paradoxes is not in that category. Plato's tactic of deliberate silence in the *Protagoras*, for example, does not result from his despair of making things any clearer. It is not really surprising, therefore, that several problems left unsolved in the dialogues of this chapter are answered in the *Republic*. We learn there that virtue can be taught, since it is taught to the Guardians, not by instruction alone, but by Socratic dialectic combined with discipline or εὐτροφία. This discipline, which the *Republic* too calls "nurture" (τροφή, τὸ τρέφεσθαι), is the early stage of an education meant only for those naturally predisposed, those with proper φύσις.[28] We learn too that all the virtues are knowledge, but not knowledge alone; courage, for example, is the rational discipline imposed by the rule of wisdom upon the spirited element in the

28. *Rep.* 402, 491d, 485-87.

soul (τὸ θυμοειδές). Moreover, courageous men who are not philosophers will not actually "know" in the proper sense of having
fully reasoned convictions. But their right opinion will, when exercised in choice, have the same effect as knowledge upon action.[29]
The general problem of the relation of knowledge to the other virtues is clarified by the doctrine that all virtue is either wisdom
alone or wisdom expressed in nonrational impulse. The *Republic*
shows, moreover, that the practical wisdom that rules behavior is
only one aspect of that virtue, only the extension into moral activity of a knowledge of the eternal Ideas and of the Good. Ultimately, virtue is not merely right behavior; it is the contemplative
union with the Ideas and the Good which right behavior facilitates
and which only death and final purification can make perfect.

Our study of the meaning of the *Laches, Charmides,* and *Protagoras* has already carried us within sight of the doctrine of the
tripartite soul. It was within the framework of this doctrine that
Plato chose to express his mature conceptions of education, politics,
and ethics. Under its influence, the ethical paradoxes of the early
dialogues undergo a kind of transformation. Some scholars, who
would prefer the word "abandonment," conclude that the doctrine
of the soul, as it appears in the *Republic*, signals a radical change
in the nature of Platonic ethics. Whether this is a change of substance or of philosophic vesture is a question that occupies the
next chapter.

29. Cf. *Meno* 98bc. The doctrine of "right opinion" allows Plato in the
*Republic* to acknowledge levels of virtue and to define courage, for example,
as a preservative of opinion (429c7-8), although opinion will become knowledge in those trained to be Rulers. It will also become clearer how Laches,
who lacked knowledge, could have fought courageously in battle. His natural
qualities, fortified by practice, were guided by the "right opinion" that to
fight for one's country is noble.

## 5. THE TRIPARTITE SOUL

If the third chapter was about the sense in which virtue is knowledge, this chapter and the next, broadly speaking, are about the sense in which it is not. As the latter implies, and as earlier chapters have already made clear, Platonic ethics embodies a qualified, not a naive, intellectualism. In the early dialogues, the qualifications are for the most part only hinted at. When they finally take systematic form, in the works of Plato's maturity, they appear as aspects of the doctrine of the tripartite soul. The pages which follow trace the expression given to this doctrine in different dialogues, beginning with the *Republic*. Special attention will be drawn to the one feature of Plato's mature thought which seems most subversive of his earlier intellectualism, viz. the appearance in his psychology of the θυμοειδές, a nonrational, regulatory psychic power.

The θυμοειδές, the "spirited element" in the soul, or the principle of anger, reflects Plato's evident conviction that there is need of a power to mediate between reason and desire and of emotions to lend vigor to moral decisions. In the *Republic* this power is conceived on the analogy of the soldier-police of the ideal state, and appears in similitude as a docile and alert lion who is ready to carry out the commands of right judgment. In the *Phaedrus* the same power is envisaged as a noble steed who pulls the chariot of the soul and holds it, in obedience to its charioteer, reason, away from unworthy objects of desire.[1] A habitual coöperation of the θυμοειδές with reason produces, through long practice, the permanent dispositions of courage and temperance, as well as that proper order in the whole soul which goes by the name of justice.

With the doctrine of a complex soul comes an apparent fragmentation of moral virtue, which is most evident in Plato's treatment of courage and temperance. Though he sometimes speaks of these as compatible and complementary aspects of a fully developed virtue, at other times he seems to imply that they are in fact contradictory tendencies. On the other hand, he appears to leave the boundary between them so unclear that he can call a man now brave, now temperate for the same reason.

All these problems are interconnected. It is the object of this chapter and the next to trace in Plato's unsystematic manner and changing forms of expression the inspiration of an essentially coherent view of man's moral life, one which the earlier dialogues have, in their more oblique fashion, already foreshadowed. This fifth chapter is concerned, in the main, with the doctrine of the tripartite soul, which Plato introduces in the *Republic* and takes up again in the *Phaedrus* and *Timaeus*. The next chapter deals with a corollary issue, viz. the way in which Plato was led, in some later dialogues, to qualify the unity of virtue and the unity of vice.

The *Republic* is as close as Plato comes to a comprehensive statement of his philosophy. In form it is a long conversation on the virtue of justice, beginning, in the manner of some early dialogues, with a dialectical examination by Socrates of some of the imperfect or erroneous notions of that virtue held by his companions. It soon turns, however, into a lengthy discourse by Socrates himself, and the original narrowness of the subject gives way before a wide-ranging exposition of politics, ethics, and education. The dialogue is a vision of the ideal state, inhabited by men and

1. *Rep.* 588d3 ff., *Phaedrus* 246a3 ff.

women whose lives are so ordered as to bring to flower what is best in their natures and prepare them for the life that lies beyond. The discussion centers upon the élite of this state, the Guardians, some of whom, as merit determines, will rise no higher than auxiliary rank, while others will become the philosopher-rulers. Throughout the argument, Socrates is open and positive to a degree that we have not seen in any of the dialogues taken up in previous chapters. Since he discusses most of the problems that those dialogues deal with, we find in the *Republic* answers to many of the questions which they left unresolved. Is virtue one or many, knowledge or nature or discipline? Can virtue be taught? The *Republic* does not resume the questions. It simply explains the unity of virtue and its multiplicity, shows how it is at once knowledge and nature and discipline, and explains in detail how it can be taught to the Guardians. No lengthy analysis of this long dialogue, already so rich in commentaries, will be attempted in these pages. But it is important that we trace out the essential lines of ethical doctrine in the *Republic* insofar as they bear on the argument of this book.

Socrates' discourse about education in the Platonic ideal state begins, not with philosophy, but with natural endowment and discipline. When he states the need for a class of Guardians he sounds for the first time a theme that will recur through the *Republic* as a basic supposition of Platonic ethics, politics, psychology, and education, viz. the balance of temperaments. Like good watchdogs, Guardians must be both fierce and gentle, and it is by asking how to discover and train such a balanced character that Socrates begins the long colloquy on education (375c6-8). Gentleness and forcefulness, he argues, complement each other, so that a man must have both; but they are also opposed, and judicious behavior requires that neither predominate. The best education will achieve this balance by grounding its young subjects in music[2] and gymnastic.

Thus far, Plato's argument might be taken as a systematic jus-

2. "Music" is a convenient but imperfect translation of μουσική, which Liddell-Scott-Jones' *Lexicon* defines as "any art over which the Muses presided, *esp.* poetry sung to music. . . . generally, art *or* letters."

tification of traditional Athenian schooling, in which a study of the poets was counterbalanced by a cultivation of physical grace, strength, and agility. But he has important changes to introduce even at this elementary level. If the customary study of the poets is to fulfill properly its purpose of shaping character, then of the many current musical modes the perfect state will require only two. Those which convey sorrow or express softness, idleness, and drunkenness will be discarded. Of the two acceptable types, one will express compulsion, misfortune, and courage, the other willingness, happiness, and temperance (399a5-c1). A like requirement will dictate the choice of rhythms, one for decorum, one for courage (399e8-11).[3] The reason for this strict selection is the fact that modes and rhythms alike influence the soul of the singer, player, or listener. Music endows the soul with a kind of grace, but only if practiced within proper limits (401d5-e1).

Musical and poetic education, therefore, is not envisaged merely as a way of developing cultivated tastes and good manners. It is an early step in the formation of the virtuous character. Music, it is true, does not instruct the intellect, but it so trains the feelings that they are attracted by the good and the beautiful and repelled by the evil and the ugly. The student feels these effects before he is capable of grasping the reason for them (πρὶν λόγον δυνατὸς εἶναι λαβεῖν 402a2). By exposing the young Guardian constantly to the modes and rhythms that naturally express courage and temperance, the teacher forms dispositions that will later grow into the fully developed virtues. All this has important implications for the doctrine of the Socratic paradoxes. Courage and temperance cannot be merely knowledge, since the well-nurtured soul already expresses both in some fashion before it can grasp the reason for its actions. The two virtues are grounded in the powers of the nonrational soul, and, though their form is a rule of reason, they have for their content blind tendencies which have been nurtured and directed from the student's early years. Socrates' phrase for the process is simpler, that music has its effect in love of the fair (403c6-7).

3. The contrast of κοσμιότης and ἀνδρεία (399e) is essentially the same as the earlier contrast of πρᾷον ἦθος and μεγαλόθυμον ἦθος (375c). κοσμιότης and πρᾳότης are both aspects of σωφροσύνη. See Rep. 430e6 and Politicus 307ab.

Gymnastic, which had earlier been described as a discipline of the body (376e3-4), has, it now appears, a place in the training of the soul too. It serves as a counterbalance to musical education, and its devotees share with those who study music the obligation to observe due measure. Those who exercise to excess become wild and harsh, while those devoted exclusively to music tend to become soft and tame (410d1-2). A harsh, fierce temperament is an effect of the spirited part (θυμοειδές), which, if trained judiciously, will make a man courageous; tameness, on the other hand, is a trait of the philosophic nature, and proper training will produce a disposition not soft but gentle and orderly. Virtue, which lies in a mean, is an attribute of the well-harmonized soul, at once temperate and courageous (410e10 ff.). Though music will soothe a too violent nature, too much of it, especially in natures already gentle, will produce enervation. Too much athletics, on the other hand, will carry a man beyond the fine point of courage to stupidity and brutishness. It is to prevent either extreme of disharmony and to keep the soul well tuned that the god has given man these two arts. But they must be used together (411e4-7).

During the first stage of the young Guardians' education, tests are given them to separate those fit to be rulers from those fit only to be auxiliaries. The tests try, in part, the effectiveness of their musical and gymnastic training. The Guardians have been taught to believe that they must always act for the best interests of the community, but there are three forces that tend to drive out this opinion. Plato designates them metaphorically as "theft," "violence," and "sorcery." Victims of "theft" have been persuaded out of their belief or have forgotten it; victims of "violence" have been changed by pain or grief; victims of "sorcery" have succumbed to pleasure or panic. The tests to which the candidates are subjected will correspond to these dangers. One kind will strain their memory and intelligence; a second will expose them to toil, pain, and anguish; a third will lead them into frightening situations to try their nerve and among pleasures to gauge their self-control. The young Guardian who acquits himself well in all will be judged to have a soul perfect in rhythm and harmony (413e2-4).

Implicit in this series of trials is a reference to the objective for which the new theory of education was first introduced, viz. the creation of Guardians both fierce and gentle, or brave and temperate. The ordeals force the aspirant to draw upon his resources in each of these qualities and upon a third, which distinguishes good Guardians from good watchdogs, strength of intellect. Moreover, if the young Guardian succumbs to one of the three kinds of temptation, whatever the conventionally recognized cause of his wrongdoing, in a deeper sense he is guilty of an act of ignorance. Persuasion, forgetfulness, pain and grief, pleasure and panic, all influence action only by depriving the agent of his right opinion. The paradox that vice is ignorance is confirmed.[4]

Political order in the Platonic Republic is to be based on a tripartite social grouping in which the highest class rules, the middle class maintains public order and defends the state against its enemies, and the lowest class engages in production and trade. The tests which have just been described will determine who will be rulers and who will be auxiliaries of the middle class. Once the tripartite order has been established, with each class fulfilling its prescribed function, it will exemplify, as Socrates explains it, all the virtues which make a state good in the full sense. It will be wise, courageous, temperate, and just (427e10-11).[5] Wisdom will be the prerogative of the ruling class and will consist in knowing how to conduct properly the affairs of the state as a whole (428b-e). Courage will characterize that part of the state which fights to defend the whole (429b1 ff.). It will correspond to the power of preserving the right conviction, given in education, about what is and is not to be feared. Courage is the preservative of this right opinion in pain and pleasure (429c7-8, 430b2-4); in the long simile in which Plato explains its nature it is compared to the quality by which

4. What the victim of these bad influences suffers is described in the phrase, "to be deprived of true opinion" (413a10). Knowledge is not actually referred to here, because the young Guardians-in-training have not yet reached the stage at which it will replace right opinion. But knowledge and right opinion are equivalent in their practical effect on behavior, as Socrates says in *Meno* 98bc.

5. The canon of four virtues adopted in the *Republic* is not a Platonic invention. For some earlier expressions of it see Helen North, "Pindar, *Isthmian*, 8, 24-28," *AJP*, 69 (1948), 304-308, and the scholarly literature there cited.

dyed wool keeps its color fast.[6] Of the two virtues that remain, temperance will be a concord or harmony, within the state, of the naturally superior and the naturally inferior, in their agreement that only the former should rule (432ab); and justice, the last and most elusive of the virtues, will be the quality by which each class of citizens tends to its own affairs, without meddling elsewhere (434c).

We have already noted that Plato's description of how the young Guardians are tested implies ethical intellectualism of a sort, since the tests are conceived as attempts to deprive the candidates of right opinion and so to confuse their moral judgment. The description of courage as a preservative of right opinion is cut from the same cloth. Since right opinion is simply a belief consistent with knowledge or wisdom, held by somebody who is unable to defend fully what he thinks to be true, the measure of courage is the wisdom of one's behavior in pain and pleasure. In the auxiliary class this is, of course, only a reflected wisdom, since the members of this class must rely on the instructions of their rulers. Nevertheless, even at this early point in the *Republic*, the arguments of Nicias in the *Laches* and of Socrates in the *Protagoras* find partial justification. It remains true, in a sense, that to be courageous is to be wise. In the later description of the full virtue of the rulers, who possess wisdom in their own persons, those arguments will receive a further vindication.

The virtues of the individual person are like those of the state, because individual and state have similar natures. The soul, like the state, has three parts. Proof of this depends on the principle that nothing can act in opposite ways at the same time with respect to the same part of itself and towards the same object (436b8-9). Since we often experience simultaneous contradictory impulses, our souls cannot be simple entities. For example, in a thirsty man who purposely refrains from drinking there are two distinct attitudes toward the same object. They must, reasons Socrates, have different sources, which he calls the appetitive principle (τὸ ἐπιθυμητικόν) and the rational principle (τὸ λογιστικόν) (439d5-8).

Whether the source of anger is a distinct third part of the soul is a question harder to settle. The story of Leontius shows that it

6. This passage is discussed in Chapter 4, above.

is at least separate from the principle of pleasure. Leontius wanted
to see the corpses of the criminals left by the executioners and was
angry with himself for having the desire. The two impulses fought
in him and his desire won (439e6 ff.). His experience is generalized by Socrates, and the principle is stated that in any conflict between reason and desire anger (θυμός) will support reason; it will
never make common cause with the desires against reason (440a8-
b7). The attachment of anger to reason is said to be constant not
only in their joint battle against the unjust impulses within a man's
own soul but also in their opposition to injustice inflicted by others.
When a man suffers deserved pain or discomfort, the nobler his nature the less anger he feels, but a victim of injustice will in his anger endure every pain and hardship until he succeeds or dies in the
attempt, or until his reason restrains him. Therefore the principle
of anger cannot be part of the appetitive principle. It is proved
separate from reason by the observation that babies show temper
long before they show sense (441a7 ff.). The soul, therefore, has
three parts which correspond to the three parts in the state, and
good politics only reflects sound psychology. The parts in the
state are the money-making, the auxiliary, and the deliberative; in
the individual they are the appetitive (ἐπιθυμητικόν), the spirited
(θυμοειδές), and the rational (λογιστικόν) (440e10 ff.).

Pausing only to crown his argument by making Homer a tri-
partitionist (441b2 ff.), Socrates concludes that they have weath-
ered the storm and are ready to say what the virtues are in men.
They will inhere in the soul as they inhere in the state. The soul,
like the state, will be governed by reason and the obedient strength
of the θυμοειδές; these will safeguard it from the seditious movements of pleasure within and the attacks of enemies from without
(442a4-b9). Courage will be found in the θυμοειδές (442b11-c3);
wisdom will be found in the reason; temperance will be the concord of all the parts in their agreement that reason must rule and
the other two obey; and justice too will be what it was in the state
(442c5-d8), viz. the restriction of each part to its proper function.

Although Socrates does not claim that these definitions give a
full account of the virtues, he makes it clear that virtue in a man
presupposes three things: a good nature, a discipline of the tem-

perament, and a right conviction (*Republic* 429-430). In his description of musical and gymnastic training, he has already explained in detail the kind of discipline needed; he will show later
in the *Republic* how prolonged instruction in mathematics and
dialectic may turn right opinion into knowledge. First, however,
he inquires into the philosopher's nature, the innate temperament
required in a philosopher and ruler, which will incline him naturally to virtuous ways (485a4-5). He concludes, after some pages,
that no man can practice philosophy well if he is not by nature of
good memory, quick to learn, dignified, pleasant, and a friend and
kin to truth, justice, courage, and temperance (487a3-5). These
predispositions, however, if not properly trained, may actually occasion the ruin of the man who enjoys them (491b7-10).[7] The
superior nature is more capable of great virtue and great vice
alike, and so the very qualities that make a man fit for philosophy
also threaten to destroy him (491e1-3). His exceptional gifts of
memory, intelligence, courage, and generosity will tempt him to
ambition and self-advancement (494a11 ff.). Therefore, to nature
must be added right instruction and prolonged discipline.

A nature of the kind required in a philosopher and ruler is not
only hard to train; it is hard to find. Men are not born with perfectly balanced temperaments. The brilliant are too often unstable,
the firm and reliable too often stupid. But the Guardians who will
pursue the highest studies must have intellectual strength combined with constancy of character. A new kind of trial, the strain
of prolonged study, now tests their endurance (503c2-504a1), and
only those found strong by nature in all the essential qualities of
the philosophic temperament are admitted to the highest studies,
which lead to the intuition of the Good.

The prerequisites of the philosopher have now been established, viz. a nature disposed to virtue, and an early training of

7. This helps to explain Plato's occasional use of the word ἀνδρεία to mean
a vice (see *Gorgias* 463a, *Rep.* 426d, and above, Chapter 1, note 13). If
ἀνδρεία is an innate disposition, susceptible of good or bad development according to one's education, then the word may be applied to a nature born brave
but ruined by bad upbringing no less than to the same nature properly brought
up. Natural bravery may end in audacity or in courage, and, although Plato
seemed before to restrict the word to the virtue of courage (430b), he uses it
here and elsewhere to mean either the natural endowment or its perversion.

the reason in right opinion, of the θυμοειδές in courage, and of the whole soul in temperance and justice. But the fullness of virtue, Socrates now intimates, has not yet been described. The discussion has taken the shorter road although the longer road is the only way to an exact knowledge of the virtues. This longer road, it now appears, is the higher education of the Guardians (504c9-d1), by which they will arrive at the greatest μάθημα. Justice and the other virtues are not the greatest; in fact, of these virtues themselves Socrates has given only an outline (ὑπογραφή 504d4-7). The highest μάθημα is the Idea of the Good, by which things become just and useful and beneficial (505a2-4). The nature of the Good is disputed. It is thought to be pleasure by the common people, knowledge (φρόνησις) by the more clever (505b6). But, asked what the object of this knowledge is, the latter answer "the Good." Their opinion, though closer to the truth than that of the common people, is still not exact. The Good is not pleasure, because there are bad pleasures. The Good is what everybody wants; no one is satisfied with the apparent good, though many are satisfied with the apparently just and the apparently beautiful (505d5 ff.). The Good is like the sun, which gives sight to the eye, visibility to the object, and existence to both (508a4-6, 509b2-4). In the same way, the Good gives truth to the Forms, knowledge to the mind, and to all things their being (509b7-8).

The importance of the doctrine of the Good, which is central to Plato's thought, cannot be overstated, but it cannot be discussed here at any length. Its bearing on Plato's ethics, however, should be noted, for it restates and generalizes some doctrines treated in earlier chapters. For example, in *Meno* 78a, all men are said to choose what they think is beneficial and good, though sometimes they are mistaken; in *Gorgias* 467d, the ultimate ends for which men strive are said to be always good, although wrong means are often chosen. The Good in *Republic* 505 ff. is the correlative of "desire" (βούλησις) in the *Meno* and *Gorgias*: in the former dialogue, "the Good is what all desire"; in the latter two, "all desire what is good." The Good is the ultimate principle of action regarded as present in that which is chosen, whereas desire (in this restricted sense) is the same ultimate principle viewed as a property of the agent. The Good is therefore the criterion of virtue too, i.e. activity is virtuous insofar as it achieves the Good, or insofar as it achieves our desire; there is no difference of meaning.

The ascent of the mind to apprehension of the Good is described in the discourse about the divided line, which follows (509d1-511e5), and in the allegory of the cave (514a1 ff.). The selected few who make the journey and reach the intuition of the Good will then have the fullness of wisdom, a quality not only foremost among the virtues but of a different order. "Now the other so-called virtues of soul, it seems, are akin to those of the body—for the fact is that when they are not already present they are instilled by habit and practice—but the virtue of wisdom more than anything has in it something divine" (518d9 ff.). It is evident now that all previous education was a preparation of the character and the mind for this higher virtue, which is, for the few who are capable of reaching it, the crown of all human activity. Keen intellects that have turned to perverse ends are the victims of neglect. If they had been educated in virtue from childhood, as Plato's Guardians will be, their minds would have come to rest at last in the vision of the Good (519a ff.), the highest human activity, the μέγιστον μάθημα.

The discussion of the Good, the divided line, and the cave is central to Plato's ontology and his ethics alike. While defining the hierarchy of reality it also provides human aspiration and moral judgment with a real goal and an objective standard. Moreover, it introduces a new dimension into human virtue and adds substantially to the sketch (ὑπογραφή) that Socrates had drawn from the model of the state and had based on the doctrine of the threefold soul. In that earlier description virtue was determined by a good nature, discipline of the irrational soul, and right opinion. It now appears that right opinion was only a temporary and imperfect condition of the reason; human virtue in the full sense must be the complete expression of the highest activity of which reason is capable. Wisdom as previously described was a correlative of the other three virtues. Its content was an opinion of the soul's highest good, and reason, which it informed, was essentially a faculty of regulation and direction. All four virtues were therefore on one level, and all referred primarily to the good of the soul. In ascending from right opinion to knowledge and to the apprehension of the Absolute Good, however, reason breaks a path away from its primary concern with the moral problems of its own mortal state. In fact, the pursuit of this upward path presumes that these issues have been solved: the appetites are quiet, the θυμοειδές is obedient, the rules of virtue are learned and accepted, if not fully understood. The contemplation of reality by those who have completed this ascent is a new activity, which will indeed provide the rational basis, now first understood by them, of their virtuous behavior. But such contemplation also has a value beyond mere practical ethics, a science which applies only to man with a body. Human virtue in the highest sense of the word is excellence in a state of perfection, and we have been told in the *Phaedo* that perfect wisdom requires escape from the prison of the body (66de, 68b). Once free of the body, moreover, and restored to its truest nature, the soul will no longer have three parts (*Rep.* 611a10 ff.) and will come to enjoy that better life for which it is meant (611b10 ff). The soul's true nature is revealed only to those who observe it in its highest activity, philosophy, in which it rises above its mortal condition and shows itself akin to the divine, the deathless, the eternal (611e1-3).

Human virtue in its perfection is knowledge and knowledge alone. This is quite clear, but it should be made equally clear that it is not a statement about practical ethics. In the flight of the soul from the body practical ethics has been left behind. As long as virtue is regarded as a struggle against imperfection it presupposes the union of soul and body, because, as Socrates says in the passage just cited, the body is the source of vice. The *Republic* is a book about justice and the other virtues insofar as they can be realized in any soul burdened with the effects and appearances of human life (612a5), and it finds four qualities essential for bringing rational order to a soul so afflicted. It is also a book, however, about a few men who will win the moral battle and go on to enjoy at intervals the contemplation which they hope to be their only activity after death. In these men the four virtues merely prepare the soul for the one virtue, wisdom. In a new sense, therefore, virtue is knowledge.[8] But what Plato does not say is that the distinction among the virtues vanishes in this life once the knowledge of the Good is reached and that consequently for the philosopher who reaches it this knowledge is the sum of moral virtue. There is no knowledge that is proof in itself against the impulses of the lower soul. If such there were and the philosopher possessed it, courage would no longer be for him an irrational power regulated by rational principle, and the stability of his soul would no longer be the effect of reason helped by the θυμοειδές. Courage, if the name were kept, would merely be wisdom judging about what might inspire fear in others; temperance would be wisdom judging about what might stir appetite in others. But the very reason for naming several distinct virtues was that the soul in the body is multiple; each of the virtues was said to correspond to the power of one part or the relationship of several parts. As long as the philosopher has a body, therefore, his soul will be divided and his virtues distinguishable. He will judge the fearful with his reason but will endure it by an effort of his θυμοειδές. He will discard the excessive claims of his appetites by rational judgment but will curb them through his θυμοειδές. The philosopher on earth has four virtues, and his soul is ruled by a double principle; in the after-life he will have one virtue and one self-sufficient ruling principle.

Whether the philosopher, who comes to know the Good after long training of his innately superior character, can ever lose this knowledge is an interesting but unanswered question. Plato does not consider the possibility, and his ideal order of things is an effort to avert all such mischances by supporting knowledge with courage, temperance, and justice. But as long as reason functions in a body which is subject to unpredictable disturbances of physiology, it is hard to see how such mischances could be absolutely excluded. Plato does admit that ideal states can suffer corruption, but he attributes this to the begetting, through no fault of the Guardians, of children of inferior nature, who inherit the government only to misuse it (546a-d).

8. This should be distinguished from the other sense in which the paradox is true, viz. that all right actions are due to knowledge (or right opinion) and all wrong actions to ignorance at the moment of choice. See Rep. 413a9-b2, Tim. 86c3, and Chapter 6, below.

This degeneration of the ruling stock and the consequent decline of the ideal polity are both characterized, in Books VIII and
IX, by a kind of disorganization. In each type of inferior constitution and in each exemplar of a dominant vice the rational part has
lost control to one of the two lesser parts. When reason rules the
soul and philosophers rule the state, the activities given precedence
and honor are those of the intellect. Since each lower part of the
soul, as of the state, has its natural objective too, which it will pursue to excess if unchecked by reason, the passage of leadership to
one or the other will change the dominant activities of the state
and of the soul. When the ἐπιθυμητικόν rules a man's soul he will
serve his appetites, or else money, the means to their satisfaction
(580e2-581a7). The θυμοειδές has its natural goals too: domination
of others, victory, honor (581a9-10). It is φιλόνικον and φιλότιμον
(581b2), and when it escapes the control of reason it will lead a
man to certain characteristic excesses, viz. envy, violence, and anger (586c7-d2).

Having described justice, the rule of reason, and injustice, the
rule of the spirited or of the appetitive principle, Socrates sums up
the whole doctrine of the soul's parts in a simile. A human soul is
like a composite animal which one might invent by putting together a many-headed monster, a lion, and a man, and by molding
them into a single creature with the external likeness of a human
being. To be unjust, in the terms of the simile, is to feed and
strengthen the monster and the lion and to starve the man, so that
he is dragged about at their whim and is unable to keep them from
each other's throat. To be just, on the other hand, is to put the man
in charge, to have him tame the monster after having made the
lion his ally (589b3-4), and to let him bring both monster and lion
into harmony with each other and with himself (588b10-589b6).
Socrates then clearly identifies man, lion, and monster with reason,
spirited principle, and appetite. Debauchery lies in giving too
much freedom to the many-headed beast; wilfulness and ill temper
are the result of excessive strength in the lion, and softness and ef-
feminacy the result of his weakness; flattery and meanness occur when the lion is turned into an ape and subjected to the monster. The common artisan, on the other hand, simply does not

have a ruling element strong enough to assert its mastery over the rest of his soul (590a5-c6).

This elaborate similitude implies that the soul of even the philosopher, who has reached knowledge of the Good, is ruled by the alliance of the θυμοειδές with reason. Socrates first expressed this doctrine when he was discussing ordinary virtue and before he revealed that a few men would attain a virtue beyond the ordinary. This fact might have led one to think that the doctrine resembles the first definitions of virtue in being a sketch true for the ordinary man but inaccurate for the philosopher. But the doctrine is repeated here (589b3-4), and Socrates implies that it is true of the philosopher as well as of the common man. A page later, he reminds his listeners once more that reason, the supreme regulatory principle, is immanent only in the philosopher-ruler, and must be imposed from outside upon the common artisan (590c8-d5). This distinction is what ultimately determines the status and worth of the ruler. But when we recall that philosopher and artisan remain alike in their possession of bodies, which are sources of potential disorder, it is clear why the virtue of both depends on the sustaining strength of the θυμοειδές. However rare temptation may be for the philosopher, however slight its allure in the face of his clear knowledge, he remains in principle a soul in a fleshly prison. In spite of this, there is a misleading tendency of some scholars to speak of the philosopher as if he were already a disembodied spirit.[9]

9. "Connaître le Bien, c'est être à la fois courageux, sage, juste, pieux, et savant" (René Schaerer, *La Question Platonicienne* [Neuchatel, 1938], p. 72). The philosopher's virtue is "homogeneous," the common man's "heterogeneous" (*ibid.*). The objection to this is that the body requires a tripartite soul, and tripartition implies a heterogeneous virtue. The theory of a self-sufficient knowledge appears also in Hans von Arnim, *Platons Jugenddialoge* (Leipzig, Berlin, 1914), pp. 8-10, where it is said that the full knowledge which is virtue cannot yield to any anger, fear, or desire. Arnim finds proof of this at *Protag.* 352b, *Theaet.* 176c, and *Laws* 689a. The first passage is discussed above, in Chapter 4, note 21. It does not assert or imply the existence of a knowledge that is identical with virtue, nor do the other two passages. *Theaetetus* 176c is not a contrast between a moral wisdom that is immune from the lower impulses and one that is not, but rather between political or technical knowledge and knowledge of the just. To call the latter knowledge true virtue, as opposed to the former, is not to say that it can *by itself* forever insure good conduct. At *Laws* 689a5 ff. the greatest stupidity is said to be the condition of a man in whom discord exists between reason and the principles of pleasure and pain. But this implies that the wisdom opposed to this belongs to a man

Their interpretation ascribes to Plato's mature ethics the same kind of simplistic intellectualism which plays so prominent a part in scholarly discussion of the early dialogues. Even in those early works, the ascendancy of knowledge was restricted, among other ways, by the acknowledgment of something called "ability." This vague notion is now at least partially clarified by the conception of a naturally strong and rigorously trained θυμοειδές.

The *Republic* is one of those great intellectual achievements in which we behold at once an individual mind come to full maturity and the common ideas of an age joined in a new synthesis. Conceived on a scale that Plato has not hitherto attempted, it carries forward trains of speculation which in the early dialogues were briefly sketched or only hinted at. It does so, moreover, while remaining faithful to the broad outlines of ethics and education which those dialogues have laid down. Far from abjuring Plato's youthful intellectualism, the *Republic* sustains it by a psychological framework whose absence in earlier works has made that intellectualism seem to many to be out of touch with reality. Virtue in the *Republic* is rational order in the soul; it is good nature, properly disciplined, and ruled by right opinion or knowledge. If virtue is often simply called knowledge, it is because regulative knowledge is the ruling element in behavior and contemplative knowledge is man's highest

---

who enjoys concord between his reason and his desires and fears. This suggests a self-sufficient knowledge far less than it does one supported by a docile and cooperative lower soul. C. Ritter, *Platon: Sein Leben, Seine Schriften, Seine Lehre* (Munich, 1910-23), 1.437-39, also defends the theory that for Plato knowledge alone is virtue, defining it as the wisdom which consists in knowing one's own nature and the supreme end of action. He anticipates the obvious objection that this means there is no need for "practice and training of the will," a supposition contrary to all experience. He replies that such practice and discipline are quite necessary but that this can be reconciled with the identification of virtue and knowledge. Practice is good for us, since we need it to create virtuous habits. Virtue is knowledge of all that is good for us, including the fact that we cannot habitually be virtuous without practice. Hence an aspect of virtue which seemed separate from knowledge is really an aspect of knowledge. But if "practice," the long training of the whole soul to work cooperatively, is necessary for virtue, then it seems perverse to deny that the resultant concord in man's tripartite nature is a part of his virtue. Yet Ritter speaks of knowledge of the Good as if it alone constituted courage and temperance: as if the difference of name merely signified a difference of object, courage being knowledge against fear, temperance knowledge against passion (*ibid.*, 2.515. Cf. Ritter's *Kerngedanken der Platonischen Philosophie* [Munich, 1931], pp. 333-34).

and best activity. This theory of education and the good life is not only the mature expression of Plato's own views but is the flowering as well of much that was typical in the intellectual life of classical Greece. The great argument, for example, on the relative merits of nature, practice, and instruction, which during the fifth century distilled passionate controversy into a triad of abstractions, and helped mold the thought of historians, philosophers, and poets,[10] finds in the *Republic* a solution that makes all three indispensable while adapting all to new Platonic meanings. The intellectual fervor, moreover, of the age of Socrates, in which human reason as expressed in the arts acquired unparalleled scope and prestige, reaches a kind of climax in Plato's ambitious scheme to reorganize society according to a new art of politics. In these, as in many other ways, the *Republic* is the fruit of Greek civilization as well as of Plato's private speculations.

The doctrine of the tripartite soul, explained at length in the *Republic*, appears again prominently in two other dialogues of later date, the *Phaedrus* and the *Timaeus*. Since this psychological scheme is so closely bound in the *Republic* to the political program of the tripartite state, Plato's retention of it in contexts where there was no compelling political analogy is at first surprising. He was the least doctrinaire of philosophers in his attachment to such schemes and definitions, as he shows in the *Republic* in his depreciatory reference to his "sketch" of the virtues (504d4-7). His continued references, therefore, in later passages, to the tripartite soul show that he must have found that doctrine unusually illuminating. What is not surprising is that he freely varied his presentation of it by introducing new details and suppressing old ones, and by showing himself in no way bound to the terminology which he had so painstakingly developed in the *Republic*. This is most evident in the *Phaedrus*, where the conception of the soul as a union of three diverse parts is transformed into a mythical narrative of man's prenatal vision of the Forms.

The myth of the *Phaedrus*, in which Socrates describes the soul's life in the other world and its view of the eternal realities, is one of the best-known passages in the dialogues. In a prolonged simili-

10. See above, Chapter 4, note 27.

tude, disembodied souls are compared to chariots which move across the heavens in the train of the gods, who lead the grand procession. Drawing each human chariot is a team of two winged horses, one of good breed, the other base, guided by a charioteer. In this figure the essential threefold division found in the *Republic* is preserved. In their journey around the heavens, where the eternal Forms are enthroned as objects of contemplation, only the chariots of the gods move with any ease. Consequently, when the gods lead the way to the highest heaven, where these Forms can be glimpsed, those chariots which correspond to imperfect souls have great trouble following (247b3-6). In their effort, some charioteers have more success than others in controlling their mettlesome teams. Those which follow the gods best are able to rise to a point where they can lift their heads into this upper region. They are carried around the course and see reality, though with difficulty. Others are less successful; they rise and fall, seeing some things and missing others. The rest of the souls have not the strength to rise at all and are lost in the melee below; they are forced to go off and nourish themselves on opinion instead of enjoying that food suited to what is best in them (247c3-248c2).

The degree of success which a soul enjoys in following the chariots of the gods is what determines its subsequent fate. Those which catch some glimpse of reality suffer no penalty, and are admitted to the cortege when it next sets out. Those that fail to see anything and, losing their wings, fall, heavy with forgetfulness and evil, to earth, come to be embodied in human form. We are to imagine, however, that even these unhappy souls have had some success in seeing the Forms on previous journeys. Among them, those who have seen the most will become philosophers, while others, less blessed, will assume lives of various ranks, of which the lowest is that of the tyrant. For all of these the future holds, as their merit determines, the promise of a return to the heaven from which they fell, or else the threat of dire punishments or subsequent incarnation in the form of a beast (248d ff.).

All those souls which have had the misfortune to lose their wings and fall to earth into the body of a man keep, nevertheless, a dim memory of their celestial vision of reality. The fact that they

have achieved human shape on earth certifies that they have had
some share in that vision (249e). They retain, moreover, their
threefold form, expressed by the two horses and the charioteer of
the myth. This memory and this threefold division will explain the
fact that the soul suffers conflicting emotions in the presence of
physical beauty on earth. Socrates explains that inner conflict of
desire and idealism by resuming the myth and by describing in
greater detail the contrast between the two horses. One, a stately
white steed, is a lover of honor, of temperance, and of modesty.
It is a comrade of true opinion, in need of no whip, but guided by
a mere command. The other is an ugly, swarthy, stunted animal,
a comrade of insolence and barely responsive even under whip and
spur (253c7-e5).

The emotions which attend pederastic love as it is experienced
by the soul on earth can now be described in the same mythical
terms which Socrates used in speaking of the earlier vision. When
the charioteer sees his beloved and the soul feels desire, the noble
horse holds itself back, overcome by modesty and obedient to its
driver (254a1-2). But its harness-mate, with lustful intent, tries
to pull the soul closer to the beloved. The memory of the charioteer is carried back to Beauty itself, which he sees again enthroned
with temperance on a holy pedestal. ʿOnly by forcing the unruly
horse to the ground and dragging him by the bit does the charioteer eventually tame him (254c5-e8). If, through continued efforts of this kind, better counsels eventually prevail and the soul's
life is brought to order and to a love of wisdom, then the lover
and the beloved enjoy a blessed life on earth: they have enslaved
the source of vice in them and liberated the source of virtue (256a8-
b3). Love, which threatened to take the form of a debasing physical indulgence, has been tamed by reason and channeled into the
pursuit of wisdom. The bond of passion which joins lover and beloved is elevated into a bond of mutual assistance and concern for
the good life.

We are evidently dealing in this myth with an adaptation of
the doctrine of the *Republic* that the soul is threefold. The charioteer represents reason in both of the aspects already noticed in the
*Republic*: in its function as the guiding element in the soul and

in its power and aspiration to rise to a vision of the Forms. The unruly horse corresponds to the ἐπιθυμητικόν. Like that power, it contains no principle of limitation and must be curbed by a force outside itself. If the noble horse is the θυμοειδές, and analogy with the *Republic* supports that correspondence, then it must be admitted that the conception of this part of the soul found in the *Republic* and that found in the *Phaedrus* do not exactly coincide. The noble horse is a source of shame or modesty and an ally of honor and temperance (*Phaedrus* 253d6, 254a2, 256a6). But its role as a source of courage, vigor, and impetuosity is less clear; it lacks the ferocity which the lion in *Republic* 588b-d suggests. None of this, however, signifies any profound change in psychological doctrine. A myth is invented to make a few points, and in doing this Plato may properly exclude details elsewhere made explicit. The myth of the *Phaedrus* describes the battle fought within the soul between the forces of pleasure and reason. The virtue tested is temperance, in the form of the subjection of appetite to knowledge. In a struggle of this sort, if we may reduce the high rhetoric of the *Phaedrus* to its simplest terms, one can detect in the soul the emotion of shame, which tends to curb reckless desire. A myth depicting this struggle will naturally confine itself to the emotions involved in it alone, and it need not allude to the fact that the soul also engages in struggles against pain or fright, for example, which call out different emotions, like fear or anger. The fact that the noble steed is not drawn to conform precisely to the θυμοειδές or to the figure of the lion does not make it less probable that Plato is thinking of the same psychological principle in all three descriptions.

It may seem that the apparent disparity cannot be so easily disposed of. There remains the obvious rejoinder that the struggle of the soul against its own baser desires in the *Phaedrus* is like the struggle of Leontius with himself in the *Republic* (439c6 ff.). The emotion in Leontius, however, which supported reason against desire was his anger with himself, and this fact stands in apparent contradiction to the analysis of motives implied in the *Phaedrus* myth. But the larger context of the story of Leontius makes Plato's choice of terms there clear. One of the major themes of the *Republic* is the correspondence between state and individual. The presence of a soldier class in the state, whose virtue is courage and which treats rebellion with disciplined ferocity, will require in the individual, by analogy, a second part of the soul whose proper virtue is also courage and which views excessive pleasure with anger. In the *Phaedrus*, where there is no compelling analogy, anger with one's self is replaced by shame. It is fair to say that the complex emotion which an inner struggle against debasing appetite calls forth can be characterized in either of these two ways.

The tripartition of the soul, which provides so convenient a framework for Plato's psychology in his middle and later periods, also raises a large problem to which there appears to be no clear answer. To put it briefly: Why is the soul divided? At *Republic* 611a10 ff., Socrates says that the cause lies in its attachment to the body, yet it appears from the *Phaedrus* myth that the soul has three parts even before birth. This seeming inconsistency can be traced even within the *Republic*, since the division of the soul before birth is implied in the myth of Er, where Socrates describes the disembodied spirits as still in need of purification. Without implying in the least that the problem is negligible, we can, I think, divine some of the reasons which led Plato to deal with it as he did. It is natural that he should have envisaged the two lower parts of the soul essentially as sources of bodily anger and appetite, since it is only by reflecting on such impulses that he could infer the existence of these parts at all (cf. *Rep.* 436b ff.). It is obviously true, moreover, that a soul cannot achieve unity *without* leaving the body: there are, in short, no living men who are complete strangers to anger and desire; and this fact implies that they all possess θυμοειδές and ἐπιθυμητικόν. To leap from this, however, to the conclusion that the soul achieves perfect unity *merely* by leaving the body is to condemn as trivial and irrelevant all efforts at self-control in this life; hence Plato concludes that mere death cannot liberate us from our spiritual disorders. Beyond this point he can only express his conviction in myth, and he does so, among other places, in the myth of Er. It appears there that the man who dies without having reached philosophic virtue may be so blind as to choose a tyrant's life in his next incarnation. Death will not cure such a man of his folly (*Rep.* 619b7 ff.). Quite apart from this, there remains the fact

that to claim that the soul can achieve unity simply by separation
from the body would be to leave inexplicable its first entry into
the body. Plato cannot explain the soul's fall scientifically, but he
shows that he is aware of that problem by stating in the *Phaedrus*
myth that souls which enter bodies are already imperfect. The
vague, metaphorical terms in which he describes their imperfection
(*Phaedrus* 248c5-8) admittedly do not explain the fact, but merely
acknowledge it. Of the soul in the body he can speak with some
precision; of the disembodied soul he must speak in myth. The
way to perfection is (1) an improvement in moral virtue, which
leads ultimately to philosophical wisdom, and (2) final liberation
from the body. It may take many incarnations to achieve both.

The interest of the *Timaeus* to students of the doctrine of tripartition is that it not only attributes the division of the soul to its
connection with a body, but it carries that division to extraordinary
lengths. According to this dialogue, the creation of the lower parts
of the soul was carried out by the sons of god in order to accom-
modate the soul to the body (69c5-d6). Not wishing to defile the
divine part of the soul, they separated the mortal part from it and
made the neck for a boundary (69d6-e4). This anatomical segre-
gation of parts was continued within the lower soul itself. Hence
the better half of the latter lies above the midriff, the worse half
below (69e5-70a2). Of these two physically separated portions of
the lower soul, the better is meant to fight against injustice both
from the outside world and from the desires of the soul's lowest
part.

To the student of Platonic psychology this account may seem
to carry to its ultimate degree the dissolution of the soul's unity
which had already been foreshadowed in the *Republic* and the
*Phaedrus*. It is easy, however, to exaggerate the significance of
the passage. Remarkable as it may seem that the *Timaeus* should
divide the soul into parts actually separated in space, this is no
more than can be expected in a context of scientific and physiological interest. The soul is discussed here merely as a source of
physical activities, and since these activities are separated in the
body their vital principles act at separate points in space and may
be said to exist outside of each other. The fact that all three prin-

ciples are one in the unity of consciousness is, for the physiologist, quite irrelevant. This single point of view shapes the whole exposition. The speaker is interested not in the soul's emotions but in the physical changes that accompany them: the action of the heart, the movement of the blood, the cooling effect of the lungs (70a7-d6). The same viewpoint accounts for the striking statement that the soul's partition is a physical separation with tangible boundaries. Plato speaks as a biologist, but he knows that in other respects the soul is one.[11]

A consistent terminology and systematic cross references would have helped the reader in comparing the *Republic, Phaedrus,* and *Timaeus.* But it is Plato's way to give neither, and so part of the critic's job is sifting what is essentially different in the passages from what is a matter of terminology and emphasis. Plato takes up a subject afresh each time he meets it, and divides and defines it according to the purpose in hand. Certain terms and convenient formulations of doctrine, like the tripartition of the soul, recur, but otherwise he begins discussions with no verbal deposit and leaves none behind. That fact, evident enough in the three dialogues that deal with the partition of the soul, will be shown again in the next chapter.[12]

11. Cf. A. E. Taylor, *Commentary on Plato's Timaeus* (Oxford, 1928), p. 496. The same physiological interest accounts for some details in the discussion of moral error a few pages later, at *Tim.* 86b1 ff. (see below, Chapter 6, n. 12). In this passage too the vices are assigned physical causes, because the *Timaeus* is more a scientific discourse than a moral one. But this interest in the effect of body on soul is not a denial of the soul's ability to affect the body.

12. In H. Raeder's scheme of development the *Phaedo,* with its simple soul, precedes the *Republic* and *Phaedrus,* with their composite soul (*Platons Philos. Entwickelung* [Leipzig, 1905], p. 214). (But see this note below.) Reginald Hackforth, *Plato's Phaedrus,* translated with introduction and commentary (Cambridge, 1952), p. 75, thinks there is no possibility of reconciling Plato's different views about the unity or multiplicity of the soul. He concludes that Plato wavers to the end between the conception of a divine soul and that of a scientific soul that is a source of motion for bodies.

W. K. C. Guthrie has tried to counter this accusation of inconsistency. In the face of Hackforth's contention that if soul is a moving principle it must itself possess motions over and above the reason which contemplates the eternal Forms (Hackforth, p. 8), Guthrie replies that the tripartite soul can also be a simple soul. As he puts it, "instead of defining nous . . . as the highest part of a tripartite soul, we can also describe it as the power of soul when all its energies are directed to the pursuit of wisdom, and every desire for the objects either of worldly desire or of sensual gratification has lost its meaning" ("Plato's Views on the Nature of the Soul," *Recherches sur la Tradition Platonicienne*

[Geneva, 1955], p. 17). R. D. Archer-Hind, in his *Timaeus* ed. (London, 1888), p. 256, addresses himself in much the same way to this point. Cf. F. A. Wilford, "The Status of Reason in Plato's Psychology," *Phronesis*, 4 (1959), 54-58, who goes on to show that it is even inexact to assume that a simple soul, free of the body, would be "all λογιστικόν" (p. 55). Reason itself, like anger and appetite, is a mode of the soul's activity in the world of time and sense. Hence in the presence of the Forms, the soul does not reason; it "sees."

The *Phaedo* is often contrasted with the *Republic, Phaedrus,* and *Timaeus* in the matter of the soul. As an account of the philosopher's death, it is naturally concerned with the soul's affliction by the body and its hope of release (81b ff., 82e ff.). It therefore dwells on the perfection desired for the soul rather than on its primeval flaws. Even so, its expression is guarded. The soul is merely "most like" the divine and the uniform and the always unchanging (80b). Cf. P. Shorey, *The Unity of Plato's Thought* (Chicago, 1903), p. 42, and J. Moreau, "Platon et la Connaissance de l'Âme," *REA*, 55 (1953), 253.

R. S. Bluck has recently suggested that the "falls" described in the *Phaedrus* myth are not original falls ("The *Phaedrus* and Reincarnation," *AJP*, 79 [1958], 156-64). He tries in this way to square the *Phaedrus* with *Tim.* 41b ff. and 69c, where Plato speaks as if souls were meant for bodies, and to explain the original connection of soul with body by invoking the *Timaeus* account. He calls attention to *Phaedrus* 247b4, where the bad horse is called "not well-trained," and he argues that this suggests bad training in a previous incarnation. But his conclusion is not warranted. The phrase quoted may simply be part of the sustained metaphor, balancing εὐήνια two lines before, and felt as no more than a natural synonym for "unruly." He also says that the heaviness and fall of the soul at 248c make one think of the similar language at *Phaedo* 81a-d and 83d, where it is an effect of incarnation. But at *Phaedrus* 248c Plato chose what looks like a deliberately vague phrase, "some mischance," when nothing prevented him from saying "the ill effects of the body" if he had meant that. Moreover, heaviness, forgetfulness, and evil are words as well suited to an original fall as to a later one. Now an original descent of some kind is part of both the *Phaedrus* and the *Timaeus* myths, since every soul in a body has previously seen the Forms in heaven (*Phaedrus* 249e, *Tim.* 41e). But no real explanation is ever offered. *Tim.* 41b ff. adds to the *Phaedrus* account only that the existence of mortal natures is needed for a perfect world (41b), that their souls are not quite pure to start with (41d), and that they enter bodies through "necessity" (42a). If one lays aside the mythical trappings, this is not irreconcilable with the *Phaedrus*, where the reference to "some mischance" connected with "forgetfulness and evil" (248c) is equally opaque. The "badly trained horse" with the ill-bred sire and dam (246b3) is a mythical expression of the mixed nature (246b1), which itself may be no more than the original impurity alluded to at *Tim.* 41d. As Bluck rightly says, "these matters are obscure" (p. 164). There are philosophical problems here that were undoubtedly obscure to Plato too. (The above comments had already been written when I first read the detailed and cogent criticism of Bluck's view that the "falls" are not original by D. D. McGibbon in "The Fall of the Soul in Plato's *Phaedrus*," *CQ*, N.S. 14 [1964], 56-63).

# 6. THE LATER DIALOGUES

## AND

## THE QUESTION OF CHANGE

Socrates had asked in the *Protagoras*, "Is virtue one thing, and justice, temperance, and holiness its parts, or are these all names of the same one thing?" (329cd) No satisfactory answer appeared in that dialogue, but it may already be clear from the preceding chapter that Plato meant to answer yes and no to the question: Is virtue one? This implies only that the problem is ambiguous and hard. But since Plato, in different passages, stresses one part or the other of his answer, passages that are really complementary seem inconsistent with one another. Virtue in some dialogues seems to be one thing, but in others it is several quite different things, which can even be ranked in value. The same problem is raised by Plato's discussions of the nature and causes of vice. At times he seems determined to reduce all forms of vice to the single fault of ignorance, but as often he seemingly lapses into the conventional view that ignorance is one thing and incontinence or rage another. Since his tolerance of conventional views apparently increases in later dialogues, not a few scholars have seen in this the evidence of a gradual but radical change in doctrine, culminating in the *Laws*, where traces of the unity of virtue are few and may perhaps be dismissed as remnants of a doctrine long since superseded. The evidence for this theory will be examined in the following pages.

Of the four virtues that are cardinal in the *Republic*, courage and temperance make an obviously contrasting pair. In popular usage the term σωφροσύνη meant "caution" as well as "moderation" (cf. Thucydides 6.79.2), and what was mere caution to one man might seem timidity to another. Therefore the problem whether virtue is one or many most often touches upon the relationship of these two. Plato virtually identifies them in the *Gorgias*; in several dialogues he speaks as if they had the same function; he calls them opposed in the *Politicus*; and in the *Laws* he calls courage the least of virtues and says that animals possess it. All this must be accounted for.

As virtues in the full sense of the word, courage and temperance are "very much alike." This is a phrase which Socrates used of justice and holiness in the *Protagoras*, but which sums up as well Plato's judgment of the relationship of the two virtues in question here.[1] Perfect courage insures temperate action, perfect temperance brave action. The perfection of each of these virtues implies a limitation of the irrational tendencies of which each is the ideal form. The courageous man will be forceful and assertive up to a point, but no further; the temperate man will be gentle and restrained, but not excessively so. They will, in fact, be the same man, who reacts differently to diverse challenges but is constantly governed by the same ideals. There are times, moreover, when the emotion called forth by a specific decision will be so complex that the act itself will seem both brave and temperate. One such example, the struggle against desire, has already been reviewed in the last chapter. For these reasons Plato sometimes calls a man

1. *Protag.* 331b5. The phrase is, of course, extremely vague, but a logically precise statement of how the virtues are related was the least of Plato's concerns. He had sketched the possibilities at *Protag.* 329c ff., and had included (at 329e4) the formula he would eventually prove right, viz. mutual entailment. The real problem for him was to show why and how the virtues entail one another, and it is solved only by thoroughly probing the nature of each at all its levels.

temperate for actions usually associated with courage and courageous for actions usually associated with temperance. What makes the two virtues compatible—indeed, in a sense, one—is simply the rule of reason over both. To see this is to return to the central doctrine of Platonic ethics, that all virtues are expressions of knowledge, and even beyond that to the central principle of Platonic philosophy, the Form of the Good. The limitation, perfection, and consequent unity that knowledge imposes upon the soul's mutually hostile[2] tendencies are simply the unity of the Good, apprehended by reason and imposed on irrational impulse.

Paul Shorey has pointed out that this dependence of virtue on the Good, which comes to its full expression in the *Republic*, can be traced in germinal form in the argument of the earlier dialogues.[3] He shows, for example, that in the latter it is Plato's habitual method to assume from the start that any virtue under examination must always be "good" or "noble" (ἀγαθόν or καλόν). Socrates will accordingly reject proposed definitions which fail to conform to this requirement. On these grounds, for example, courage cannot be merely steadfastness (*Laches* 192c), or temperance merely shame (*Charmides* 161a). According to *Meno* 87d the first thing to be said about virtue is that it is a good, and speculation about its nature will have to take that fact into account. At *Protagoras* 349e it is agreed that virtue is entirely a noble thing, and this sets the inquiry on the right track. To assume, in this fashion, that the virtues are all "good" dispositions of man's soul is to assert their unity in the broadest terms. Admittedly, the terms "good" and "noble" are merely blank counters in the discussion. They remain so until the Idea of the Good itself is introduced in the *Republic*, and it becomes clear that the unity of the virtues as "good" dispositions means that they are all expressions of an ultimate rational principle (*Rep.* 509b). It requires only a step beyond this to assert that they cannot be fully understood, only "sketched," until the Good itself is understood (*Rep.* 504a ff., especially 504d6).

There is a passage in the *Gorgias*, at 507a5-c3, in which Soc-

2. Courage and temperance are so described at *Politicus* 306b. See this Chapter, below.
3. Paul Shorey, *The Idea of Good in Plato's Republic*, in *Univ. of Chicago Studies in Class. Philology*, No. 1 (Chicago, 1895), p. 208.

rates goes further than he ordinarily does in early dialogues toward making the above line of argument explicit. By using the notion of goodness, Socrates maintains in this passage that the conception of temperance contains implicitly that of a fully rounded virtue. If the temperate soul is good, he argues, then it will do what is proper concerning gods and men. Now to act properly towards men is to be just; to do so in one's relations with the gods is to be holy. Consequently, the notion of temperance implies justice and holiness. It even implies courage, for the temperate man will not behave improperly with respect to the things which he pursues or avoids. Whether he is faced with antagonists in the shape of other men, or pains, or pleasures, he will always pursue or flee them in the way he ought and will stand his ground when he ought. Therefore, the man who is temperate will also be just, courageous, holy, and, in brief, a completely good man.

If the temperate man is brave, then for the same reasons the brave man will be temperate. Plato often says that courage enables a man to fight not only against outside enemies but against his own pleasures too. When Socrates first tries to elicit from Laches a definition of courage, he points out that he wants to characterize not only the brave infantryman but also the brave cavalryman, or the man brave at sea, or in disease and pain, or in politics. These extensions of the idea are not unusual, but Socrates goes on to say that he has in mind not only those brave in pain but those brave in the face of desire and pleasure as well (*Laches* 191e4-7). He evidently thinks of courage as a check on desire, although the obedience of desire to the right rule is usually called a mark of temperance. The basis for this extended use of courage is more than the unity of virtue in the principle of reason and of the Good, although this alone would justify the extension. It is rather that the suppression of desire is seen as a victory of good impulses over bad. Therefore, since a man's desire subsides because his better impulses fight it down, he is called courageous; since the result of this struggle is a harmony in his soul, he is called temperate too.

In the *Republic* the extended use of the term "courage" is to be expected, because the analogy of the state would have suggested it anyway. It is the characteristic virtue of the soldier class, and that class has two duties: repelling attacks of enemies, and crushing revolt. Their courage is the power of preserving in all circumstances the right opinion about the fearful, and the phrase "all circumstances" covers pains, pleasures, desires, and fears (429c9-d1, 430a7). Later, this definition of courage in society at large determines by analogy the definition of courage in the individual (441d1-4), which is also said to meet two threats, the open hostility of pain and the treachery of pleasure (442b11-c3).

The essential unity of the virtues as diverse forms of rational order in the soul invites such identifications as those just mentioned. But at times it serves Plato's purpose to stress their distinctness as expressions of temperament and habit. The passage which treats this question most clearly and most discursively is found in the *Politicus*, where the Stranger undertakes a discussion of the art of statesmanship. One of the bases of that art, he explains, is an awareness that there is in some way an opposition between courage and temperance (306b9-11). This appears to be a way of saying that good qualities of soul fall into two large and contrasted categories. The first includes vigorous traits, like rapidity and forcefulness of mind, body, and voice (306e4-5), which are called collectively ἀνδρεία. The second includes gentle, slow, orderly traits, and these are called collectively σωφροσύνη (307ab). Excesses in either set of qualities are given opposite names too. Actions too sharp, too quick, and too rough are called arrogant and frenzied; those too heavy, too slow, and too gentle are judged cowardly and sluggish. The "temperate" and the "courageous" qualities do not mix with each other in actions of the sort mentioned, and the very men who possess each set of traits oppose each other (307c).

This opposition of temperaments concerns the statesman because it affects the welfare of the community over which he exercises command. The gentle incline to be peaceful in the extreme, and their unwarlike ways leave them at the mercy of those who would attack and enslave them and the whole state. The aggressive involve their countries in continual war, which leads no less surely to destruction or enslavement (307e1-308a). The statesman's art lies in using these opposed temperaments for the good of the state and in preventing them from destroying it. After executing, exiling, and disfranchising those whom an evil nature utterly perverts and enslaving the stupid and the abject (308e-309a), the statesman takes those who incline to courage and to decorousness and weaves them as warp and woof into the fabric of the state. He binds them with bonds both divine and human: divine for the immortal part of the soul, human for the mortal (309c1 ff.). The divine bond is true opinion, which makes the courageous soul gentle and keeps it from brutishness, and which makes the decorous soul truly temperate and prudent and saves it from silliness (309de). It is applied to the immortal part of the soul, the reason. The human bonds are those of marriage and procreation and are applied to the temperament, the soul's mortal part. The statesman must join in marriage vigorous temperaments with gentle ones. He must see to it that the natural tendency of like to marry like does not produce in the one group soft children and spineless grandchildren, and in the other a corresponding heightening of vigor ending in frenzy (310c-e). He must, finally, entrust the government to men who combine both natures or to committees composed of both types, and in all ways mingle the two to achieve a balanced society (310e-311a).

This is in large measure a restatement of doctrines already found in the *Republic*, where virtue was said to be a product of nature, training, and right opinion or knowledge. The arrangement of marriages, for example, which lays so much emphasis on heredity, is also a concern of the *Republic* (459d6-e3). In the passage from the *Politicus*, however, unusual stress is laid on inborn character, and therefore on the eugenic responsibilities of government. The role of the statesman is to encourage the birth of balanced natures and to mingle men of contrasting natural endowments in a balanced community. He is consequently envisaged as a kind of weaver, who is heavily dependent on the quality of the threads at his disposal. Apart from all this, the passage involves the remarkable supposition that temperance and courage are actually opposed, in spite of the fact that Plato elsewhere insists on their unity. This is widely held to be evidence of a radical reform in doctrine.[4] But the disparity simply proves that elsewhere Plato is more often interested in the philosophical doctrine that all virtues are subject to the rule of reason, whereas here he is concerned with a specific issue of statecraft. Virtue is one as shaped by reason and many as grounded in diverse impulses. Eugenics need concern itself only with the latter.

That the two kinds of temperament are opposed and the ideal character combines both is a common theme in the dialogues, and the Stranger in the *Politicus* is by no means alone in asserting it. A balanced soul is the purpose of early education in the *Republic* (410e10), where the soul both temperate and brave is said to be "well tuned." According to the *Laws* (731b3-4) every man must be spirited but as gentle as possible too. Iccus of Tarentum, a paragon of excellence (*Laws* 840a2), possesses courage joined with temperance. Theaetetus is eulogized by Theodorus because he combines the two natures better than any other young man he has ever met (*Theaetetus* 144a1 ff.). He is quick to learn, gentle, and at the same time courageous, an exceptional combination. Yet those who have good, sharp minds and memories are usually hot-tempered and, properly speaking, are more frenzied than courageous, whereas more dignified characters are sluggish and forgetful. Theaetetus, on the other hand, combines all good traits. In fact, he fits closely the description given in the *Republic* of the kind of man suited to become a philosopher-ruler (503c2 ff.). It is

4. Lewis Campbell, in his ed., *The Sophistes and Politicus* (Oxford, 1867), p. 174, said that 306bc was certainly a modification of the view taken by Socrates in the *Protagoras*, "the simple unity of virtue." J. B. Skemp has gone further in saying that the psychology of the *Republic* is "explicitly supplanted in the *Politicus*" (trans. *Plato. The Statesman* [London, 1952], p. 239). "The accord of the several 'virtues' in δικαιοσύνη or righteousness is, of course, the cardinal doctrine . . . in the first half of the *Republic*. . . . We now make what seems a frontal attack on this position," i.e. in the *Politicus*. "It is equivalent to declaring eternal conflict between the warrior and civilian classes" (p. 223). *Politicus* 306 is one of the landmarks in H. Raeder's account of evolving Platonic doctrine, in which virtue becomes progressively more fragmented (*Platons Philos. Entwickelung* [Leipzig, 1905], p. 399). The passage itself, however, makes it clear enough that the courage and temperance in question are actually traits of temperament and not developed virtues. This extension of meaning is by no means unexampled (see above, Chapter 1, note 13). Paul Friedländer explains the passage well in *Platon*, II, *Die Platonischen Schriften* (1st ed.; Berlin, 1930), pp. 24, 555.

no accident that in praising so highly his natural gifts of soul Theodorus should also remark that he bears a marked physical resemblance to Socrates.[5]

There exist in the *Laws*, the latest of the dialogues, a number of passages which are regularly quoted to prove that Plato in old age gave up the belief in the unity of virtue away from which, supposedly, he had long been drifting. The best known of these occurs in Book I, in the puzzling attempt to "rank" the virtues. To explain the context of this "ranking" we must go back almost to the beginning of the dialogue. The *Laws* has opened with a discussion of Clinias' theory that all states are organized for the purpose of success in war. The Athenian Stranger, who leads the conversation, proposes to test this theory by making a general principle out of it and by developing several analogies. He shows, for example, that a similar hostility seems to determine the relations of village with village, of house with house, of man with man, and, finally, of a man with himself (626a-d). A man is constantly doing battle with himself and will find in this struggle either the first and best of all victories or the most degrading of all defeats (626e2 ff.). In consequence of this battle the individual becomes either his own master or his own slave, and the same alternatives await the result of a similar conflict in the state or in the household (626e-627d5). Now the judge who restores peace among brothers in a household can do so in any of three ways: by killing the malefactors, by making them submit willingly to be ruled by their good brothers, or by reconciling the two groups to live together as friends. The third way, says the Stranger, is the best. But it looks to peace as an ideal and argues against the primacy of war, the hypothesis being tested by the conversation (627e-628a). On a political level, the man who guides the life of the state should consider the problem of war within the state (στάσις) more worthy of his attention than that of war from without. His main purpose, in short, will be to achieve

---

5. The belief that virtuous action draws support from strong natural impulses held in equilibrium appears in a different form at *Laws* 646e4 ff. Here the balance is said to involve being fearless and fearful at the same time. The Athenian Stranger means by this to commend the fear of disgrace, which is the same thing as shame, and to disparage the fear of impending evils. As 647d1-3 indicates, this is another way of praising the balanced temperament, which inclines equally to courage and to temperance.

the supremacy of better men within his state, since this is more important than the supremacy of the state over its foreign enemies. His goal can be reached in one of two ways. The worse method is to destroy the dissidents; the better is to reconcile them with their rulers in peace and friendship. The highest good, therefore, at which the lawgiver will aim, is not war and not civil strife, but peace and friendliness (628a-c); it is not even that victory of the state over itself mentioned before, because this victory is not unqualifiedly good, but is merely at times regrettably necessary. So ends the first part of the argument. Its conclusion has been a rejection of Clinias' opening suggestion that the needs of war should determine the laws of a state. Laws are meant ultimately for peace, not for war.

The discussion of the virtues, which follows, runs parallel to the preceding comments about politics. It is essential to keep this in mind, because the conclusions of the earlier passage are implied in the later one; one might say they are simply expressed in a new way. This second part of the argument gets under way with a quotation by the Athenian of a poem of Tyrtaeus, who said that the man who has almost all other goods but is not brave in war is a man of no account. Tyrtaeus, it is decided, was referring not to civil war but to war against outside enemies and was praising those who excelled in the latter (629a-e). The Athenian, on the contrary, maintains that the man brave in time of sedition far surpasses one who resists foreign enemies. The superiority of the former, he says, is like the superiority of justice, temperance, wisdom, and courage, taken all together, over courage alone (630ab). In the war of which Tyrtaeus speaks there are many mercenaries ready to die fighting, most of whom are reckless, unjust, violent, and unwise to an extreme (630b4-7). The good lawgiver will want to encourage the greatest virtue, which is loyalty in danger, or justice in the full sense (630c6). The courage which Tyrtaeus praised, although properly honored by him, is no higher than fourth among the virtues (630c8). Consequently, Clinias, in making war the objective of lawgiving, had reduced the lawgiver's concern to a part of virtue, and that the least part, whereas his true concern is with the whole of virtue (630e). The purpose of law is the provision of good things, of which there are two kinds, human and divine. The human goods, which are inferior to the divine, are four: health, beauty, strength, and wealth, in that order. The divine goods also number four. The greatest is wisdom, which rules. The second is temperance with wisdom.[6] The third is justice, compounded of these two and courage. The fourth is courage (631cd).

This listing of the virtues in order of precedence is at first sight a surprising procedure. Wisdom is naturally first, but it is strange that Plato should treat it and the others as separable ingredients in a mixture and then value what looks like the fully rounded quadripartite virtue of the *Republic* third. It not only seems to contradict our understanding that the presence of one virtue implies the presence of all the others, but it compels us to explain: Why *this* mixture and *this* ranking?

The reason for the primacy of wisdom is given a few lines later: the other three divine goods are directed by it (631d5-6). The reason why the other three are ranked in the order given is much harder to assess. But it can be found, I think, in the judgments about courage immediately preceding and in the earlier discussion about the goals of legislation for the state as a whole. The courage that is ranked fourth is evidently the daring disposition that often goes with injustice and arrogance, the strong natural vigor wrongly trained or not trained at all, not the virtue properly so called.[7] It is a good because it serves a good purpose in war and could have been shaped into a real virtue. It is least among the goods of the soul just as preparation for foreign war is least among the goals of legislation. The lawgiver is to think such preparation less im-

6. At 631c7 I read νοῦ (Eusebius) rather than νοῦν (Mss., Stobaeus) with Schanz, Burnet, England, and most others. The textual point does not really affect the interpretation. Unless wisdom were present, at least implicitly, temperance would hardly be ranked second. But it is better made explicit.

7. Cf. above, Introduction, n. 13. Two other passages in the *Laws* show this limited use of the word. In 661de the Athenian Stranger speaks of a man who has health, wealth, despotic power, strength, *courage*, immortality, and freedom from evils, but who also has injustice and arrogance. In 963e he gives the reason why wisdom (φρόνησις) and courage, both virtues, are called by different names. It is, he says, because the term "courage" concerns fear, which wild beasts and children experience, for a soul becomes courageous "by nature and without reason." Wisdom, on the other hand, implies the use of reason.

portant than suppressing sedition and achieving civil harmony. Of these two, civil harmony, which implied friendship and peace, was called more desirable than victory of the better element in a civil war, because such a victory, though it brought order, implied unrest. So too, among goods of the soul, temperance with wisdom is rated higher than justice, compounded of temperance, wisdom, and courage. The reason is the same: "temperance with wisdom" here means the virtue of a soul which enjoys the placidity that comes from a friendship of its three parts; whereas justice, the effect of wisdom and temperance joined with courage, characterizes a well-ordered soul in which strong emotions imply some danger of disorder. The mention of courage implies this, since the need for that virtue is always the presence or imminence of evil. I suggest that this is what Plato means by the odd statement that temperance with wisdom ranks higher than a combination of these with courage.

The attention of scholars has been drawn to this section of the *Laws* because it seems to many to provide incontrovertible evidence that Plato here abandoned some of his most characteristic earlier teachings. To others, these gradations in virtue have appeared virtually unintelligible, quite apart from their incompatibility with earlier doctrine. Consequently, at least one scholar goes so far as to suppose that the present text is the result of an inexpertly abbreviated argument, if not an actual confusion of several versions.[8]

8. This is Gigon (see this note below). Gerhard Müller, *Studien zu den Platonischen Nomoi* (Munich, 1951), pp. 16-17, concludes his discussion of the passage with a frank statement that the whole thing lacks clarity, that it cannot be reconciled with the theory of virtue in the *Republic*, and that this kind of ranking of virtues excludes their unity. This is one of the passages which force him to the conclusion that the system embodied in the *Republic* exists in the *Laws* only as fragments and lifeless phrases. "Wir stehen vor einem verfallenen Gebäude" (p. 21). Another fragment lies at 963e (see note 7, above), a statement about courage in "flagrant contradiction" with *Laches* 197a and *Protag.* 350c ff. (*ibid.*).

Olof Gigon, "Das Einleitungsgespräch der Gesetze Platons," *Mus. Helv.* 11 (1954), 201-30, shows an equally critical view but takes issue with Müller on one detail. Gigon points out that 630b5 ff. does not concede an irrational courage to mercenaries (in contradiction to the doctrine of the earlier dialogues) but says only that they are qualified for battle. They possess none of the four virtues; the list of their qualities at 630b, daring, injustice, wantonness, and foolishness, "is evidently an antitype" to the list courage, justice, temperance, and wisdom (p. 221). But we exchange one contradiction for an-

But the problem seems this hopeless only if we demand an un-Platonic exactitude of terminology from the passage. *Meno* 88b might also seem to have implied the fragmentation of virtue in speaking of courage and temperance with and without νοῦς. As for ἀνδρεία, most mercenaries may be denied a claim to any virtue at *Laws* 630b6-7, but they have the natural temperament, however undeveloped or warped, for at least one virtue, courage. They are "daring." By a loose but common enough usage in Plato, this inborn temperament itself is referred to at 630b2 and 631d1 as "courage." It is troublesome too that justice is called the "greatest virtue" at 630c3-6 and the only concern of the good lawgiver, that this concern is then equated with "all of virtue" at 630e, that justice appears as one virtue among four at 630a8, and finally that it is ranked third at 631c8. But none of this creates a problem of substance. Even in the *Republic* justice is spoken of in terms that make it the chief virtue, the one whose presence makes the other virtues possible (433b, 442d) and which can stand for virtue in general at the conclusion of that dialogue (612b-614a). On the other hand, it is also spoken of as the equal of the other three virtues and different from them (433d). The reason why, in spite of this, justice in the *Laws* is finally given only third rank has been explained above.

The passage at *Laws* 631c is undeniably difficult, and Plato has chosen an unusual and compressed way of making his point. The

other, he says. At 630a8-b2 Tyrtaeus' hero is said by implication to be courageous. Yet at 630b3-8 the same hero, caricatured as a mercenary, is denied every virtue. On the other hand, at 630a8 and 631c8 justice is one virtue among several, and not the first, but at 630c4-6 it is the greatest. The ranking of the virtues at 631c is so complicated, he decides, that no amount of interpretative effort can make it fully intelligible. Gigon surmises that behind the present scheme may lie a rational arrangement which Plato has muddled, viz. (1) wisdom, (2) wisdom and temperance, (3) wisdom, temperance, and courage, (4) these three and justice. But this, he adds, cannot be proved (p. 230).

Herwig Görgemanns' *Beiträge zur Interpretation von Platons Nomoi* (Munich, 1960), is a commendable effort to combat Müller's view of the *Laws* and to explain the dialogue instead as an attempt to make philosophical principles practical and detailed. The most obvious merit of Görgemanns' work is his opposition in principle to overly logical analysis of passages written in informal style (p. 118). He sees, for example, that the "courage" ranked fourth at 631cd is the "natural," not the philosophical virtue, although he admits that the ranking of "divine goods" is too difficult to explain as a whole (p. 129).

solution I offer, however, makes that point intelligible by reference to its context. There is no need to argue at length, in support of this solution, that Plato intends an analogy between the state and the individual: he says so at 626e-627a. We might expect, therefore, in the terse and obscure ranking of "divine goods" in the soul, some reference to the familial and political doctrine developed at 627d-628e, where communities are ranked by their degree of unity. An explanation which is supported by that analogy has every likelihood of being correct.

Though we can perhaps reconstruct the reasoning which led Plato to rank the "divine goods" as he does, it is still arguable that the procedure of *Laws* 631c implies a willingness to fragment virtue that is rare in his earlier works. As a reminder of his increased tendency in the *Laws* to exasperate his readers with more frequent and more rapid shifts of terminology, the argument would not be entirely false. But if it confidently assumed a consistent new doctrine, it would miss the mark. At 633cd we read that courage must fight against pleasure and desire as well as against fear and pain,[9] a statement which puts us suddenly in the presence of an old and familiar viewpoint. In short, two pages after the term "courage" has been shrunk to its narrowest dimensions and demoted to the lowest position on the scale of moral values, its scope is again enlarged in a way that takes us back to the *Laches*. This is not the only passage which rebukes our pretensions at establishing a distinct "late" ethical doctrine.[10] One of the statements quoted to prove that Plato eventually came to detach courage from the other virtues is found near the end of the *Laws*, at 963e: "A soul becomes courageous by natural endowment and without the help of reason." But within a page or two there occurs a remark which

9. The attribution to both courage and temperance of resistance to pleasure has been censured as illogical. Friedländer defended it against Zeller and Bruns as no more illogical than the identical overlapping in *Rep.* 430a, e (*Platon*, II, pp. 636 ff.). Müller (*Studien*, p. 17) has criticized him on the grounds that the overlapping in the *Republic* involves two elements of a unified virtue, both of which share the function of preserving knowledge, but that in the *Laws* fragmented virtues are involved which ought to be consistently distinguished if at all. But this argument is double-edged. The survival of the doctrine that courage fights pleasure serves as well to prove that Plato has not given up his old beliefs about the unity of virtue.

10. But see Raeder, *Platons Philos. Entwickelung*, p. 399.

puts that comment into its proper perspective: it is not enough for the Guardians to know how the virtues differ, but they should also know how they are one (965cd). Plato has not explained why they are one, contenting himself with the remark that the Guardians must know why. But for this omission he gives a good reason, one which is a distant echo of Socrates' reluctance to speak directly of the Good in the *Republic*, viz. that to explain this would be no easy matter (963d).

If virtue is knowledge, then vice is ignorance, and at times Plato clearly says as much. But whether this opinion was a doctrine of his early years which he later discarded or an unchanging conviction is a disputed question. His statements on this problem have played their part in the fertile controversies about the development of his ethics.[11] His doctrine of vice must obviously reflect his doctrine of virtue, and one might with some justification draw one's conclusions from the latter. But since Plato devotes several passages to a discussion of the nature of vice and its various kinds, there is more substantial evidence at hand. These passages are *Republic* 444a ff., *Timaeus* 86b ff., *Sophist* 227d ff., and *Laws* 860c ff. For the sake of clarity I shall first baldly summarize the four passages and then discuss the doctrine of each in comparison with the others. This will allow us to weigh the significance of their many differences in terminology and emphasis. In spite of these variations, the passages, I believe, are in essential harmony. Plato never ceased to believe that vice is ignorance, but it was not always his primary concern to stress that fact. This is why, although the *Republic* and the *Timaeus* maintain the doctrine, the *Sophist* and the *Laws* give the appearance of denying it.

In *Republic* 444a ff. Socrates has decided that justice in the soul is the proper arrangement of the soul's parts, the lower in subjection to the higher, with each doing its proper work. Just and fair action is what helps to produce and what preserves this condition of the soul; unjust action is what dissolves it. Wisdom ($\sigma o\phi\iota a$) is the knowledge ($\epsilon\pi\iota\sigma\tau\eta\mu\eta$) which presides over the former action; ignorance ($\dot{a}\mu a\theta\iota a$) is the opinion which presides over the latter. Injustice, on the other hand, is a kind of discord ($\sigma\tau\dot{a}\sigma\iota s$) of the

11. See below, note 18.

soul's three parts, a meddlesomeness and interference of one with another, a rebellion of part against whole. Such a disturbance is what we identify as injustice, incontinence, cowardice, ignorance (ἀμαθία), and, in short, all vice (444b6-8).

Timaeus 86b ff. is a discussion of diseases of the soul caused by conditions in the body. Folly (ἄνοια), the explanation begins, is a disease (νόσος) of the soul, and it is of two types, madness (μανία) and stupidity (ἀμαθία). Madness is an excess of pleasures or pains; such excesses are the worst diseases of the soul, for they cause a man temporary impairment of his thought and perception (86c). For example, a man whose "seed is overabundant" is subject to a kind of frenzy most of his life. His madness, called sexual incontinence, is not voluntary, but a disease of the soul caused by a physical condition. In fact, no variety of incontinence in pleasure is voluntary, though people call it that, for no one is voluntarily wicked. The soul suffers much from the body's pains as well as from its pleasures. Diseases of the soul are caused by different humors, acid, salt, bitter, and bilious, when they cannot find an outlet from the body. The nature of the soul's infirmity depends upon the part of the soul to which these humors are carried (86e5-87a7).[12]

12. At this point Timaeus adds a condemnation of those corrupt societies where the young can find no lessons to cure them of their moral ills. He concludes that the blame for these ills lies not so much with those who suffer from them as it does with their parents and with those responsible for their upbringing. The fact that it diminishes personal responsibility for wickedness by appealing to heredity and environment seems to A. E. Taylor to be one reason for putting this dialogue in a special category. In his Commentary on Plato's Timaeus (Oxford, 1928), he argues: (1) that the Timaeus as a whole is an example of fifth-century Pythagorean doctrine and is Platonic only to the extent that Plato would have been ready to "accept most of it" (p. ix); (2) that 86b ff. is one of the passages that Plato would not have accepted, because it "makes moral freedom and responsibility illusory" (p. 611). Taylor makes a distinction between two theories of choice. The first is the Platonic theory, that " if a man chooses at all, he chooses the alternative which seems to him best. Choice is always 'determined' by the agent's estimate of good." The second is "scientific" determinism, according to which "my 'choices' express my character and . . . this character in turn has been partly 'inherited' at birth, partly moulded by the interplay between my 'inherited' endowments and the characters of others who have influenced me" (p. 612). Taylor finds the two doctrines incompatible and sees the second one here at Tim. 86b. But the Timaeus does not espouse scientific determinism. It does lay stress on the physical and environmental influences on character formation, as one might expect in a scientific dialogue. It does not, however, exclude other influences;

The remedies which restore good health to the soul, a worthier subject than the mere inspection of its ailments, are taken up next. Since what is good is always beautiful or noble, and since the beautiful cannot exist without symmetry, then the restoration of goodness to the soul will be tantamount to a creation in it of symmetry. In matters of health and disease and of virtue and vice, no symmetry is more basic than that between soul and body. A man lacks it when he has a strong soul in a weak body or a weak soul in a strong body. In either event, he is a bit like a person whose legs are too long or who is otherwise deformed: not only is he ugly, but he is inefficient and clumsy too. In much the same way, when the physique is too weak to sustain the soul's activities, the body suffers. On the other hand, when a body too large and strong is joined to a small, weak intellect, the result is stupidity (ἀμαθία 88a7-b5). To get proper symmetry of body and soul one must exercise both. The bookish student must do gymnastics, and the man used to physical exertion must cultivate "music" and philosophy; each can then hope to be καλὸς κἀγαθός.

*Sophist* 227d ff. contains part of the Eleatic Stranger's attempt to define the "sophist" by dichotomies, and this happens to involve a classification of vice. The sophist, it is said, practices purification. Of this there are two kinds, of soul and of body. Purification of soul is the removal from it of evil, which can be of two sorts, the first like a disease (νόσος) in the body, the second like a deformity (αἶσχος). Disease is a discord (στάσις), a dissension, because of some corruption, between things naturally allied; deformity is the presence of disproportion, which is always ugly (228a). Now in the souls of the wicked, opinions are at variance with desires, anger with pleasures, reason with pains, and, in short, everything with

---

indeed, its brief exhortation at 87b6-8 implies that a man can to some degree form himself. Moreover, the passage, though scientific, adheres to the Platonic doctrine that "choice is always 'determined' by the agent's estimate of good" (Taylor's phrasing. I postpone to Chapter 7 the question whether "determined" is a proper term here). The three terms ἄνοια, μανία, and ἀμαθία imply that the body's ills and the environment corrupt choice by impairing the mind. That is to say, they affect "the agent's estimate of good."

F. M. Cornford, who refutes Taylor's explanation of this passage convincingly in *Plato's Cosmology* (New York, 1957), pp. 344-47, points out too that physical determinism would be an anachronism in the *Timaeus*.

everything else. But all these should be in concord. Therefore wickedness (πονηρία) is a discord and disease of the soul. On the other hand, a soul can suffer disproportion too (ἀμετρία), which is the cause of ignorance (ἄγνοια). When a moving object misses its goal we attribute its failure to a lack of proportion, and ignorance is merely the derangement of a soul moving towards truth when it swerves away from understanding (228c10 ff.). The foolish soul, therefore, is deformed and ill proportioned (αἰσχρὰν καὶ ἄμετρον).

There are, then, two kinds of evil (κακία) in the soul. The first is called wickedness by the common people and is a disease. It includes cowardice, intemperance, and injustice (228e), or, in another summation a few lines later, insolence, injustice, and cowardice (229a). The other type of evil the many call ignorance (ἄγνοια), but they are not willing to acknowledge it as κακία (228d10-11) when it occurs alone in the soul. The remedy for deformity in the body is gymnastics, for disease in the body, the medical art. For the corresponding deficiencies of the soul the remedies are the art of punishment for discord in the soul and the art of teaching (διδασκαλική) for ignorance. Now there are at least two kinds of ignorance. The lesser varieties, taken together, are cured by ordinary instruction in the crafts. The greatest variety is stupidity (ἀμαθία), the false belief that one has knowledge (229c), and it outweighs all other kinds.[13] Moreover, it is in some way a fundamental cause of all intellectual error. The branch of the art of teaching designed to remove this greatest ignorance is education

13. The "greatest stupidity" (ἀμαθία) described at Laws 689a ff. does not correspond to what is described in similar terms here. In the Laws it is attributed to one who hates what he believes to be fair and good and loves what he believes wicked and unjust. The condition there referred to (also designated ἄνοια at 689b3) is evidently one in which the soul's lower parts oppose reason. It exists not only in individuals but in states too when the lower classes disobey their rulers. Unlike the ἀμαθία of Sophist 229c and Tim. 88b, the type in question in the Laws passage is not the lack of right opinion through a fault of intelligence. Though in other dialogues Plato reserved his sharpest judgments for a subdivision of the latter, viz. the conceit of wisdom (cf., apart from the Sophist, Apol. 21c and Philebus 48c ff.), he here omits the whole category. His motive lies in the political analogy. In the context he wishes to attribute the downfall of states to the disobedience of the masses (Laws 689b4-5). When the comparison of state and individual appears, therefore, his special condemnation descends on the opposition of pain and pleasure to right opinion. In short, the needs of the political discussion limit the scope of his remarks on ethics.

(παιδεία), of which there are two kinds. The first, practiced by fathers upon errant sons, is the art of admonition. But some teachers believe that admonition takes great trouble to achieve little, because all ἀμαθία is involuntary and a man who thinks himself wise in something will never wish to be instructed in it. These teachers try to remove ἀμαθία in another way, by questioning a man until he sees that his opinions contradict one another. When he understands this he will be angry with himself and gentle with others and will finally be freed from his stubborn self-assurance.[14]

A final discussion of the causes of vice appears at *Laws* 86oc ff. It is hard, comments the Athenian Stranger, to make laws to punish injustice, since the ordinary distinction between willing and unwilling offenders, which dictates the size of the penalty, means nothing if all unjust acts are involuntary. If the lawgiver is to keep his belief that no man errs willingly and yet distinguish between two kinds of crime, he must find another ground of distinction. The solution is to divide injuries into two aspects: (1) the injury proper, (2) the injustice, if any. The injury proper is to be remedied by

14. G. B. Kerferd, "Plato's Noble Art of Sophistry," *CQ*, 48, N.S. 4 (1954), 84-90, maintains that this passage is less important than usually thought for a study of Plato's ethical thought. The article was written to contest the views of Hackforth and Dodds, explained in note 18 below. Kerferd thinks that "for the special purposes of the present dialogue he [i.e. Plato] is using the popular view of the matter which distinguished wrongdoing from ignorance" (p. 88). Although I agree, on grounds explained below, that Plato does not here repudiate the doctrine that vice is ignorance, I think some of Kerferd's reasons are wrong. According to him, the phrase κατὰ τὴν ἀνθρωπίνην δόξαν at 229a6 suggests "that it is not the teaching of Plato, but simply popular opinion, which would punish πονηρία by κολαστική. On the other hand, ἄγνοια is definitely stated to be the result of a popular classification, and the Stranger adds that οἱ πολλοί refuse to regard it as vicious when it occurs by itself in the soul (228d10-11)" (pp. 87-88). Now, in the first place, Theaetetus' reply at 229a6 means, "It is likely at any rate, as far as human opinion allows one to say." (Cf. the use of ἀνθρώπινος at *Apol.* 20d8 and *Phaedo* 107b1.) This is certainly an assent and not a report of what the common people think. The doctrine, moreover, is a suggestion of the Stranger not attributed by him to anyone else. In the second place, 228d10 does not mean that ἄγνοια is the result of popular classification. The distinctive popular doctrine is contained in the δὲ clause, the rejection by the common people of κακία as an epithet of ἄγνοια. Although they call the affliction ἄγνοια (like the Stranger), they refuse to call it κακία. He *does* call it κακία (227d13) and to this extent is not purveying popular doctrine at all. N. B. Booth, "Plato, *Sophist* 231a," *CQ*, 50, N.S. 6 (1956), 89-90, offers some good general objections to Kerferd's view. He points out that the notion of στάσις in the soul is a corollary of the doctrines of the tripartite soul and the multiplicity of virtue in the *Republic*.

compensation and restoration of the impaired friendship. Where injustice too is present, the guilty person must be cured; he must not only pay for the injury but also be compelled never or hardly ever to repeat his offense. Incurables will be executed (862c-e). A mere injury, then, is external and accidental; an act of injustice is the symptom of a fault in the soul.

Clinias, one of the listeners, asks for a clearer explanation of this distinction between injustice and injury and of their confusion with the other pair of terms, "voluntary" and "involuntary" (863a3-6). The Athenian Stranger replies by enumerating three causes of wrongs (ἁμαρτήματα 863c1): anger, pleasure, and ignorance. Ignorance is of two kinds: simple ignorance, a source of slight errors, and the compound ignorance of one who does not know but thinks he does, a source of great errors. Common speech recognizes a difference between ignorance and the other two causes: men are said to get the better of pleasure or anger, or to be bested by them, but these terms are not applied to ignorance. Nevertheless, all three will often induce a man to do the opposite of his own wish (863e2-3). In the light of this, what, then, is the proper use of the terms "just" and "unjust," "voluntary" and "involuntary?" Injustice, the Athenian Stranger concludes, is the tyranny of anger and fear, pleasure and pain, envy and desire in the soul, whether it cause injury or not. To judge from 863e2-3 (paraphrased above), this means that injustice is an affliction of the contentious, the pleasure-loving, and the ignorant alike.[15] The lower impulses can tyrannize the

15. The common interpretation is that wrongs done in anger or pleasure are here called unjust but wrongs done in ignorance are not. This is then usually taken to mean that a man who abides by his conscience, however erroneous, is a just man. Such is the stated view, or implication, of E. B. England, The Laws of Plato (Manchester, 1921), 2.403; G. M. A. Grube, Plato's Thought (London, 1935), pp. 228-29; R. Hackforth, "Moral Evil and Ignorance in Plato's Ethics," CQ, 40 (1946), 119; Constantin Ritter, Platons Gesetze: Kommentar zum Griech. Text (Leipzig, 1896), p. 283; and the great majority of other scholars. It is generally acknowledged, however, that such a doctrine contradicts Rep. 444a1-b8, where all injustice is attended by ignorance, and ignorance is a form of injustice. The common interpretation of Laws 860c ff., therefore, implies a radical change from Plato's earlier views.

My objections to this interpretation are as follows:

(A) It is clear from the way in which the passage begins and ends (863a3-6, 864a6-8) that it is meant to satisfy Clinias' request by explaining the distinctions already drawn between injury and injustice and between voluntary and involuntary. There is even a verbal reminiscence of Clinias' words at 863a4-6 (ἥδιον δ' ἂν ἔτι σαφέστερον ἀκούσαιμεν . . . διαπεποίκιλται) when the Stranger begins his résumé (σαφῶς ἂν διορισαίμην οὐδὲν ποικίλλων 863e6). Moreover, the two conditions finally described at 863e5-864a8 are (a) tyranny by the soul's lower impulses and (b) a condition which causes what is commonly and wrongly called an "involuntary injustice" (864a7). Now the whole passage was motivated by the popular use of this last phrase (861b4-5). Plato substitutes for it the notion of "mere injury." The coincidence of phrasing, moreover, between 862a5-6 and 864a7-8 confirms that both these passages make the same point, i.e. they divide offenses at law into injustice and injury. There is no room whatever for a third category to fall between these two, viz. the deliberate and wrong but just action of the erroneous conscience.

(B) The crime caused by the erroneous conscience will not fall into the category of mere injury either. The latter is a purely external accident, for which external penalties, compensation or ritual purification, are prescribed. Plato has in mind, for example, accidental killings in the public games (865a) and wounds due to chance (879b1-3).

(C) Offenses due to an erring conscience must then fall under the heading of injustice, and this is where Plato puts them. Ignorance, though it is not said to impair a man's self-mastery in the usual sense, is nevertheless one of the three causes which turn a man against his own real wishes (863d6-e3). The other two are anger and pleasure. The emphatic phrasing πάντα δέ γε at 863e2 shows that the Stranger, as he moves into his summary, is grouping the three together. A moment later he states in different words the principle of this grouping: they are all injustice. Anger and pleasure cause (and ignorance, by implication, permits) tyranny in the soul.

I argued in favor of this interpretation in "Plato and the 'Good Conscience': Laws 863e5-864b7," TAPA, 88 (1958), 81-87, and I have since noticed that it is consistent with the views presented, but not defended in detail, by A. Jagu in "La Conception Platonicienne de la Liberté," in Mélanges A. Diès (Paris, 1956), pp. 133-34. My view was criticized by Herwig Görgemanns (Beiträge, pp. 136-40). Görgemanns maintains three points in disagreement with it:

(1) Ἄγνοια is not an injustice. My reasons for thinking otherwise are stated above.

(2) By ἄγνοια Plato means an ignorance of ways and means, causing mere injury. In this he agrees with Müller (Studien, p. 58). But there is a decisive objection to this. A "mere injury" is an accident; it can issue by chance from a state of mind that is "best for the whole life of men" (864a6). On the other hand, whatever Plato means by "simple ignorance" in 863c1 ff., his description of the ignorant assurance which comes with a conceit of wisdom is strongly reminiscent of Sophist 229c-230e, not to mention Apol. 21c5-7. Concerning this kind of ignorance, which must be treated by the laborious Socratic method, and which can turn a man against his own wishes (863e2-3), thus placing him in the predicament of the tyrant of Gorgias 467b, one can hardly say "dass sie 'technisch,' nicht sittlich ist" (Görgemanns, p. 140).

(3) δόξης τῆς ἀληθοῦς . . . ἔφεσις (864b7) means the "(Verwirklichungs-) Streben von . . . wahrer Meinung," which happens to produce an injury (p. 140). Now it is true, as Görgemanns says, that this phrase must refer to ignorance, for the word δεδήλωται shows that 864b1-7 is a repetition of the threefold classification at 863b1-c2. Regarding this ignorance, however, as one of technique, not moral truth, he takes δόξης as subjective genitive with ἔφεσις rather than objective genitive. This must be wrong, if the ignorance is moral. The phrase then means "an (unsuccessful) aiming at true opinion."

soul either directly, by their own violence, or indirectly, by the submission to them of an intellect unaware of its proper end. The just act, on the other hand, is that which is in accord with a man's "conviction of the best," in whatever way cities or individuals think they can achieve it.[16] As long as this conviction rules in a man's soul, even if he injures someone unintentionally, such an act is just, though it is commonly called an "involuntary injustice." The Athenian Stranger then restates the three causes of wrongdoing: (1) anger and fear, which come from pain; (2) pleasure and desire; (3) ignorance.

The reader will have noticed a great disparity of terminology in these four passages. In the *Republic* moral defect is called a number of things, all equivalent: injustice (ἀδικία), "a sort of discord" (στάσις τις), vice (κακία), disease (νόσος), deformity (αἶσχος), and weakness (ἀσθένεια). Moreover, such a defect, however designated, is always associated with stupidity (ἀμαθία). In the *Timaeus* all moral defect is designated folly (ἄνοια) or disease (νόσος) and divided into madness (μανία) and stupidity (ἀμαθία). In the *Sophist* vice (κακία) is divided into (1) disease (νόσος), also called discord (στάσις) or wickedness (πονηρία), and (2) deformity (αἶσχος), also called disproportion (ἀμετρία) and equated with ignorance (ἄγνοια). Stupidity (ἀμαθία) is one subdivision of ignorance. In the *Laws* the causes of wrongdoing are listed as three: anger, pleasure, and ignorance (ἄγνοια). The verbal inconsistencies are great. The word νόσος is twice used as a generic term for vice and once as a subdivision of it; αἶσχος is now used to mean any kind of vice that is not νόσος, and is then used as a synonym for νόσος; ἀμαθία now means one kind of ἄγνοια, which in turn is one kind of κακία, then means ignorance in general, which is only one kind of vice, and then it is said to preside over all vice.

Either Platonic doctrine changed kaleidoscopically or, as I think, the four classifications are simply not meant to be commensurable. Such wide variation in the use of terms can be expected.

16. τὴν δὲ κτλ. (864a1-3), as (C) of the previous note indicates, cannot allude to ignorance. The δόξα τοῦ ἀρίστου is therefore the conviction which has the best for its object, and the next clause (read τοῦτό γ᾽ for τούτων, after Hermann) means simply that not everyone will decide to achieve the best in the same way.

For Plato they are not part of a rigid terminology but common words used in civilized conversation, and any distinctions made for clarity of discussion in one passage need not be assumed in another. The identification in the *Republic*, for example, of νόσος and αἶσχος, so carefully distinguished in the *Sophist*, is quite reasonable in the absence of a dialectic need to make a distinction. In the *Republic*, injustice is νόσος because it involves the unhealthy predominance of a lower impulse, and αἶσχος because evil and disorder are ugly. In the *Sophist*, on the other hand, Plato needs two terms to distinguish between a turmoil caused by unruly passions and a lack of symmetry caused by a defect of intellect. He chooses νόσος and αἶσχος, which are suitable and clear in the context.

In two of the passages all vice is a kind of ignorance. The *Republic* says simply that over all unjust action presides ἀμαθία. The *Timaeus*, which characterizes all vice as folly or lack of sense (ἄνοια), divides it into two kinds. When due to passion or pain it is called madness (μανία), a distortion of reason caused not by innate incapacity but by an absence of that tranquillity which reason requires in order to judge well. This tranquillity is the proper disposition of the seats of desire and fear. The other kind of folly is stupidity (ἀμαθία), a lack of development in the intellect itself. The importance of the *Timaeus* passage is that in it Plato explains why he regards vice as essentially an affair of the mind, a lack of good sense. Intemperance, though its source is in the body, can affect behavior only through clouding the reason. The madman, so called, whose soul is made diseased and senseless by the body (86d1-2), has no share in reason when pleasure or pain overwhelms him: λογισμοῦ μετασχεῖν ἥκιστα τότε δὴ δυνατός (86c3). This impairment of reason is what makes the offense "involuntary." It is implied that other emotions can blind the reason too, bad temper, cowardly fear, and rashness (87a5-6, 86e3-5). Bad humors in the body can even affect the mind directly and permanently, making it forgetful and dull (87a7). In short, the aberrations of the "madman" and the constitutional defect of the stupid confirm the doctrine that vice is essentially unreasonable behavior.

Why, then, does Plato imply in the *Sophist* and *Laws* that some defects of the soul are reducible to ignorance but others are not?

The reason is that in the *Sophist* the standpoint is pedagogic and in the *Laws* juridical, and the standpoint is what determines the method of division. In the one dialogue the Eleatic Stranger wants to isolate and define the function of the sophist by dichotomy. He divides moral defects into those requiring chastisement and those requiring instruction. For the defect that instruction remedies there is no more natural term than ignorance. It would be true but irrelevant in the context to point out that chastisement is also meant to remove ignorance in another, purely Platonic, sense of that word and that it ultimately improves the mind, though it acts directly upon the lower parts. This would only introduce another principle of division. The choice of terms in the *Sophist* is well suited to explain the fact that the arts designed to remedy vice must be of two kinds, and this is what it is meant to do.

The classification of vices in the *Laws* is likewise remedial in intent. The purpose of the best laws, Plato has said in a passage just preceding (862d4 ff.), is to make a man hate injustice and love—or at least not hate—justice; they effect this purpose by words and actions, pleasures and pains, honors and penalties, fines and rewards. Laws are meant to cure the individual, if possible, and the society. A lawgiver's division of the causes of crime will therefore be designed to suggest the treatment or punishment suited to each offense.[17] He need be concerned with ignorance only insofar

17. The long section that begins at 865a confirms the purely legal interest of the theory of vice in the *Laws*. It deals with crimes of murder and physical injury and distinguishes between voluntary and involuntary crimes. Among the latter Plato includes, e.g., accidental killings (865a). For these, certain light penalties are prescribed as purifications. In a class between voluntary and involuntary and resembling both are killings done in anger. Of these there are two kinds (866d ff.): (1) sudden crimes of anger done without forethought and followed by repentance, (2) deliberate and planned murders of revenge. Of these two, the impulsive act resembles the involuntary and the planned act the voluntary. Therefore the latter act is punished more heavily (867b). Finally, there are voluntary crimes, due to injustice in the full sense, premeditated, and caused by yielding to pleasure, desire, and envy (869e). The use of "voluntary" (ἑκούσιον) and "involuntary" (ἀκούσιον) here is legal and not philosophical, i.e. it classifies crimes as injuries and not as injustices. The involuntary injury is not an injustice at all. The voluntary injury and the injury done in anger, hence more or less voluntary, are acts of injustice. As such they are both involuntary. A deliberate crime can be both voluntary and involuntary because it has two aspects: there is a wish to injure; there is no wish to do evil as such. (Cf. the reference to voluntary and involuntary lies at *Laws* 730c.)

as it is caused by defect of intellect and may be cured by instruction; that ignorance, in another sense, is an element in every offense is not to the point. In varying the meaning that he gives in different passages to the word "ignorance" (ἄγνοια, ἀμαθία), Plato does no more than he does with the other terms αἶσχος and νόσος, noted above. Here, as almost everywhere else, he uses common words to express his doctrines and uses them with some freedom.[18]

18. The usual way of explaining discrepancies between Plato's earlier and later pronouncements on virtue and vice has been to say that his views changed. This interpretation was made classic by Eduard Zeller in his *Die Philosophie der Griechen*, 2. Theil 1. Abth. (4th ed.; Leipzig, 1889), 746-48. Socrates, said Zeller, thought virtue was simply knowledge and could be implanted by instruction. Plato at first believed this too, but he later came to see the importance of the nonrational. T. Gomperz, *Griechische Denker* (2nd ed.; Leipzig, 1903-9), 2.239-40 and 285-86, espoused the same theory and dismissed Plato's continued repetitions of the maxim "No man errs on purpose" as the vestiges of a lost faith. Hans Raeder devoted a book to a defense of the theory of development, *Platons Philos. Entwickelung*, and had Plato gradually slough off Socratic intellectualism (pp. 96-97, 99, 210-11, 215, 402). The main stages are: the use of right opinion as a substitute for knowledge in the *Meno*, the tripartition of the soul in the *Republic*, and the statement that ignorance is only one cause of wrongdoing in *Laws* 860c ff. (Cf. Gomperz, 2.522-23.) One can find substantially the same arguments in: Max Pohlenz, *Aus Platos Werdezeit* (Berlin, 1913), p. 103; Andreas Leissner, *Platonische Lehre von den Seelenteilen* (1909), p. 29; Fritz Seidel, *Intellektualismus und Voluntarismus in der Platonischen Ethik* (Weida i. Th., 1910), pp. 9-10, 36-37, 43-45, 63, 96, 105-6; M. Croiset (ed.), *Hippias Mineur, Alcibiade, Apologie de Socrate, Euthyphron, Criton* (Paris, 1920), p. 22.

The theory still finds many defenders. E. R. Dodds, in "Plato and the Irrational," *JHS*, 65 (1945), 16-25, argues that in his later works Plato "no longer makes ignorance the sole cause of wrongdoing, or increased knowledge its sole cure" (p. 18). The evidence that he "comes to recognize an irrational factor within the mind itself, and so gradually develops a deeper view of moral evil as being the result of psychological conflict" Dodds finds thoroughly worked out for the first time in *Sophist* 227d-228e. He sees it even in *Tim.* 86b ff. "where a wide range of emotional disorders, including sexual excesses, irritability and despondency, rashness and cowardice, and even forgetfulness and stupidity, are attributed by Plato to bodily causes over which the victim has no control. . . .Here surely Plato's thinking has swung to the opposite pole from the intellectualism with which he started" (p. 19). Yet the *Timaeus* passage shows unmistakable traces of the intellectualism which Dodds thinks has vanished (see text above). R. Hackforth, in an article devoted to the four passages discussed above (*Rep.* 444b ff., *Tim.* 86b ff., *Sophist* 227d ff., *Laws* 863b ff.), calls the later doctrine of the *Sophist* and *Laws* an overcompensation for what Plato acknowledged to be an error in his earlier theory: first he stressed the role of ignorance in wrongdoing too much; then he stressed it too little ("Moral Evil and Ignorance," pp. 118-120).

There have been other ways of solving the apparent discrepancies in Plato's statements about virtue and vice. One way is simply to acknowledge the simultaneous existence of two unreconciled tendencies, (1) Socratic intel-

The last sentence sums up much of the argument of this chapter. It is no easy matter to discuss adequately so complex a subject as virtue and vice, and Plato therefore tends to deal with one aspect at a time. He varies his presentation from dialogue to dialogue, showing little concern in one for what he has said in any of the others. He is no more concerned to reconcile verbal divergences in different passages than he would be to merge the images of the chariot and the lion into a composite metaphor of the soul. A metaphor makes a point, approximates a truth, and can then be discarded for another. A definition or a particular way of analyzing a subject is hardly more sacrosanct. What will throw a flood of light on one problem may only obscure another. These convictions, or something like them, underlie Plato's determinedly unsystematic manner of writing philosophy. Beneath that manner, he remains faithful, even in his latest works, to the general principles of ethics laid down in the early Socratic dialogues. The ethical paradoxes survive to the end in substance, and occasionally in form, but the will to astonish, inherited from Socrates, which Plato expressed through them, has been tempered with the years.

---

lectualism, and (2) the common-sense view that emotion and habit count for something. This has been maintained by Otto Apelt, *Platonische Aufsätze* (Leipzig, 1912), p. 192; Francesco Guglielmino, *Preconcetti Teorici e Realismo in Platone* (Catania, 1936), p. 32 in particular; and Raphael Demos, *The Philosophy of Plato* (New York, 1939), p. 321. It was Paul Shorey who argued with most telling effect against the uncritical use of any theory which assumes contradiction or change. He claimed instead that Plato's dialogues display "the naturally varied expression of a homogeneous body of opinion" (*The Unity of Plato's Thought* [Chicago, 1903], pp. 4-5). Not all editors magnify insignificant variations in wording. See, e.g., R. D. Archer-Hind's ed. of the *Timaeus* (London, 1888), p. 323. The recent book by John Rist, *Eros and Psyche, Studies in Plato, Plotinus, and Origen* (Toronto, 1964), supposes Plato's gradual acceptance of restrictions on the Socratic doctrine that virtue is knowledge (pp. 143-56). Plato came to realize, e.g., that "habit is the key to morals for the majority of mankind" (p. 147) and that there is a kind of virtue which is governed by right opinion rather than by knowledge. Nevertheless, given the proper qualifications, it remains true that "Plato held up to the end of his life that for the philosopher virtue is knowledge" (p. 156).

# 7. INTELLECT,
# WILL, AND EROS

If we are right in concluding that Platonic ethics embodies a unified set of doctrines, then it should be possible to draw together in a single comprehensive summary all its ostensibly inharmonious components. These fall, roughly speaking, into two groups, one associated with Plato's youth, the other with his full maturity and old age. They are, respectively, the Socratic paradoxes and the doctrines connected with the partition of the soul. Now that they no longer need be regarded as logically incompatible, they can be seen instead for what they really are: two different ways of presenting the complex and original ethics which Plato built upon the intellectualism of Socrates. In short, they are alternative pedagogic techniques. The paradoxes are an affirmation of the rational unity of human nature and human action; the partition of the soul is an acknowledgment of the irrational multiplicity of both. What they teach in combination can be reduced to a pair of complementary propositions: virtue is knowledge, and it is more than knowledge.

The ordinary man of philosophic bent who harbors no Platonic prejudice would see in the second of these two propositions a rough summation of what common sense and introspection have always told him. It would probably involve for him a reference to the will. Yet if he looked for an affirmation of the importance of will in Plato, he would be disappointed, or at most would find a few references which left its freedom, even its existence, in grave doubt. This is a problem as vexing and as subtle as any in Platonic ethics, enlivened but scarcely illuminated by the flatly contradictory statements of scholars in mutual disagreement. Yet anyone who pretends to explain the meaning of Plato's intellectualism cannot ignore it. We shall therefore take it up as the last, and perhaps most interesting, of the many problems with which this study is concerned. In exploring its implications we shall rediscover, from a new direction and with a fresh point of view, a well-known aspect of Platonic thought which this book has so far neglected, the doctrine of Eros, or Love.

We begin, then, with a summary of Plato's position by amplifying, in the light of the conclusions reached in earlier chapters, the two complementary statements already mentioned.

Virtue is knowledge because, in the first place, a man's nature is made primarily for knowledge. This means simply that knowledge as a value takes precedence over all other activities of which he is capable. On earth, it is true, even the best and most fortunate man will be constrained by the demands of the body to devote only a fraction of his time to pure intellection. But the ideal state to which he aspires, the perfect model which gives meaning to his existence, is that of a bodiless soul. To such a soul only the activity of knowledge remains, since no effort need be expended in controlling a body and acceding to its requirements. Man in a state of perfection, then, is pure intelligence, and his activity is purely intellectual. Since virtue is merely excellence of activity, his virtue in the ideal order is knowledge.

Dialectic and contemplation occupy much of the philosopher's time on earth, and to that extent the paradox that virtue is knowledge is true for him even before his soul wins its freedom from the body. But it is true in another sense too, and true for every man, since all virtuous activity in this life which is not itself knowledge is an expression of knowledge. The reason for this is that every man's conscious activity is always fully consistent with his knowledge or opinion at the moment of choice. This is not to say that what he knows or believes fully determines what he does. It means only that any decision is the immediate expression of what he knows or believes at the moment he makes the decision. In other words, the state of his emotions may help decide his course of action, but it will do so only by influencing what comes to his mind when he makes his practical judgment. The average decision may be influenced by emotions and habits, by pressure and persuasion, by the digestion and the circulation, and finally by intellectual capacity and the permanent fund of knowledge. In the process of reaching a decision all of these will interact,[1] and the final distillate will be a practical judgment of the reason: "This is the best course of action." Whatever form such a judgment may take, it is always implied in any conscious choice, and often expressed. Whether an action is virtuous, therefore, depends entirely on whether the practical judgment is correct; and since the practical judgment is merely a summary expression of what one knows or believes at the instant of decision, expressed in its relation to a single possible act, virtue is knowledge.[2] Some men, it is true, who lack knowledge in the proper

1. The word "interact" is used here in a way that will require qualification later in this chapter.

2. The whole question of knowledge in Platonic ethics was given an interesting turn by the appearance of John Gould's book *The Development of Plato's Ethics* (Cambridge, 1955). Gould proposes to disprove the "widely held" current theory that what Socrates believed was simply that "knowledge of moral facts involves morally correct behaviour" (p. 4). He begins with the words ἐπιστήμη and ἐπίστασθαι, which often mean, he says (1) "knowing how" to do something, (2) confidence, subjective certainty. These meanings, moreover, are for him the essential ones in the Socratic and Platonic identification of virtue and ἐπιστήμη. "Since ἐπιστήμη does not imply contemplation of an object, but understanding, in the sense of an ability to act, it remains a purely subjective 'faith.' It retains this characteristic, or so I believe, in Plato's early dialogues" (p. 15). Gould thinks that the implication of *Gorgias* 472b6 ff. is "that the business of a philosopher is simply to produce conviction in those with whom he talks. . . . 'In fact,' Socrates claims [to Callicles at 487e1 ff.], 'when you and I agree, we shall finally possess the truth'" (p. 18). The word ἐπιστήμη represents "a moral assurance, perhaps without objective justification, but sufficient to make action follow" (p. 21). If the last phrase seems to contradict the well-known fact that many steal, for example, who know they ought not to, this only means that they "had not, in fact, attained ἐπιστήμη." Ἐπιστήμη involves the "ability to react instinctively . . . to various moral sit-

sense of the word, act virtuously on the basis of right opinions learned from parents, teachers, or rulers. But this only means that their decisions express other men's knowledge, not their own.

On the other hand, virtue is more than knowledge, because moral excellence in the form attainable on earth is complex in its genesis and in its nature. It cannot be otherwise as long as the soul is associated with a body. This imprisonment of the soul in

---

uations" as much as "the explicit and conscious formulae which might express a man's intellectual attitude toward the same situations" (p. 52).

Now ἐπίστασθαι without a doubt often means "knowing how to do something." But the rest of Gould's theory is open to serious objection. Socrates at *Gorgias* 472b6 ff. does not define his business merely as producing conviction in Polus. This is how he defines his *method*, as opposed to the "courtroom" method of Polus, who (says Socrates) tries to make his point by counting off those who agree with him. Socrates' business, more properly defined, is to convince Polus of the truth and the reality, a point emphatically made here (472a1, b6; cf. 479e8). The reason why Polus' method cannot guarantee truth is given, viz. the availability of false witnesses (472a1). The superiority of Socrates' method for finding truth is not explained. But the practice of his elenchus here and elsewhere readily discloses its advantage: it clarifies logical relationships and so exposes falsehood. The later remark, made by Socrates to Callicles at 487e1 ff., that their agreement will guarantee the truth is patently branded as sarcasm (Callicles has "good will" and "wisdom," 487a3, e4). G. Vlastos has exposed a more basic weakness in Gould's theory. The definition of ἐπίστασθαι as confidence or subjective certainty is clear in Herodotus in less than 15 per cent of its occurrences (in the verbal form), and hardly anywhere else in Greek literature. Gould offers no examples in Attic. Its irrelevance to Plato's ethics is shown by the elenchus itself, the purpose of which is to correct false beliefs. This certainly implies that "knowing how" to be moral depends on "knowing that" such and such is right or wrong ("Socratic Knowledge and Platonic 'Pessimism'," *Philosophical Review*, 66 [1957], 226-38, esp. 226-28). Vlastos also doubts that ἐπιστήμη, even as confidence and "know-how," could make a man "so invulnerable to 'rage, pleasure, grief, love, terror' " that he would never act contrary to it under stress (p. 231). Gould, in other words, does not escape the objection to Arnim's theory (see Chapt. 5, note 9, above). R. E. Allen has pointed out with justification that Gould's explanation of the elenchus has introduced anachronistically into Plato the contemporary notion of the "persuasive definition," which is actually a disguised recommendation that redirects attitudes by redefining terms ("The Socratic Paradox," *JHI*, 21 [1960], 259-60). John Rist, *Eros and Psyche, Studies in Plato, Plotinus, and Origen* (Toronto, 1964), pp. 115-42, has a lengthy and critical discussion of Gould's theory.

A. Vergez describes Platonic morality as a technique of techniques, i.e., as the knowledge how to apply all other techniques. But he insists, correctly, that it is an expression of reason and the Good ("Technique et Morale chez Platon," *R. Philos.*, 146 [1956], 9-15). The role of knowledge in Platonic ethics is also discussed ably by J. Moreau, in his article "Platon et la Connaissance de l'Âme," *REA* 55 (1953), 249-57. Moreau stresses the central importance of rational judgment in the moral act but perceives that this "intellectualism" does not deny the conflicts of the inner moral life (pp. 255-56).

the body is described sometimes as a cause (*Republic* 611a10 ff.),
sometimes as an effect (*Phaedrus* 248c2 ff.) of man's imperfect nature. The practical result and the evidence of this imperfection is
the presence in his soul of three distinct kinds of activity, rational,
assertive, and appetitive, each of which demands a separate principle, or part of the soul, as its source. Man's multiplicity of nature
tends to hinder the exercise of reason, his highest activity, since it
makes him the occasional, if not the constant, victim of fear, anger,
and appetite. For a man to act well, therefore, he must not only
know the good but he must also control the disruptive influences
within him. In fact, knowledge could not exist without such control, since uncontrolled emotion would cloud the judgment. On the
other hand, proper control of one's lower impulses presupposes
knowledge (although that knowledge need be present only in the
mind of a teacher or parent) since emotional discipline must be
exercised according to rational rule.

This mutual dependence of knowledge and discipline means
that for man on earth virtue is complex: it is always an expression
of reason, but it involves regulation as well as cognition. Reason
must exercise and mold the lower impulses in order to create in
them permanent dispositions to follow its commands. The creation
of these dispositions will therefore be the first step in the education
of the young. Not all will undergo such a discipline with profit,
but only those who already possess a certain inborn nobility of
character. The first component of virtue is therefore a good nature,
which Plato usually describes as gentleness balanced by vigor.
The man who possesses these qualities is already, in a loose sense,
both temperate and courageous. Commonly, however, these natural qualities are excessive or defective before education, as they
are in a man who has been badly educated. It is the purpose of
musical and gymnastic training to correct any such disproportion
and, by enforced habit, to channel natural impulses towards virtuous ends. When this training is complete, the student can be
said, in a stricter sense, to possess temperance and courage, and
the attachment of each of his soul's parts to its proper end will also
make him just. If intellectually qualified, he is then ready to ex-

amine, by long and arduous intellectual study, the purposes which underlie the order in his soul and in the state. He is, in short, ready to replace right opinion with knowledge. His eventual achievement of this knowledge is the final step in the perfection of his virtue. At this last stage he will possess the virtues of temperance and courage in the form of natural tendencies governed by a rational discipline whose ultimate purpose he understands and is capable of defending in argument. But to describe his perfected virtue as knowledge alone would be to overlook the excellence of moral character without which his knowledge could not exist.

If we turn our attention from the permanent dispositions of the good man to his particular actions, we find the same need to introduce qualifications into the stark simplicity of the paradox that virtue is knowledge. Briefly, each individual virtuous act is an expression of character as well as of judgment. If a man makes a correct choice, it is not only because of intellectual capacity and his fund of knowledge or right opinion, but also because his courage and temperance have prevented the cowardly or irascible or pleasurable impulses in him from clouding his reason in its exercise of judgment. In the struggle among conflicting motives which precedes this judgment, these two virtues appear in different ways. A man is courageous when he resists the impulse to be afraid of danger or pain, and he is no less courageous when he resists the impulse to pleasure. He is temperate when he quells excessive anger or rashness, but he is also temperate when he allows his desires to subside. The two virtues will often seem only two different aspects of the same thing. In the internal moral struggle of anger and desire, for example, or of shame and desire, one virtue is the inevitable complement of the other: a man is brave because he opposes desire, and he is temperate because his desires subside. If he possesses one of these virtues fully, he will possess the other too. Wisdom remains the primary virtue, since every good act is always a wise act, whether directed by knowledge or by right opinion. But Plato's concern in all periods with the conditions and prerequisites of moral conduct show his unalterable belief that every life wisely lived is also a series of triumphs of temperance, courage, and justice, and not of wisdom alone.[3]

Plato's ethical intellectualism radically influenced even his conception of the soul's first movement toward virtue. One of the teachings which he owed to the collective wisdom of Greece was the admonition of the Delphic Apollo, "Know thyself." Self-knowledge, already endowed with moral implications in the usage of poets and wise men who preceded Plato, became for him in a peculiar way the source of virtue. When Socrates went about Athens interrogating politicians, poets, and artisans, his attack was directed not primarily at dishonesty, cowardice, or intemperance, but at that ignorance which allowed these to flourish, and above all at the self-delusion which was its worst form. The Athenians of each class whom he questioned, as he says at *Apology* 21b ff., were unaware of their own ignorance and were unwilling to have it pointed out to them. The fundamental virtue, the seed from which all others might eventually grow, and which remained the only form of wisdom that Socrates claimed for himself, was the freedom from this self-delusion. For this reason, he conceived of his divine mission as above all the liberation of men's minds from the heavy incubus of an ingrained, self-sustaining ignorance. This liberation held the same priority for him and for Plato as conversion, the sinner's response to divine grace, came to hold for Christians. Moreover, in

3. This point has been overlooked by Gerasimos Santas, who in "The Socratic Paradoxes," *Philosophical Review*, 72 (1964), 147-64, maintains that Plato's account of the relation of knowledge to conduct is "far more plausible than it is usually supposed to be" (p. 164). He confines his discussion to the *Republic* and earlier dialogues, principally the *Meno* and *Gorgias*. The main shortcoming of his treatment is that he claims to have reconciled Platonic doctrine with the facts of moral weakness (see pp. 147, 148, 159, 164) but actually has not. Assailing the "traditional interpretation" that Plato taught " 'If one knows what is virtuous, one will do what is virtuous,' " he interprets the Platonic "moral paradox" instead to mean "that if a man knows what is virtuous (and what is not) and also knows that it is always better for one to behave virtuously, then he will always do what is virtuous and will not even desire to do otherwise" (pp. 158-59). Thus stated, he says, "the Platonic thesis, that knowledge is sufficient for virtue, no longer contradicts the fact of moral weakness" (p. 159). But the common objection to Platonic doctrine still remains unanswered, viz. that a man who knows all the relevant ethical facts will not always behave virtuously if he is subject to overwhelming passions. Santas at one point shows an awareness of this difficulty and seems to imply that Plato simply did not meet it (p. 163). But this is tantamount to saying that the paradoxes hold true only for those in whom reason already rules unchallenged.

the command engraved at Delphi, and in the oracle proclaiming that none was wiser than Socrates, Plato could claim for it the sanction of a direct divine utterance. In his later works he continues to regard the false conceit of knowledge as a separate and peculiarly vicious kind of ignorance, for which the treatment remains the same, the Socratic elenchus.[4] It is characteristic of Plato that the fundamental and primary movement of the soul toward virtue, under the stimulus of Socratic questioning, is described as a dawning of knowledge.

In the face of an intellectualism so radical, the modern reader may ask, "Does Plato recognize the existence of the will?" Of more importance, "Does he believe in freedom of the will?" The summary just concluded makes that question seem unavoidable, because it apparently leaves no room for the spontaneous and self-determined movement toward the good which embodies for most of us what is essentially meritorious in good conduct. According to Plato, no man does wrong on purpose, no man desires evil. We have, in short, no choice between good and evil as such; we always choose what to us seems good and reject what seems evil. If we choose rightly, it is because we have knowledge or true opinion at the moment of choice; if wrongly, it is because we have false opinion at that moment. A man, if he is aware of the good, will do wrong only if anger, fear, or desire temporarily cloud his awareness; hence all wrongdoing is carried out in ignorance, permanent or momentary, of the good. Platonic education produces good men by giving them knowledge of the good and by preventing temporary lapses of this knowledge.

It is only a step from this to the conclusion that Plato is a determinist. We must always do what we think is best; we can never do what we think is wrong. Knowledge or opinion determines our choice absolutely. To an extent, we may change our opinion by our actions, but these actions in turn are always determined by the opinion we have when we act. In no smallest deliberate deed can we do what does not agree with our knowledge or opinion of the

4. See *Sophist* 229c-230c, *Philebus* 48c ff. I do not, of course, suggest that the Delphic maxim "Know thyself" was originally meant in a strict Socratic sense or that the oracle foresaw the interpretation that Socrates would put on its compliment to him.

good at the moment in question. Our knowledge or opinion, more-over, depends in turn upon our desires and emotions, our native in-telligence, and our perceptions. In *Timaeus* 86b ff. Plato attributes moral error to ills of the body, to parents' neglect, and to society's bad example. These produce "madness," i.e. temporary loss of knowledge or right opinion, and ignorance, an habitual lack of either. Evidently, then, our every act is determined by heredity and environment. There is apparently no freedom and no spon-taneity. In fact, there is no real choice: in any situation only one alternative is ever possible. So might we argue.[5]

5. "Intellektualismus und Determinismus sind die psychologische Grund-voraussetzungen der Ethik des Sokrates und, wenn ich ihn recht verstehe, auch des Platon" (C. Ritter, *Platon: Sein Leben, Seine Schriften, Seine Lehre* [Mu-nich, 1910-23], 1.437; cf. 2.533). Ritter takes up the question of free will in the last pages of his *Kerngedanken der Platonischen Philosophie* (Munich, 1931) and concludes that Platonic doctrine on the point shows a contradiction. Although Plato had elsewhere proved determinism "in a strict scientific man-ner," he chose at *Rep.* 617e to assert human responsibility. Ritter is sympa-thetic to Plato's dilemma, which he compares to the attempts of Christian theologians to reconcile free will with Divine omnipotence. Moreover, he adds, though what a man does is determined by his convictions, they are, after all, his own convictions, and responsibility is rightly imputed to him, not to God.

Julius Stenzel has written sympathetically about Plato's intellectualism. He explains its origin by the absence in Plato, and to a degree in all classical Greek culture, of a certain kind of subjectivity ("Das Problem der Willensfrei-heit im Platonismus," *Die Antike*, 4 [1928], 293-313). He lays great stress on the different scope of the idea of knowledge in Platonic and in modern Euro-pean thought. For Plato, knowledge, when expressed in a practical judgment, already implied choice or commitment. In considering moral action, therefore, all his attention fell on the content or nature of the act, none on the move-ment of the ego toward the act, unless this movement was arrested by pleasure or other strong emotion (p. 296). But such emotion he regarded as a constraint upon one's ability to act. Plato did not know the modern psychological phe-nomena of "Nicht-tun, Bloss-wollen, Nur-denken" in a man not under con-straint (pp. 296, 301). Choice and knowledge alike were movements toward the real and the good. That one's choice might be of anything but the known good, Plato never considered; that one might have to convert the self after train-ing and teaching it, would imply a sense of subjectivity foreign to him. When one strips away the obstacles that divert the βούλησις of *Gorgias* 467de, its free acts will be completely predictable. Platonic freedom is conformity with the laws of the universe (p. 312).

This whole presentation was vigorously attacked by F. Guglielmino, who argued in effect that Stenzel was using "freedom" in a Pickwickian sense ("Il Problema del Libero Arbitrio nel Sistema Platonico," *Archivio di Storia della Filosofia Italiana*, 4 [1935], 197-223). Guglielmino saw in this ideal of *Nicht-widerstreben*, and of unity with the *Weltgesetzlichkeit*, a kind of circumlocu-tion for the word "determinism," whose candid use by Ritter he approved (Guglielmino, pp. 212, 222). Cf. R. D. Archer-Hind (ed.), *Timaeus* (London, 1888), p. 324, who also equates Platonic intellectualism with determinism.

Whatever the apparent implications of Platonic doctrine, he is not explicitly a determinist: he does not speak of man as a helpless victim of forces beyond his control. Man is victimized but not helpless. The *Timaeus* passage is not a denial of personal responsibility but a list of influences that curtail it; these are to be overcome, not accepted. In fact, the passage ends with an assertion of personal responsibility (87b6-8).[6] Plato nowhere denies that men really control their own moral destinies. If he does not repeatedly emphasize that they do, it is because the great issue for him is not *whether* men are free to become good, but *how* they can become good. He seizes upon the possibility as a fact and tries to define the means and the goal. (The question, "Can virtue be taught?" does not raise a doubt about man's ability to improve himself, but about the ability of society or another person to do it systematically.) The impassioned pleas for virtue that Plato so often has Socrates utter are most naturally understood as being directed to an audience of men who have a real power to change their lives. One of these pleas comes at the end of the *Gorgias*, when he calls Callicles to a life of virtue "and to this contest, which I hold more important than all earthly contests" (526e3-4). Callicles, and all men, must choose virtue now, in anticipation of that day of judgment when they will no longer be able to help themselves (526e5). The passage clearly implies that self-help is possible now.

6. I do not find in the *Timaeus* or elsewhere the complete absolution from personal responsibility which L. Robin attributes to Plato here. "La maladie propre à l'âme, la 'déraison,' qu' elle soit folie ou ignorance, a *toujours* une origine physiologique" (italics added; *La Morale Antique* [Paris, 1938], p. 154). Robin suspects determinism not only here, but also in the references to Necessity in the myth of Er, a doctrine which ill accords, he says, with the insistence of that myth on man's responsibility (pp. 157-60). Guglielmino thinks that the limitations on personal responsibility admitted at *Tim.* 87b, and the admission that some vice is incurable (cf. *Laws* 862e), mean that destiny limits the freedom of some men and condemns others to unavoidable wickedness ("Il Problema del Libero Arbitrio," pp. 219-22). According to Guglielmino, this amounts to determinism in the common sense of that word. But his argument is not convincing, for several reasons: (1) To say that the power of choice is strained in the presence of passion is not to say that it is extinguished. (2) Part of a man's duty is to strengthen his soul in the intervals between temptations. (3) If the misuse of choice eventually makes a man incurable, the fault is largely his own. A. E. Taylor sees determinism at *Tim.* 86b ff., but he thinks Timaeus does not give Plato's own views (*Commentary on Plato's Timaeus* [Oxford, 1928], pp. 611-12). See above, Chapter 6, note 12.

Plato's explicit statements of human responsibility come in passages where the purpose is to exculpate God of blame for evil. At *Timaeus* 41e ff., where the creation of man is described, a distinction is made between what belongs to human nature by necessity and what is conditional. Necessity requires, for example, that the first birth be alike for all, that eventually the souls be born in bodies, that they have sensation, desire mixed with pleasure and pain, fear, anger, etc. Certain eventualities are not said to be dictated by necessity, e.g., whether men will master their emotions and live well, or the opposite. God laid down rules and penalties at the beginning in order that he might be free of blame for the future wickedness of each man (42d2-4). This had to be done since, as 42e3-4 states, a man can be the cause of evil to himself. Moreover, the narrative implies that a man exercises his responsibility *during* each life (42b3, c1-2). *Laws* 904b-d also delineates the responsibility of God and of men. God created the soul and decided where to consign souls after they had proven themselves virtuous or wicked (904b6-8). This decision is imposed on man by fate (904c8 ff.). But man is the cause of his own virtue or vice (904b8-c4, c7, d5).

The well-known words of Lachesis in the myth of Er belong here too. "The blame belongs to him who chose; God is blameless" (*Rep.* 617e4-5). Unlike the *Timaeus* myth, however, this part of the myth of Er devotes itself almost exclusively to the choice of a life before birth, and there has always been some uncertainty about its implications for freedom of choice during life. The soul in the other world chooses a life that will then belong to it by necessity (617e2-3). Its chosen daemon will see to it that the life is fulfilled, and a ceremony ratifies the now irreversible decision (620e). The patterns of lives offered for choice are described at 618ab, and their elements are listed again at 618c6 ff. It seems probable that they are meant to include only what is morally indifferent, e.g. reputation, beauty, strength, high birth, ancestral virtue, and their opposites, as well as wealth and penury, disease and health, private and public station, cleverness and dullness.[7] It is true that some

7. There is an obvious objection to this last statement, which must be considered. Some of the lives are "tyrannies" (618a), and the first soul chooses the greatest tyranny (619bc), in which it is fated, among other unnamed evils,

lives are better and others worse, according to whether they lead a man to justice or injustice (618d7 ff.). A man, moreover, is said to commit evil after he falls into tyranny (619a4). But crimes and injustice are not themselves said to be fated or objects of prenatal choice. When Plato, at 619a5, recommends that a man choose a life that embodies the mean among the things mentioned, he ap-

that he will eat his children. It looks at first as if Plato means that a soul can bind itself before birth to a life of the grossest crime. The connotations of "tyranny" elsewhere in the *Republic* tend to support this inference. But the tyrannies among which the souls choose are actually described as stations in life, some permanent and others temporary (618a5-6), involving sufferings rather than despotic acts. Some end in poverty, exile, and beggary (618a6-7). The greatest involves eating one's own children. This is, significantly, the only "action" of the tyrant specifically named from among those "actions'" which a choice of tyranny apparently entails (619a3). But it is a typical example of extreme suffering, not of deliberate crime (cf. the myths of Thyestes and Tereus, and the stories of Cyaxares and Harpagus at Herodotus 1.73 and 1.119). The theological problem which this detail of the myth is best suited to answer is the kind posed by the story of Oedipus the "tyrant." No specific reference can be proved or need be present, but Plato, committed as he was to the goodness of God (*Rep.* 379a-e), could not have tolerated in his theology the shadow of doubt cast by the speech at *Oedipus Coloneus*, 960 ff., a play produced when he was a young man. If Oedipus could not justly be blamed for his monstrous deeds, as Sophocles has him argue convincingly, then the suggestion let drop at 964-65 of that play may be the answer: what happened pleased the gods, who had perhaps some ancient grudge against his family. *Rep.* 619c4-6 might serve as a résumé of this speech.

R. S. Bluck thinks that "according to the *Republic* . . . the outward and *visible* events of . . . life were not, apparently, within the control of the soul that lived it," and he includes among these "the crimes an incarnate soul may commit through force of circumstances" ("Plato, Pindar, and Metempsychosis," *AJP*, 79 [1958], 413). Plato's point, he says, seems to be that a soul can still pursue wisdom and virtue. "Even if so doing may not be able to alter one's actions during this life, yet it may help to mold the desires of the soul in such a way as to affect its destiny hereafter" (*ibid.*). Dom David Amand, *Fatalisme et Liberté dans l' Antiquité Grecque* (Louvain, 1945), p. 6, finds in the myth of Er "un déterminisme rigoureux, qui fixe en détail toutes les actions extérieures . . . de notre vie." Yet man is free, he adds, to choose his destiny before birth, and free during life to be internally virtuous and happy (pp. 32-33). I doubt, however, that Plato meant that *all* outward events of a life have been decided at birth. Not only is it hard to imagine a change of belief or desire with no influence on action, but Plato's παραδείγματα do not seem to be exact blueprints. For example, the wrongdoer can still be influenced to look for a good teacher (618c). J. A. Stewart, *Myths of Plato* (London, 1905), has gone further than Bluck or Amand in defining the scope of Necessity. He tries to clarify it by an appeal to the ideas of Kant and Schopenhauer. The prenatal choice of a life is a mythical expression of a "transcendental idea," viz. the freedom of the "noumenal" as distinguished from the "phenomenal" self. The human character on earth unfolds according to a "necessary law" (p. 172). But all this wrongly implies that Plato's Necessity is equivalent to the modern scientific conception of unalterable and pervasive physical law.

parently sums up the process referred to at 618c6 ff., viz. striking a proper balance between wealth and poverty, strength and weakness, and so forth. All of these have an influence on virtue (618c7-8), and certain combinations of them (like the "greatest tyranny") would seem to make virtuous conduct very difficult indeed. They restrict the scope of free choice during life much more than any modern believer in free will would allow, for Plato includes in men's fate not only their heredity and environment but also—for some men at least—their ultimate stations in life.

But scope remains for influencing one's future while yet on earth. A man should learn how to distinguish the good from the bad; he should find a teacher who will make him able always and everywhere to choose the best that is possible (618c). He should choose the mean and shun extremes in this life and in the next (619a). After he has made a sensible choice of life, he should then live strictly (619b4). If a man on earth shows a wholesome love of wisdom, it will affect his fortunes (619d8), and the listeners to the myth, if they are persuaded by it, may find salvation (621c1).[8]

8. The ordinary man's belief is that some things in his life are decided by God but that many things are decided by himself. Ernst Wüst has cited passages from Greek authors to show that this was also the ordinary classical Greek view ("Von den Anfängen des Problems der Willensfreiheit," *Rhein. Mus.*, 101 [1958], 75-91). Among the references are: *Odyssey*, 1.32 ff. and Solon, frag. 8 (Diehl), both of which say that man should not blame the gods for ills of his own making; the Choices of Achilles, Heracles, and Paris; Aeschylus, *Prometheus Bound*, 1071-79; and the weighing of decisions by Homeric heroes, like that of Hector at *Iliad*, 22.99 ff. Lionel Pearson, *Popular Ethics in Ancient Greece* (Stanford, 1962), cites *Odyssey*, 9.302 and Book 9 *passim*, as well as 6.145-47, to prove that Homeric heroes had the freedom to make decisions (pp. 6, 208-210). The scope of fate in Homer is by no means settled among scholars. Denys Page has recently stated his view that in the *Iliad* man "can only do what destiny has predetermined for him," in *History and the Homeric Iliad* (Berkeley, Los Angeles, 1959), p. 302. He cites *Iliad*, 19.86 ff., where Agamemnon blames the gods for his own misdeeds. But L. A. Post had already shown the fatuousness of Agamemnon's excuse and the mere courtesy in Achilles' acceptance of it (19.270 ff.). Priam, likewise, at *Iliad*, 3.164 is being polite to Helen, as is Odysseus to Ajax at *Od.*, 11.558 ff. One can be rude by saying, "The gods made you what you are," as at *Iliad*, 1.178 ("The Moral Pattern in Homer," *TAPA*, 70 [1939], 158 ff.). It is more important that Zeus disapproves of all of these ways of speaking, which are current in both the *Iliad* and the *Odyssey*. His opinion should carry some weight (*Od.*, 1.32 ff.). See the discussion of this problem in E. L. Harrison, "Notes on Homeric Psychology," *Phoenix* 14 (1960), 77-80.

Max Pohlenz's book *Griechische Freiheit* (Heidelberg, 1955) has put Greek ideas about free will in good general perspective. The Greeks took human

To acknowledge all this is not to say that Plato took an explicit stand on the question of freedom of the will. The last phrase, in fact, cannot even be translated into Platonic Greek.⁹ It is true that "freedom" and "will" can often be translated separately. "Freedom" is ἐλευθερία, a social term which Plato, like us, used in a psychological sense. It describes the state of the democratic man, whose desires have free rein (*Rep.* 561a4) and whose freedom is like that of a democratic city (562b12, e1). But this usage, to be exact, is a misuse of "freedom" to mean "anarchy" (560e5). True freedom of soul is praiseworthy. It is one of the spiritual adornments of the philosopher (*Phaedo* 115a1), or it can be merely the result of the soul's liberation in old age from its former despots, the passions (*Rep.* 329c7). When passion is enslaved, that part of the soul which produces virtue is freed, and blessedness results (*Phaedrus* 256b). This statement should be compared with Socrates' remarks in Xenophon's *Memorabilia* 4.5.3 ff. and 4.5.11, where freedom is simply the ability to sort out and do what is best, as opposed to incontinence, which is slavery to the passions. As Plato uses the word, then, "freedom" is either the ability of the passions to seek their own ends uninhibited by reason, or, more properly, the power of reason to seek its end unhampered by passion. Nowhere does

freedom so much for granted, he says, that the philosophical question, "Does anything at all ever lie in man's power?" never occurred to them in the classical period (p. 132). Plato believed in freedom, he thinks, but saw in the myth of Er that it was somehow restricted by innate characteristics (pp. 133-34).

9. R. I. Lambrechts thought that Plato's equivalent of the free will was θυμός, which seemed to him to mediate the claims of reason and desire (*Dissertatio Philosophico-Litteraria Exhibens Platonis Sententiam de Animi Libertate* [1858], pp. 51-52). This mediation by an independent θυμός would make untenable Plato's other doctrine that a man always does what his reason judges best. Lambrechts admits this and imputes the contradiction to Plato (p. 46). But θυμός is not an independent arbiter. Though it sometimes opposes reason it never does so in alliance with desire, and when functioning properly it always sides with reason (*Rep.* 440ab, 441a, 589b, *Laws* 863b1-4, 865 ff.). Lambrechts' error combines mistranslation with anachronism. A. Fouillée thought that the *Hippias Minor*, since it defends the doctrine that no man does wrong on purpose, was a polemic against freedom of the will, and Socrates was the first determinist (*Platonis Hippias Minor* [Paris, 1872], pp. 70-71). One still finds this inference occasionally drawn. See D. Mayor, "El 'Intelectual' de Hoy Predibujado en Platón ¿Los Diálogos Platonicos Terminan Insolucionados?" *Humanidades* (Santander), 1 (1949), 242. Mary H. Wood, who at times uses "will" to refer to the βούλησις of *Gorgias* 467a ff., decides that the closest translation for the "Good Will" may be σωφροσύνη (*Plato's Psychology in its Bearing on the Development of Will* [London, New York, 1907], p. 46).

the word mean freedom to choose between good and evil. On the other hand, the word "will," as used in the term "free will," is absent from Plato's language too. When Wilamowitz uses "Wille" to translate θυμοειδές, and A. E. Taylor declares that "will" has nothing at all to do with θυμοειδές, but belongs in the λογιστικόν, the reader is warned that there are profound ambiguities to be overcome.[10] But Wilamowitz evidently means by "will" an abiding capacity to overcome temptation, and Taylor means a source of rational choice, and each is a legitimate application of the modern word. "Will" might also be used to translate βούλησις in the sense in which the verb βούλεσθαι is used at *Gorgias* 467a ff. But in none of these senses is "will" an independent faculty to choose between good and evil. The θυμοειδές is properly subordinate to reason, and βούλησις always has the good for its object. Plato names no power in the soul which means "will" in the sense required.

The question still unresolved is whether Plato implicitly denies the existence of such a power. It was seen above that his analysis of deliberate action as a reflection of knowledge seems to imply that men's decisions are never more than indirect expressions of their heredity and environment. On the other hand, Plato constantly assumes that individual responsibility exists and can be exercised in this life. We might leave the matter at that and impute a contradiction to him. But the imputation would be unfair. The intellectualist analysis outlined at length earlier in this chapter is an attempt by Plato to answer two questions: (1) What induces a man to do wrong? (2) By what means can a man be taught to do right? The answers provided by that analysis are: (1) unreasonable dispositions in the soul and in society; (2) the creation of a rational order in both. In order to explain the unreasonable dispositions (the vices) and the rational order (virtue) Plato must speak of the soul as something made up of three separate parts and of virtue as four different things. Now when the soul is divided into parts one must speak of its actions as interactions. Thus: passion in the appetitive part causes a loss of right opinion in the rational part;

10. Ulrich von Wilamowitz-Moellendorff, *Platon* (2nd ed.; Berlin, 1920), 1.392; A. E. Taylor, *Plato, the Man and His Work* (4th ed.; London, 1937), p. 38.

the absence of right opinion causes a misdeed. If one asks, "Is the misdeed freely chosen?" in the modern sense of the phrase, one asks a question which the analysis was not meant to answer. The ground of individual responsibility for evil, which Plato asserts in his role of theologian and assumes in his moral exhortations, is not discoverable in the analysis he makes as an educator and legislator.[11] It is present in the whole soul, but not in any of its three Platonic parts. This is not a paradox. The Platonic parts do not exhaust the soul's powers. Aristotle, for example, found them unsuitable for the biologist.[12]

Those who find determinism in Platonic ethics note the fact that what we choose is always what we think right, and that this knowledge or opinion is influenced by our heredity and environment. But what we think right is also what we choose to think right. A right practical judgment cannot be reached without attention to its premises, and this attention can be given or withheld. To reply that the allotment of attention is itself a decision based on previous knowledge is to embark on an apparently infinite regress. Which ultimately determines the other, choice or knowledge? The question, I believe, is meaningless. There is no order of primacy between the two functions, because in the concrete they are identical. To choose is to judge an act as the best alternative among those within one's power. Any choice is a conclusion reached from known premises; any practical judgment is a choice imputable to the agent. When confronted by two courses of action, we will always choose the alternative we think better, but we are free to choose either alternative.

It is often said that genuine freedom must include the power to choose what we know is the worse alternative.[13] An experience

11. J. Jérôme upbraids Plato because "il n'a pas établi nettement que l'homme était en outre le principe (ἀρχή) de ses actes," and goes on to say that rewards and punishments have no justification "si nos actes n'ont pas en nous leur principe" ("La volonté dans la philosophie antique," *Laval Théologique et Philosophique*, 7 [1951], 256). But common beliefs are rarely established with any "netteté" until they are seriously challenged. The only challenge that Plato had to face, the occasional blaming of the gods for men's ills, was met by him with clear statements of individual responsibility.

12. See F. Solmsen, "Antecedents of Aristotle's Psychology and Scale of Beings," *AJP*, 76 (1955), 162.

13. "Pour qu'il ait liberté vraie, il faut que l'homme puisse choisir, en

pleine conscience, ou le bien ou le mal" (A. Jagu, "La Conception Platonicienne de la Liberté," in *Mélanges A. Diès* [Paris, 1956], p. 130). Plato lacks
this conception, in spite of his many affirmations of human responsibility, and
therefore, according to Jagu, "sa doctrine est incohérente" (p. 132). Raphael
Demos thinks that "freedom which has any moral significance must include
the ability to see the good and yet reject it." This ability will be expressed in
"the choice between reason and desire." But in Plato, "the human soul is the
seat of a dual determinism—mechanical and teleological . . . [and] the conflict between the two settles itself" (*The Philosophy of Plato* [New York,
1939], p. 334). Theodor Gomperz also finds two kinds of determinism in Plato,
but he regards them as two phases of Plato's development. At first Plato
thought that all actions depend on knowledge; later (*Laws* 860d ff.) he acknowledged that some actions are determined by vice (*Griechische Denker*
[2nd ed.; Leipzig, 1903-1909], 2.522-23). Guglielmino, who thinks that Plato
is normally a determinist, though not a consistent one, says that *Laws* 689a
implies the freedom to reject what one judges good ("Il Problema del Libero
Arbitrio," p. 212). So it does, but this need only mean that strong passions can
overcome moral convictions by clouding them (the doctrine of *Tim.* 86b ff.).
The *Laws* passage is discussed above, in Chapter 6, note 13. Otto Apelt also
returns a verdict of incoherence against the Platonic doctrine of the free will,
which he says exists in Plato in two forms. A freely willed act, in the strict
sense, is dictated by the pure understanding independently of all outside influences. It proceeds from the βούλησις of *Gorgias* 467a ff. But this "metaphysical freedom," says Apelt, is an abstraction, never found in reality, and
misapplied by Plato and Socrates to real life in the formula "No man freely
wills injustice." In a looser sense, an act is freely willed if it is the result of
unreasonable passions. Such an act is based on "psychological freedom," the
power of choosing between rational and physical desire (*Platonische Aufsätze*
[Leipzig, 1912], pp. 191-92). Now Apelt's "metaphysical freedom" is apparently the type whose genesis is described at *Phaedrus* 256b3 ff. But his "psychological freedom" corresponds to no phrase or doctrine of Plato, since it
means that we could reject what we believed at the moment of choice to be
the right and reasonable decision. Moreover, to say that no man freely wills
injustice (in Plato's sense) is not to misapply "metaphysical freedom" to real
life. Plato means only that the wish for good, though often blinded and mis-
directed by desire, is always the source of choice.

Robert E. Cushman, *Therapeia, Plato's Conception of Philosophy* (Chapel
Hill, 1958), tries to transform Plato's intellectualism into voluntarism in such
statements as, "there is no achievement of knowledge which is not conditioned
by a prior decision about the Good, or, more specifically, about what is worth
knowing" (pp. 270; cf. 249, 269). This "decision," however, is said to be
entirely the result of a certain balance in the affections. Knowledge "is an
*event* which takes place in the mind when certain inward as well as outward
conditions prevail or, what is the same thing, when the total orientation of
the soul is right with respect to available reality." This orientation "has to do
with the inner balance of affective forces" (p. 147; cf. 248). Having denied to Plato any conception of autonomy (pp. 66, 149), Cushman envisages
the soul as the field where affections vie to achieve supremacy and where
knowledge can occur only when the proper ones prevail. In this process, not
only does knowledge presuppose choice (p. 270), but "choice will follow the
prevailing passion of the soul" (p. 205, n. 1). He maintains, to be sure, that
there is always freedom of choice: a man has no one to praise or blame for
his decisions but himself and his own affections (pp. 185, 205, n. 1). Yet it
is clear to Cushman himself that his interpretation excludes the kind of freedom

which seems to correspond to this is common in the presence of great passion or fear. Euripides testifies to it at *Hippolytus* 380-83. It can also be present in acts of apparently pure devilishness. One can even use Plato as a witness against himself, since Leontius speaks as if he knows his decision is wrong (*Rep.* 440a). Plato's position is defensible if by "what we think good" he means what we accept at the moment of choice as our standard of behavior, whether or not we *call* it "good." When Huckleberry Finn deliberately "takes up wickedness" (as he puts it) by helping a runaway slave, he does not try to square his terminology with his standards. So too, if passion temporarily alters our opinion of the value of an act, it is natural that in speaking of it we should still apply society's or our own former terminology. We are more apt to do so if experience has taught us that we will soon remorsefully resume the old standard (like Leontius). Socratic questioning, however, would reveal the present intrusion of a new standard. Examples will make this clearer. "Murder is never right, but it's the only solution now." "Yielding to this temptation is unforgivably wicked, but it's worth it this one time." "One ought never to resort to violence, but he must be taught a lesson." In each of these decisions, the second clause expresses what the speaker really thinks is the greater good. The occasional choice made for "no reason at all" may disguise a decision to choose spontaneously, which itself implies a standard. Otherwise, it is a purely unthinking reaction and not a choice in the proper sense. The reflex and the nervous tic are not "chosen." Somewhat different is the judgment, "This is good, and therefore I shall not do it." "Good" here expresses a conventional standard which the speaker does not accept. The Platonic doctrine that no man wishes evil implies as a strict corollary that a man who does evil on the ground that it is evil has simply mistaken evil, the word and the thing, for good. His choice is not

---

that would make Socratic dialectic intelligible, since "dialectic . . . at one and the same time is designed to induce and yet itself presupposes a suitable condition of character" (p. 150). He calls this a weak link in Plato's theory. But the weakness lies in his own assumption that moral choice in Plato is separate from knowledge and prior to it. Actually the validity of intellectual dialectic as an instrument of conversion rests on the fact that choice is expressed *through* knowledge.

a real and absolute rejection of good, but only an extreme form of ignorance. This way of explaining self-confessed and deliberate wickedness will strike many people as incredibly perverse reasoning. Beyond a certain point, differences so profound are not arguable, since every man feels that he is the best judge of what he can choose. Plato's own judgment is that to choose a known evil is no more possible than to believe a known falsehood.[14]

In rejecting the belief that Plato is a determinist, we have not yet entirely disposed of the original question, "Does he recognize

---

14. There have been other ways of explaining the choice of Leontius. N. R. Murphy, *The Interpretation of Plato's Republic* (Oxford, 1951), p. 48, concludes from it that when Plato says everything we do is for the good "we must admit that he is here speaking of a presumed wish rather than of one that is actually operative always in particular persons." But if this means that some men do not always act for the good then it is simply not Platonic doctrine.

David Gallop, in "The Socratic Paradox in the *Protagoras*," *Phronesis*, 9 (1964), 117-29, remarks of the argument at *Protag.* 356-357 that "Socrates gets his opponents to agree that the action recognized as pleasantest is always *preferable*, and concludes that the pleasantest action, once recognized as such, will necessarily be *preferred*. Yet this would be true only if men always did act rationally; and to assume that they do is only to beg the whole question over again from the start" (p. 129). In the sense that Plato never attempts in this dialogue or elsewhere to demonstrate that a man simply cannot choose what he judges the worse of two alternatives, Gallop's conclusion is soundly based. Socrates' opponents either admit this principle after a review of examples (as Polus does at *Gorgias* 468) or phrase their denial in a way that is inconsistent with their other beliefs (as at *Protag.* 355a5-b3). But this is not quite to beg the question. Since we do not find in the dialogues an interlocutor who simply and resolutely claims that evil is sometimes his τέλος, the question is, properly speaking, never raised.

There is an extensive literature about the will in Plato, much of it in the form of *obiter dicta* and hence apt to be overlooked. Among these, the brief but penetrating remarks of Th. Deman, in *Le Témoignage d'Aristote sur Socrate* (Paris, 1942), pp. 108-10, deserve special commendation. Other works whose views are of interest but have not been discussed here are: Arthur W. H. Adkins, *Merit and Responsibility, A Study in Greek Values* (Oxford, 1960), pp. 302-303; I. M. Crombie, *An Examination of Plato's Doctrines*. 1: *Plato on Man and Society* (London, 1962), pp. 275-80; Henri Daudin, *La Liberté de la Volonté* (Paris, 1950), p. 5; Hermann Gauss, "Das Problem der Willensfreiheit bei Platon," *Festschrift K. Joel* (Basel, 1934), pp. 70-87; C. Librizzi, "Il Problema del Libero Arbitrio in Platone," *Sophia*, 16 (1948), 190-94, 319-25; Paul Shorey, *The Unity of Plato's Thought* (Chicago, 1903), pp. 10-11. My own article, "Modern Philosophy and Platonic Ethics," *JHI*, 19 (1958), 451-72, tries to show that the issue has often been clouded by the intrusion of modern terminology and modern issues. Discussion of the problem of human freedom as it affects Plato's political philosophy is a principal topic of Ernst Moritz Manasse's *Bücher über Platon*. 2: *Werke in englischer Sprache, Philosophische Rundschau*, Beiheft 2, Sonderheft (Tübingen, 1961). See pp. 73, 175, 203, 228, and my review in *Gnomon*, 35 (1963), 765-70.

the existence of the will?" Since there is no Platonic term equivalent to the modern term "will," the answer might seem to be an unqualified no. This would be true but unenlightening; what we really want to know is how Plato conceived of those phenomena which we cover by the term in question. Part of the answer is already clear. No Platonic word denotes individual responsibility conceived as a faculty, which is what we mean by the "free will." Yet Plato evidently believed in such responsibility. Two of his terms, moreover, coincide in usage with the English word "will" far enough to allow a translator the occasional liberty of using the latter as their English equivalent. These are βούλεσθαι and θυμοειδές. The former, when it does not mean simply "wish," denotes the abiding desire for the good or for happiness which underlies all our conscious and purposeful actions;[15] the latter is the source of those

15. Plato's use of βούλεσθαι and βούλησις has been examined critically in an article by Norman Gulley, "The Interpretation of 'No One Does Wrong Willingly' in Plato's Dialogues," *Phronesis*, 10 (1965), 82-96. He has undertaken to show: (1) that this paradox is interpreted in an "awkward" way in the *Gorgias*; (2) that an earlier, less strained interpretation found in the *Protagoras* is probably the original "Socratic" version; and (3) that the "Platonic" interpretation, found in dialogues from the *Gorgias* on, moves, in the late dialogues, close to determinism. I shall take these points in order.

In the *Gorgias*, Gulley finds "surprising" (p. 89) and in need of explanation Socrates' statement at 510a3-5 that the wish not to do wrong is not a sufficient defense against doing wrong. Plato "is here pressing too far the analogy between moral behaviour and the practice of professional skills" (p. 90). This is so, he argues, because the question raised in the *Gorgias* whether or not the life of a tyrant is a good or happy one "is obviously the question of whether or not such men know what the 'right' aim, or what the 'really' good is, and not the question of whether or not they have practical skill or expertness in assessing the means to a generally accepted end" (pp. 86-87). To this degree the analogy of virtue with, say, running a race well (in which all runners wish to win) is misleading, since not all men wish to be just. The runner's wish does not insure success, but the wish to be just should imply knowledge of what justice is and should therefore insure just action (the inference rejected at 510a3-5). Hence, he argues, it would have been more "natural" for Plato to say that the unjust man wishes what he thinks good and not what is really good (p. 91). To correct this alleged awkwardness, Gulley asks us to interpret the thesis that no one does wrong willingly "in the hypothetical form that no one acts against what he *would* wish to do if he knew what was 'really' good" (p. 89; italics mine).

In spite of Gulley's skillful argument, it is worth taking seriously Plato's decision to phrase his thesis categorically rather than hypothetically. Plato wants to emphasize here, as elsewhere, that a "desire for the truly good" is something all men have all the time. As Socrates says at *Rep.* 505d5-8, δίκαια μὲν . . . πολλοὶ ἂν ἕλοιντο τὰ δοκοῦντα . . . ἀγαθὰ δὲ οὐδενὶ ἔτι ἀρκεῖ τὰ δοκοῦντα κτᾶσθαι, ἀλλὰ τὰ ὄντα ζητοῦσιν. That is, not all men seek the good qua justice,

indigant emotions whose function it is to support the judgments of reason.

There still remains the well-recognized use of "will" by some

---

yet all seek it qua good. Even tyrants desire something they fail to achieve (*Gorgias* 466e1, 467b2), and this is their own good (468a-d). The analogy of the poor runner with the unjust man admittedly limps (Gulley is right here) because the former understands clearly what it is to win the race, whereas the latter does not understand the nature of the good. But his soul grasps it after a fashion, ἀπομαντευομένη τι εἶναι, ἀποροῦσα δὲ καὶ οὐκ ἔχουσα λαβεῖν ἱκανῶς τί ποτ᾽ ἐστίν (*Rep.* 505e1-2). This point is especially important in the *Gorgias*, since only the presence in Polus and Callicles of a real desire for the good, whose nature they "divine," makes worthwhile Socrates' attempt to win them over. It is the "desire for the truly good" which Polus acknowledges at 475e1, when he answers that he would not accept the worse and more ignoble of two alternatives. Cf. Callicles' admission at 499e-500a. Yet this real desire is clearly an insufficient defense for them against wrongdoing, and Socrates' later statement to that effect at 510a3-5 is therefore not "surprising." (The mention of "practice" at 509e2 indicates that Plato has in mind a further qualification, discussed above on p. 92.)

Gulley bases his remarks about the *Protagoras* mainly on 358cd, where Socrates says that no man voluntarily pursues what is bad or what he supposes to be bad. As Gulley says, "this is a radically different application" of the distinction "voluntary-involuntary" from Plato's normal use of it (p. 93). Elsewhere (e.g. in the *Gorgias*) Platonic doctrine has it that no one voluntarily pursues what is really bad, whether or not he judges it to be bad. "Hence [in the *Protagoras*] the thesis that no one does wrong willingly is the thesis that no one willingly does what he knows or believes to be wrong. It does not mean that no one does what is 'really' wrong willingly" (p. 94). But once the terminology is untangled, the "Socratic" doctrine of the *Protagoras* is not so different as Gulley claims from the "Platonic" doctrine of the *Gorgias*. At *Protagoras* 358cd, ἑκών means "acting without constraint." Elsewhere (e.g. at 345de) it often means "acting in conformity with one's permanent desire to achieve good." Gulley observes this but fails to point out what it implies, viz. that the "Socratic" and "Platonic" doctrines are equivalent. They are, respectively: (1) no one, if unconstrained (ἑκών), pursues what he judges bad; (2) no one who is acting in genuine accord with his permanent desire to achieve good (ἑκών) pursues what is really bad. In general, terminological inconsistency is too frequent in Plato to be a safe indicator of real changes in doctrine. A similar shift in the *Laws* from a Platonic to a conventional use of "voluntary" is discussed in Chapt. 6, n. 17 above.

Gulley finds in later dialogues an increasing tendency to admit that ignorance of the right moral principles is not only involuntary but also not blameworthy, that it is in fact "outside 'what is in our power'" (p. 95). "Thus the *Sophist*," he says, "assumes that it is not punishable (229a-d). The appropriate discipline for the correction of ignorance is education" (p. 95). But Plato's proposal in the *Sophist* to use the elenchus on the ignorant does not, as Gulley supposes, absolve them of blame. The procedure described at *Sophist* 230b ff. is precisely that practiced by Socrates on Callicles, who is warned that stern judgment awaits him in the hereafter (*Gorgias* 527a). Gulley also cites *Timaeus* 86de as a passage which teaches that "ignorance is not blameworthy" (p. 95). But that very passage precedes an assertion of personal responsibility, at 87b6-8. (See above, Chapt. 6, n. 12, and Chapt. 7, n. 6.)

authors to mean appetency or conation in general, whether rational or not.[16] The Platonic conception which most nearly approximates this is Eros, "love." Two Platonic dialogues, the *Symposium* and the *Phaedrus*, deal with Eros as a principal theme, and it is clear in each that Plato regards sexual love as only one aspect of it. To the effort of explaining its nature he devotes two of the most eloquent and famous passages in his dialogues, the conversation of Diotima and Socrates in the *Symposium* and the great myth of the *Phaedrus*.[17]

Socrates, called upon in the *Symposium* to deliver a speech about Eros after each of his companions at the banquet has done so, begins instead by questioning Agathon, the previous speaker. Agathon's speech has been a high-flown and unqualified panegyric of love. Though all the other banqueters have received it with enthusiasm, Socrates shows politely disguised disapproval. Love, he points out in his questioning of Agathon, is a desire for something absent, specifically a desire for the beautiful and the good. Therefore, it lacks both (200e-201c). To explain this paradox, he recounts a conversation he claims to have had with Diotima, a wise woman of Mantinea, at a time when he himself was ignorant, as Agathon now is, of the nature of love. What Diotima taught him was that Eros lies somewhere between the beautiful and the ugly, just as right opinion, for example, lies between wisdom and ignorance. Eros is not a god, since the gods, being already happy and beautiful, possess what he lacks (202cd). He is not a mortal either, but instead is a great δαίμων, a denizen of that intermediate world where communication passes between the divine and the human. A child of Poverty and Resource, he shares in the nature of each. Unlike the gods, who are wise, he is merely a lover of wisdom, φιλόσοφος. He also differs, therefore, from those who are in the

16. See Alexander Bain, *The Emotions and the Will* (3rd ed.; London, 1875), p. 303 ff.

17. The reader will find useful general discussions of Platonic Eros in F. M. Cornford, "The Doctrine of Eros in Plato's *Symposium*," in *The Unwritten Philosophy and Other Essays*, ed. W. K. C. Guthrie (Cambridge, 1950), pp. 68-80; Paul Friedländer, *Plato I, An Introduction*, trans. Hans Meyerhoff (London, 1958), pp. 41-58; Thomas Gould, *Platonic Love* (New York and London, 1963); G. M. A. Grube, *Plato's Thought* (Boston, 1958), pp. 87-119; Werner Jaeger, *Paideia: the Ideals of Greek Culture*, trans. Gilbert Highet, II (Oxford, 1947), 174-97.

strict sense ignorant, who think they are noble (καλοὶ κἀγαθοί) and wise but actually are not (203e-204a). This love of wisdom is an aspect of his love of the beautiful, since wisdom is a thing of the highest beauty.

When Socrates asked Diotima of what use Eros was to men, she replied by explaining how mankind shares in the universal impulse of love. The object of Eros is the beautiful, or more precisely, the possession of the beautiful. If for the word "beautiful" (καλόν) one substitutes "good" (ἀγαθόν) it will be clear that what Eros really aims at is happiness (204e). This desire is common to all men; they all wish to possess the good forever. Custom, it is true, has limited the word "love" to one form of desire, but properly speaking it is all desire for what is good and for happiness (205d). This seems such an extraordinary expansion of the word's normal meaning that Diotima feels compelled to justify it by appealing to the analogy of the word "poetry" (ποίησις), originally and properly any kind of "making," but now restricted by usage to musical-metrical creation (205bc).

Diotima repeats that Eros aims at *eternal* possession of the good (206a). This determines the form of its expression, which is the act of "begetting in the beautiful," the mode in which mortal nature shows the desire for immortality that love implies (206b-207a). This desire is found in animals in the instinctive behavior of mating and in the nourishment and protection of the young, all of which insure the preservation of the species. Even the life and continued existence of the individual human being is the result of the continuous regeneration of bone, flesh, and hair, the constant appearance and disappearance of habits, dispositions, opinions, desires, pleasures, pains, and fears, and the nourishment of knowledge by study. All this is evidence of Eros and of the desire of mortal nature to share in immortality. The love of fame is another form of the same instinct. This extraordinary enlargement of the notion of Eros is in no way meant to reduce all its forms to a single level of value. Diotima does not preach surrender to the vital instincts, but rather their control by reason. In her scheme, some forms of love are higher than others and some lovers therefore more worthy than others. To make that point, she divides the class of lovers into those who are "pregnant" in body and those "pregnant" in soul. The former seek women who will bear children to them, finding here what they think is immortality and happiness. But those pregnant in soul seek out companions fair in body and in soul, with whom they can beget spiritual children far more beautiful and lasting than children of the flesh. Their activity results in the creation of virtue.

The highest mysteries of love have not yet been touched upon, and Diotima begins to speak of them with a solemn assertion of their difficulty and importance. In the domain of Eros, she explains, there is a hierarchy which corresponds to the levels of progress in the soul's advance to perfection and in the gradual education of its instinctive desire of the beautiful. A man begins, when young, with the love of a fair body and the creation, in this companionship, of noble discourse. Then he grows aware of the singleness of the beauty that all bodies share, and later he comes to realize that the soul's beauty surpasses that of the body. He will therefore prefer to hold ennobling conversation with those who are fair in soul, even if gifted with only slight physical beauty. Then the beauty of customs and laws and of knowledge itself attracts him. Finally, when his mind has ranged freely over the whole "sea of the beautiful" and he has taken part without stint in philosophical converse of all kinds, there will come a sudden wonderful vision of an eternal, changeless, pure, and unqualifiedly beautiful nature, the source of whatever beauty lies in anything else. This is the Beautiful itself, the ultimate μάθημα, the last step in the soul's progress in Eros. To rest in the presence of this beauty, in communion and contemplation, is to reach—if any man can—immortality (209e-212a).

The defense of Eros in the myth of the *Phaedrus*, which has already been discussed with reference to the tripartition of the soul, involves a new imaginative point of view and supplements the earlier account of the *Symposium* in several ways. Eros in the *Phaedrus* is not merely a universal desire, but a divinely inspired form of madness in a class with divination, the prophetic frenzy of cursed souls seeking relief, and poetic inspiration (244a-245c). The explanation of its nature which Socrates here undertakes involves a mythical description of the pre-existence of the soul and the vision it once had of reality before it fell into a mortal body. Socrates compares the soul to a two-horse chariot of which one horse is docile, the other hostile to the commands of the charioteer. Erotic attraction he explains as a memory, aroused by the sight of a beautiful person, of Beauty itself, once seen in the company of the gods before the soul's descent into a body. The occasion of this prenatal vision was a visit to the plain of Truth, in the regions beyond the heavens, where the soul gazed upon the eternal realities and there found its best nourishment and sustenance.

The vision described in the *Phaedrus* has much in common with that earlier description of the final stage of erotic perfection in the *Symposium*. But certain differences cannot be ignored. The *Symposium*, for example, concentrates exclusively on the Form of the Beautiful, making it the central reality which gives even to wisdom its hold on human aspiration (204b). To behold αὐτὸ τὸ καλόν is the climax and end, the τέλος, of human activity (211b-d). In the later treatment of this same subject in the *Phaedrus*, the very words in which the objects of knowledge are referred to, ἀλήθεια and τὰ ὄντα, as well as the fact that they are plural, show that the point of view has shifted. What the chariot-soul sees is true being (οὐσία ὄντως οὖσα), impalpable and without color or shape. This includes justice itself, temperance, knowledge, and other things of the sort that truly are (τὰ ὄντα ὄντως 247cde). The object of this vision, taken as a whole, is Truth (248b-249b). Beauty is one of many realities, distinguished only because it is visible on earth, in the derivative beauty of physical things, through the sharpest of our senses, sight. The memory of beauty consequently arouses strong emotion in a way no other reality can match and gives to that Form its special association with love. But this is in a way accidental: if wisdom were visible, it too "would arouse wonderful loves" (250bcd).

It is clear from these two passages that Plato allows himself considerable freedom in the way he describes the object of Eros. At one time its primary object is beauty, and it is attracted to wisdom and the other virtues only because they share in beauty. At another time this primacy of beauty seems only apparent; the other Forms are in their own right capable of arousing love but have found no clear earthly likeness through which to impress the soul, as beauty has. In one passage, without apology, ἀγαθόν is substituted for καλόν (*Symp.* 204e), and a definition is produced which explains Eros as all desire for what is good and for happiness. Finally, in the *Symposium*, the μάθημα of beauty is called the τέλος of human aspiration (211bc); yet in the sixth book of the *Republic*, where Plato will return to the subject of ultimate reality, he will use virtually the same language of the Idea of the Good, the μέγιστον μάθημα (504d-505a).

These difficulties can be clarified if not, in the full sense of the word, solved. They tend, in the first place, to be magnified in translation. The term καλός is not adequately translated as "beautiful," though that English word is normally its closest equivalent and has been used for it in the preceding pages. But καλός can mean as well "noble," "fine," or "good." It unites moral and aesthetic meanings in a way that no comparable English term does; when it occurs only context can tell which meaning predominates. In Socratic dialectic it is often found in arguments where the translation "beautiful" would be quite out of place and where ἀγαθός would have served as well. In the *Laches*, for example, courage is called a καλόν, and in the *Protagoras* the same word is applied to all virtue.[18] In short, τὸ καλόν and τὸ ἀγαθόν are overlapping conceptions. There is no more striking evidence of this than the discussion of the Good at the end of Book 6 of the *Republic*. At 505b, a point at which the Idea of the Good has just been carefully distinguished from all extraneous and subordinate realities, Socrates suddenly uses the phrase καλὸν καὶ ἀγαθόν as if it denoted a single idea. A few pages later, the Good is said to be pre-eminent in κάλλος. To substitute ἀγαθός for καλός, therefore, as Diotima does at *Symposium* 204e, is not as logically presumptuous as it would be to replace "beautiful" with "good" in English. The worst we can say of Plato's procedure is that it avoids the hard problem of deciding precisely how the two words are related.

The fact that the terms καλόν and ἀγαθόν can often be interchanged must imply the identification, in some measure, of the realities they denote. There are some indications that Plato would

18. *Laches* 192c, *Protagoras* 349e.

have agreed. In the progress of the soul away from a preoccupation with the physical and the transient, the ultimate goal is τὸ καλόν or τὸ ἀγαθόν, depending on whether one reads the *Symposium* or the sixth book of the *Republic*. To object that one passage describes a progress in love and the other a progress in knowledge and virtue is to overlook the fact that love, in this highest form, is the pursuit of both knowledge and virtue and that the two passages, therefore, chart one course. But if love and learning, in the philosopher's life, are aspects of the same activity, then their objects, the Beautiful and the Good, form a single reality. Like the identification of the virtues, this last statement demands qualification, since in fact the words καλός and ἀγαθός are not invariably interchangeable. However, in leaving us an implication of their unity, Plato has left us no commentary to explain it. Furthermore, even at this profound level of his thought, he has not made a consistent use of terminology. In the *Symposium* the question, "Why is wisdom loved?" received the answer, "Because it is τῶν καλλίστων" (204b). In the *Phaedrus*, the same question might have been raised at 250d, when wisdom is described as intrinsically lovable. But to have answered it in the same terms would have been impossible, granted the momentary assumption of the passage that wisdom and κάλλος are mutually exclusive entities united only in the fact that both are forms of truth and reality. Yet Plato had certainly not given up his belief that wisdom is a καλόν and an ἀγαθόν. Therefore, when he ascribes to κάλλος at 250cd a unique attractiveness and clarity which sets it apart from all other realities, he has in mind the aesthetic sense, "beauty," not the moral sense, "good." The problem of their relationship remains to trouble us. Plato, characteristically, will not explain it. Instead, he dramatizes it in the discourse of Diotima, where the span between the physically beautiful and αὐτὸ τὸ καλόν, at once beautiful and good, marks the upward course of the philosopher's life.

The theory of Eros, in which Plato unites with a single sweep of imagination the attraction of physical love and the study of philosophy, cannot be divorced from the ethical principle that no man wishes evil and all wish the good. Eros is this same universal wish, conceived as the vital energy of our conscious and unconscious lives, extended to the animal kingdom, and touched with passion. This is why, at *Symposium* 205a, Diotima, while speaking of Eros, momentarily lapses into the language of *Gorgias* 466b ff. in the phrase πάντας τἀγαθὰ βούλεσθαι. The object of desire, whether called τὸ ἀγαθόν or τὸ καλόν, is the same in both passages, and in both it is ultimate in the order of means and ends. This is made clear in the *Gorgias* by the insistence that βούλεσθαι is properly applied only to ends, and especially to the ultimate end, εὐδαιμονία or happiness (470e). Similarly, at *Symposium* 205a, the question, "Why does a man want to be happy?" is regarded as fruitless, because in adducing that motive the inquiry, as Diotima says, seems to have achieved a τέλος.

The terminus of desire appears in a different guise in the *Lysis*, as the πρῶτον φίλον (219d), or as the "real φίλον," in which all other so-called φιλίαι find their purpose (220b). Like the object of βούλησις in the *Gorgias*, this lies at the end of a linked series of "loved" objects, each of which is loved for the sake of the next in sequence. The example of a cup of wine which is φίλον only because it will restore the health of a beloved son (219e) could easily be translated into the terminology of *Gorgias* 467c ff. This and other passages make it clear that the motive for φιλία, which is reducible to the desire for the πρῶτον φίλον, is the same as that elsewhere called Eros or βούλησις. At *Lysis* 216d, Socrates "divines" that what is neither good nor bad is φίλον to the good and beautiful. This simply puts into other terms the relationship of Eros, which lies between the good and the bad, to the object of its desire, the good and the beautiful (*Symp.* 200e ff.). One result of this intermediate position of Eros is that he is a "philosopher," not ignorant, but not yet wise. As the formation of the word itself implies, "philosophy" is an expression of φιλία as well as of Eros. This is made explicit at *Lysis* 218ab, which, like other passages from that dialogue, reproduces in different terms an argument of the *Symposium*. It corresponds to *Symposium* 203e-204a: in each passage the name "philosopher" is denied both to the wise and to those who are so ignorant as to think they know what they do not know. Apart from the fact, evident in these examples, that many arguments using Eros are essentially identical to others using φιλία, the terms are at times used almost interchangeably. At *Lysis* 221e, ἔρως, φιλία, and ἐπιθυμία all have as their object τὸ οἰκεῖον. Four lines later, the three words reappear together in the verbal form, and at 217e φιλία is again associated with ἐπιθυμία. At *Symposium* 179e, 209c, and at *Phaedrus* 241c, 255b, Eros is a form of φιλία. Finally, as Grube has pointed out,[19] if the *Lysis* is not in some sense about Eros, then the dramatic setting, with all its talk of the relationship of Hippothales and Lysis, is singularly irrelevant.

Plato, chary as ever of establishing a technical terminology, varies his choice of βούλεσθαι, φιλεῖν, and ἐρᾶν according to the associations he wants to create, the field of experience he wishes to include, the intensity of emotion he hopes to suggest. The discussion in the *Lysis*, for example, begins with parental love, and for this φιλία is the most appropriate word. As a term of general ethical usefulness, βούλεσθαι was no doubt better suited than ἐρᾶν or φιλεῖν to denote the desire for happiness and the attachment to the good. Not all human activity is passionate, and Eros can be applied to humdrum pursuits like money-making only in passages of emotional intensity or poetic exaltation. *Symposium* 205d is one of these. Most behavior results from the unemotional calculation of preference, and what lies at the root of the resulting choices is more aptly called a "wish" than a "love."

Eros was by usage the most limited of the three conceptions, and Plato adapted it to his purposes only by doing violence to its normal meaning, at *Symposium* 205a-d. But once established in its special Platonic sense it was singularly well adapted to Plato's notion of human nature and the philosophic life. This life, in which men's natural drives were channeled into the search for knowledge, involved conversation with handsome young men in the common pursuit of virtue. Many Socratic dialogues, the *Lysis* and *Charmides* included, are themselves examples of this ideal, and the repetition of the phrase ὦ παῖ καλέ in the great speech of the *Phaedrus* (243e, 252b) is a reminder that this dialogue too illustrates the very subject with which it is concerned. Such a conversation always implies for Plato a passion that might have become sensual but has instead been diverted into the pursuit of wisdom. In the

19. Grube, *Plato's Thought*, p. 92, n. 1.

terms of the *Symposium*, the love of a fair body is transformed into the love of those realities which are not only beautiful but changelessly so. This role of personal friendship in Platonic philosophy, the reflection of Greek tolerance of homosexual sentiment,[20] is one reason for the prominence Plato gives to Eros. Another is the creativity of love, so familiar in its sexual form, which has an obvious analogy in the philosopher's effort to create virtue. In Plato's unifying imagination, these became two among many expressions of the single desire for immortality, a desire shown equally in the wish for children, in the search for lasting fame, and in the attempt to reach personal communion with the one, unchanging reality which lies beyond change and destruction. Even the prolongation of a man's physical existence by growth and his mental integrity by study, since it is a kind of temporary defiance of death, became in Plato's mind a form of Eros. This conception of a single psychic energy underlying growth, sex, ambition, and knowledge tends to break down the boundaries which separate the three parts of the soul. Yet it does not invalidate or contradict the doctrine of tripartition. The principle of Eros simply belongs to the person as a whole, not to any single part. Even in the *Republic*, where the strict separation of psychic function influences the whole discussion, Plato envisages a desire that can be channeled from the pleasures of the body to the improvement of the soul (485d).

Eros, the holy madness which inflames the philosopher with desire for eternal reality, may seem hard to reconcile with Platonic intellectualism as summarized earlier in this chapter. In that summary the philosophic soul ruled its emotions by a principle of calculation and prepared itself for a perfection which would consist in the unhampered observation of eternal truth. Faced with the chill placidity of that ideal, we might have wondered at first whether to call it the triumph of order or of senescence. Had the philosopher, perhaps, simply won before his full course of years the equanimity of Cephalus, to whom old age brought happy release from the passions that had agitated his youth (*Rep.* 329c)? Eros forestalls the judgment which the example of Cephalus might have

20. The cultural basis for this tolerance is well explained by Ronald B. Levinson, *In Defense of Plato* (Cambridge, Mass., 1953), pp. 81-100.

suggested to us, that reason flourishes by the suppression of vitality. Instead, philosophy is revealed as an expression of desire, channeled in a single stream towards the one object which can fully satisfy it. Plato so frequently speaks of desire as the antithesis of reason that his readers can hardly be blamed for divorcing the two. The *Republic*, which names the meanest part of the soul "the seat of desire," τὸ ἐπιθυμητικόν, seems to damn desire as a many-headed monster, a troublesome and dangerous redundancy, while in τὸ λογιστικόν it enthrones the cold and detached principle of calculation. That picture must be changed in the light of the *Symposium* and the *Phaedrus*. Even in the *Republic*, desire can be converted from the sensual or the venal to higher objects, while in the full doctrine of Eros it turns out to be essential, in a positive way, to the good life.

The polar opposite of wisdom, the profound ignorance which thinks it knows, is therefore not only the stultification of knowledge but the corruption of Eros too. This is the meaning of *Lysis* 218 and of *Symposium* 203d-204a, where the love of wisdom is said to belong neither to the wise nor to the ignorant in the proper sense of those two words. The wise do not need wisdom; the ignorant do not desire it; but Eros, in the mythological language of the *Symposium*, is a lover of wisdom all his life. Socrates, whose soul was fired with this daemon spirit, spent his life trying to inflame others with it too. Their emergence from self-satisfied ignorance, earlier described as a dawning of knowledge, can now be seen as something more, a quickening of that best of loves called philosophy.

# BIBLIOGRAPHY

What follows is a partial list of the modern scholarly works dis-cussed or cited in the notes. It has been prepared with a prejudice in favor of the more recent and the more useful, although it includes as well a few important older works. Since much is excluded, read-ers in search of full bibliographical data on a short title encountered in the notes and not represented here or in the list of abbreviations are advised to look in the index under the author's name. They will find that the earliest reference in the notes to any book or ar-ticle is unabbreviated. Those who want further guidance in Pla-tonic bibliography will find it in the survey by Harold Cherniss, "Plato 1950-1957," *Lustrum*, 4 (1959) and 5 (1960); in an earlier survey by Thomas G. Rosenmeyer, "Platonic Scholarship: 1945-1955," *Classical Weekly*, 50 (1957), 173 ff.; in the notes to the latest editions of Friedländer's *Platon* (listed below); and in the annual volumes of *l'Année Philologique*.

Allen, R. E. "The Socratic Paradox," *JHI*, 21 (1960), 256-65.
Amand, David. *Fatalisme et Liberté dans l'Antiquité Grecque.* Louvain, 1945.
Bambrough, Renford. "Socratic Paradox," *Philosophical Quarterly*, 10 (1960), 289-300.

Bluck, R. S. *Plato's Phaedo*, translated with introduction and notes. New York, 1955.

——. "The *Phaedrus* and Reincarnation," *AJP*, 79 (1958), 156-64.

——. "Plato, Pindar, and Metempsychosis," *AJP*, 79 (1958), 405-14.

——. (ed.). *Plato's Meno*. Cambridge, 1961.

——. "Plato's *Meno*," *Phronesis*, 6 (1961), 94-101.

Böhme, Joachim. *Die Seele und das Ich im Homerischen Epos*. Leipzig and Berlin, 1929.

Burnet, John (ed.). *Plato's Phaedo*. Oxford, 1911.

Calogero, Guido. "Gorgias and the Socratic Principle *Nemo Sua Sponte Peccat*," *JHS*, 77, Part I (1957), 12-17.

Cole, Andrew T. "The Anonymus Iamblichi and His Place in Greek Political Theory," *HSCP*, 65 (1961), 127-63.

Cornford, Francis M. *Plato's Cosmology, The Timaeus of Plato*, translated with a running commentary. New York, 1957.

Cushman, Robert E. *Therapeia, Plato's Conception of Philosophy*. Chapel Hill, 1958.

Deman, Th. *Le Témoignage d'Aristote sur Socrate*. Paris, 1942.

Dodds, E. R. "Plato and the Irrational," *JHS*, 65 (1945), 16-25.

——. *The Greeks and the Irrational*. Berkeley and Los Angeles, 1951.

——. (ed.). *Plato. Gorgias*. Oxford, 1959.

England, E. B. (ed.). *The Laws of Plato*, 2 vols. London, 1921.

Festugière, A.-J. (ed.). *Hippocrate, l'Ancienne Médecine*. Paris, 1948.

Fraenkel, Hermann. *Dichtung und Philosophie des Fruehen Griechentums*. New York, 1951.

Friedländer, Paul. *Platon*. 1st ed., 2 vols. Berlin and Leipzig, 1928-30; 2nd ed., 3 vols. Berlin, 1954-60; 3rd ed., vols. 1 and 2. Berlin, 1964- .

——. *Plato*, translated into English by H. Meyerhoff. Vols. 1 and 2. London, 1958- .

Fritz, Kurt von. "Νοῦς and Νοεῖν in the Homeric Poems," *CP*, 38 (1943), 79-93.

——. "Νοῦς, Νοεῖν, and Their Derivatives in Pre-Socratic Philosophy (excluding Anaxagoras)," *CP*, 40 (1945), 223-42; and *CP*, 41 (1946), 12-34.

Gallop, David. "Justice and Holiness in *Protagoras* 330-331," *Phronesis*, 6 (1961), 86-93.

——. "The Socratic Paradox in the *Protagoras*," *Phronesis*, 9 (1964), 117-29.

Gigon, Olof. "Das Einleitungsgespräch der Gesetze Platons," *Mus. Helv.*, 11 (1954), 201-230.

Görgemanns, Herwig. *Beiträge zur Interpretation von Platons Nomoi.* Munich, 1960.

Goldschmidt, Victor. *Les Dialogues de Platon. Structure et Méthode Dialectique.* Paris, 1947.

——. "Sur le Problème du 'Système' de Platon," *Rivista Critica di Storia della Filosofia,* 5 (1950), 169-78.

Gomperz, Theodor. *Die Apologie der Heilkunst,* Sitzungsberichte Kaiserl. Akad. Wien, Philos.-Hist. Classe, 120 (1889), IX. Abhandlung.

——. *Griechische Denker.* 2nd ed., 3 vols. Leipzig, 1903-1909.

Gould, John. *The Development of Plato's Ethics.* Cambridge, 1955.

Greene, William Chase. "The Spoken and the Written Word," *HSCP,* 60 (1951), 23-59.

——. "The Paradoxes of the *Republic,*" *HSCP,* 63 (1958), 199-216.

Grube, G. M. A. *Plato's Thought.* London, 1935.

Guglielmino, Francesco. "Il Problema del Libero Arbitrio nel Sistema Platonico," *Archivio di Storia della Filosofia Italiana,* 4 (1935), 197-223.

Gulley, Norman. "The Interpretation of 'No One Does Wrong Willingly' in Plato's Dialogues," *Phronesis,* 10 (1965), 82-96.

Guthrie, W. K. C. "Plato's Views on the Nature of the Soul," *Recherches sur la Tradition Platonicienne.* Geneva, 1955.

Hackforth, Reginald. "Hedonism in Plato's *Protagoras,*" *CQ,* 22 (1928), 39-42.

——. "Moral Evil and Ignorance in Plato's Ethics," *CQ,* 40 (1946), 118-20.

——. *Plato's Phaedrus,* translated with introduction and commentary. Cambridge, 1952.

Harrison, E. L. "Notes on Homeric Psychology," *Phoenix,* 14 (1960), 63-80.

Havelock, Eric A. *The Liberal Temper in Greek Politics.* New Haven and London, 1957.

Heinimann, Felix, "Eine Vorplatonische Theorie der Τέχνη," *Mus. Helv.,* 18 (1961), 105-30.

Hoffmann, Ernst. "Die Literarische Voraussetzungen des Platonverständnisses," *Zeitschrift für Philos. Forschung,* 2 (1947), 465-80.

Jaeger, Werner. *Paideia,* translated into English by Gilbert Highet. 3 vols. New York, 1939-44.

Jones, W. H. S. *Philosophy and Medicine in Ancient Greece,* with an ed. of περὶ ἀρχαίης ἰητρικῆς, Suppl. Bull. Hist. Medicine, No. 8. Baltimore, 1946.

Kerferd, G. B. "Protagoras' Doctrine of Justice and Virtue in the 'Protagoras' of Plato," *JHS,* 73 (1953), 42-45.

Kleingünther, Adolph. ΠΡΩΤΟΣ ΕΥΡΕΤΗΣ, *Untersuchungen zur Geschichte einer Fragestellung, Philologus* Supplementband 26, Heft 1. Leipzig, 1933.

Knox, Bernard M. W. *Oedipus at Thebes.* New Haven and London, 1957.

Levinson, Ronald B. *In Defense of Plato.* Cambridge, Mass., 1953.

McGibbon, D. D. "The Fall of the Soul in Plato's *Phaedrus,*" *CQ,* N.S. 14 (1964), 56-63.

Magalhâes-Vilhena, V. de. *Le Problème de Socrate. Le Socrate Historique et le Socrate de Platon.* Paris, 1952.

———. *Socrate et la Légende Platonicienne.* Paris, 1952.

Manasse, Ernst Moritz. *Bücher über Platon, 2: Werke in englischer Sprache, Philosophische Rundschau,* Beiheft 2, Sonderheft. Tübingen, 1961.

Merlan, Philip. "Form and Content in Plato's Philosophy," *JHI,* 8 (1947), 406-30.

Miller, Harold W. "*On Ancient Medicine* and the Origin of Medicine," *TAPA,* 80 (1949), 187-202.

———. "*Technê* and Discovery in *On Ancient Medicine,*" *TAPA,* 86 (1955), 51-62.

Müller, Gerhard. *Studien zu den Platonischen Nomoi.* Munich, 1951.

Nestle, Wilhelm. "Intellektualismus und Mystik in der Griechischen Philosophie," *Neue Jahrbücher für das klassische Altertum,* 49 (1922), 137-57.

———. *Vom Mythos zum Logos.* 2nd ed. Stuttgart, 1942.

North, Helen. "A Period of Opposition to Sôphrosynê in Greek Thought," *TAPA,* 78 (1947), 1-17.

O'Brien, Michael J. "Plato and the Good Conscience: *Laws* 863e5-864b7," *TAPA,* 88 (1958), 81-87.

———. "Modern Philosophy and Platonic Ethics," *JHI,* 19 (1958), 451-72.

———. "The 'Fallacy' in *Protagoras* 349d-350c," *TAPA,* 92 (1962), 408-17.

———. "The Unity of the *Laches,*" *Yale Classical Studies,* 18 (1963), 131-47.

———. Review of Manasse, *Bücher über Platon,* 2 (listed above), *Gnomon,* 35 (1963), 765-70.

———. Review of Snell, *Scenes from Greek Drama* (listed below), *AJP,* 87 (1966), 233-37.

Onians, Richard B. *The Origins of European Thought about the Body, the Mind, the Soul, the World, Time, and Fate.* Cambridge, 1954.

Pearson, Lionel. *Popular Ethics in Ancient Greece.* Stanford, 1962.

Pohlenz, Max. *Griechische Freiheit.* Heidelberg, 1955.

Reinhardt, Karl. "Hekataios von Abdera und Demokrit," *Hermes,* 47 (1912), 492-513.

Rist, John. *Eros and Psyche, Studies in Plato, Plotinus, and Origen.* Toronto, 1964.

Ritter, Constantin. *Platos Gesetze. Kommentar zum Griechischen Text.* Leipzig, 1896.

———. *Platon. Sein Leben, Seine Schriften, Seine Lehre.* 2 vols. Munich, 1910-23.

Robinson, Richard. "Plato's Consciousness of Fallacy," *Mind,* 51 (1942), 97-114.

Santas, Gerasimos. "The Socratic Paradoxes," *Philosophical Review,* 72 (1964), 147-64.

Schaerer, René. *La Question Platonicienne.* Neuchatel, 1938.

Schottländer, R. "Nus als Terminus," *Hermes,* 64 (1929), 228-42.

Schwyzer, Ed. "Beiträge zur griechischen Wortforschung," in *Festschrift Paul Kretschmer* (Wien, Leipzig, New York, 1926), pp. 244-51.

Shorey, Paul. *The Idea of Good in Plato's Republic,* Univ. of Chicago Studies in Classical Philology, No. 1. Chicago, 1895.

———. *The Unity of Plato's Thought.* Chicago, 1903.

———. "Φύσις, Μελέτη, Ἐπιστήμη," *TAPA,* 40 (1909), 185-201.

———. *What Plato Said.* Chicago, 1933.

Skemp, J. B. *Plato. The Statesman,* translated with introduction and commentary. London, 1952.

Snell, Bruno. *Die Ausdrücke für den Begriff des Wissens in der Vorplatonischen Philosophie,* Philologische Untersuchungen, No. 29. Berlin, 1924.

———. "Das frühste Zeugnis über Sokrates," *Philologus,* 97 (1948), 125-34.

———. *The Discovery of the Mind,* translated by Thomas G. Rosenmeyer. New York, 1960.

———. *Scenes from Greek Drama.* Berkeley and Los Angeles, 1964.

Spoerri, Walter. *Späthellenistische Berichte über Welt, Kultur, und Götter,* Schweiz. Beiträge zur Altertumswissenschaft, Heft 9 (Basel, 1959).

———. "Zu Diodor von Sizilien 1, 7/8," *Mus. Helv.,* 18 (1961), 63-82.

Sprague, Rosamond Kent. *Plato's Use of Fallacy.* London, 1962.

Stenzel, Julius. "Das Problem der Willensfreiheit im Platonismus," *Die Antike,* 4 (1928), 293-313.

Sullivan, John P. "The Hedonism in Plato's *Protagoras*," *Phronesis,* 6 (1961), 10-28.

Tarrant, Dorothy. "Plato as Dramatist," *JHS,* 75 (1955), 82-89.

Taylor, A. E. *Commentary on Plato's Timaeus*. Oxford, 1928.
———. *Socrates*. London, 1935.
———. *Plato, the Man and His Work*, 4th ed. London, 1937.
Tuckey, T. G. *Plato's Charmides*. Cambridge, 1951.
Vlastos, Gregory (ed.). *Plato's Protagoras*, translated by B. Jowett, revised by Martin Ostwald. New York, 1956.
———. "Socratic Knowledge and Platonic Pessimism," *Philosophical Review*, 66 (1957), 226-38.
Webster, T. B. L. "Some Psychological Terms in Greek Tragedy," *JHS*, 77, Part I (1957), 149-54.
Wilamowitz-Moellendorff, Ulrich von. *Platon*, 2nd ed., 2 vols. Berlin, 1920.
Wilford, F. A. "The Status of Reason in Plato's Psychology," *Phronesis*, 4 (1959), 54-58.
Wüst, Ernst. "Von den Anfängen des Problems der Willensfreiheit," *Rhein. Mus.*, 101 (1958), 75-91.
Wundt, Max. *Der Intellektualismus in der Griechischen Ethik*. Leipzig, 1907.
Zeller, Eduard. *Die Philosophie der Griechen in ihrer Geschichtlichen Entwicklung*, 2. Theil, 1. Abth.: *Sokrates und die Sokratiker, Plato und die Alte Akademie*, 4th ed. Leipzig, 1889.
Zucker, Friedrich. "Verbundenheit von Erkenntnis und Wille im Griechischen Sprachbewusstsein Beleuchtet durch Erscheinungen aus der Bedeutungsentwicklung von ἄγνοια, ἀγνοεῖν, ἀγνόημα," in *Studies David M. Robinson*, vol. 2 (St. Louis, 1953), 1063-71.

# INDEX

The works of ancient authors are listed under the authors' names. Under "Plato," the more important discussions of Platonic passages are in boldface type. Greek words are indexed separately at the end.

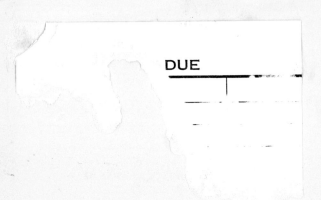

DUE